JUXTAPOSING LEGAL SYSTEMS AND THE PRINCIPLES OF EUROPEAN FAMILY LAW ON DIVORCE AND MAINTENANCE

Edited by

Esİn Örücü and Jane Mair

 intersentia

Antwerpen – Oxford

Distribution for the UK:
Hart Publishing Ltd.
16C Worcester Place
Oxford OX1 2JW
UK
Tel.: + 44 1865 51 75 30
Fax: + 44 1865 51 07 10

Distribution for Switzerland and Germany:
Stämpfli Verlag AG
Wölflistrasse 1
CH-3001 Bern
Switzerland
Tel.: + 41 (0)31 300 63 18
Fax: + 41 (0)31 300 66 88

Distribution for North America
Gaunt Inc.
Gaunt Building
3011 Gulf Drive
Holmes Beach
Florida 34217-2199
USA
Tel.: + 1 941 778 5211
Fax: + 1 941 778 5252

Distribution for other countries:
Intersentia Publishers
Groenstraat 31
BE-2640 Mortsel
Belgium
Tel.: + 32 3 680 15 50
Fax: + 32 3 658 71 21

Juxtaposing Legal Systems and the Principles of European Family Law on Divorce and Maintenance
Esin Örücü and Jane Mair

© 2007 Intersentia
Antwerpen – Oxford
http://www.intersentia.com

ISBN 978-90-5095-577-5
D/2007/7849/43
NUR 822

PREFACE

Following the publication of *Principles of European Family Law Regarding Divorce and Maintenance Between Former Spouses* by the Commission on European Family Law (CEFL) that was set up in September 2001 with a team of specialists from twenty-two jurisdictions to carry out research in the field of comparative family law, it was considered worthwhile to produce an edited volume to assess the reality of legal systems in view of the Principles, and the Principles in view of the reality of these legal systems.

The CEFL hoped to create a source of inspiration to legislators in the process of modernising their national family laws. "Functional equivalence" was sought and both the "common core" and "better law" approaches were adopted. The drafters chose "the best", "the more functional" and the "most efficient" rules, their touchstone being the modernisation of the law. So, these CEFL Principles are not merely restatements of family laws in Europe, but contributions towards the establishment of a European Family Law.

Only by empirical testing of the Principles in a number of legal systems can one demonstrate whether they are acceptable and/or are regarded as an improvement on existing national laws. For our purposes, after an introductory overview, it was deemed appropriate first to re-test the Principles in a sample of legal systems already considered by the CEFL: France, one head of the civilian tradition; Scandinavia, a variation on the civilian theme; England, the mother of the common law tradition, Scotland, a mixed jurisdiction that has gained popularity within the European Union as a model; and then, to test the Principles in the untested: Malta, a new EU member with a conservative background; Estonia and Lithuania, two new EU members with a socialist background but different socio-cultures; and Turkey, a country bridging two cultures and aspiring to membership of the EU.

The final part of the volume is a comparative assessment of our findings. One study looks at the Principles as harmonious ideals, the other looks at the shortfalls in the ideals as presented and the obstacles to harmonisation.

EsİN ÖRÜCÜ and JANE MAIR
1 March 2007

LIST OF AUTHORS

Dr Ruth Farrugia
Advocate and Senior Lecturer in Civil Law, University of Malta

Ms Joëlle Godard
Lecturer in Law – University of Edinburgh

Ms Triin Göttig
LL.M. (Kiel); Research Fellow of Civil Law, University of Tartu, Estonia

Ms Liis Hallik
mag. iur.; Adjunct Instructor, Institute of Law, University of Tartu; Counsellor of the Civil Chamber, Supreme Court of the Republic of Estonia

Dr. Gaël Henaff
Maître de conférences à l'Université de Rennes 2, France

Prof. Dr. Urpo Kangas
Professor in Civil Law, Faculty of Law, University of Helsinki, Finland

Dr Inga Kudinaviciute-Michailoviene
Lecturer in Civil and Commercial Law, Mykolas Romeris University, Lithuania

Dr. Jane Mair
Senior Lecturer in Law, University of Glasgow, School of Law, Scotland, UK.

Prof. Dr. Esin Örücü
Professorial Research Fellow and Professor Emerita of Comparative Law, University of Glasgow, Professor Emerita of Comparative law, Erasmus University Rotterdam and Visiting Professor of Comparative Law, University of Yeditepe, Istanbul, Turkey.

Dr. Rebecca Probert
Lecturer of Private law, University of Warwick, England.

Dr. Triin Uusen-Nacke
Adjunct Instructor, Institute of Law, University of Tartu; Counsellor of the Civil Chamber, Supreme Court of the Republic of Estonia

TABLE OF CONTENTS

DIVORCE SYSTEM AND MAINTENANCE OF FORMER SPOUSES IN SCANDINAVIAN COUNTRIES

ENGLAND AND WALES JUXTAPOSED TO THE EUROPEAN PRINCIPLES OF FAMILY LAW

COMMON PRINCIPLES AND PURPOSES? SCOTS LAW AND THE COMMISSION ON EUROPEAN FAMILY LAW

PART TWO – DIVERSITY IN THE NEW MEMBERS OF THE EUROPEAN UNION: CAN THERE BE ONE WAY FORWARD?

THE POSITION IN MALTA JUXTAPOSED TO THE PRINCIPLES OF EUROPEAN FAMILY LAW: DIVORCE AND MAINTENANCE

DIVORCE AND MAINTENANCE BETWEEN FORMER SPOUSES IN ESTONIA AND THE CEFL PRINCIPLES

Triin Göttig, Liis Hallik and Triin Uusen-Nacke 129

THE PRINCIPLES OF EUROPEAN FAMILY LAW PUT TO THE TEST: DIVERSITY IN HARMONY OR HARMONY IN DIVERSITY?

INTRODUCTORY OVERVIEW

COMMON CULTURES AND DIVERSE LAWS – COMMON LAWS AND DIVERSE CULTURES

Esin Örücü and Jane Mair

1. INTRODUCING THE TOPIC

Why was it that until recently, comparative lawyers worked in such a limited field, the field of private law that did not extend even to family law, and family lawyers were predominantly involved in their own domestic laws? Family law, regarded as culturally defined—the so-called "cultural constraints argument"[1]—was not seen to be appropriate for much meaningful comparison. Today things have changed and family law has now moved to the foreground. Shared values are seen to form the basis of developments in Europe, and the belief that universalism trumps exceptionalism is in the essence of these developments. Consequently, the view that family law does not lend itself to comparison let alone harmonisation, has been superseded. Even courses entitled Comparative Family Law are offered in universities. Furthermore, the pragmatic and cosmopolitan approach to family law has meant that not only can this area be approached comparatively but that most aspects of it can be harmonised.[2]

In our day, similar principles that apply to divergent societies are emerging as a result of changing social, religious and economic conditions that transcend the so-called "common law – civil law divide", "local context" and "cultural iden-

---

[1] For a thorough analysis of the "cultural constraints argument" in relation to family law see ANTOKOLSKAIA, MV, *Harmonisation of Family Law in Europe: A Historical Perspective – A Tale of Two Millennia*, European Family Law Series, Volume 13 (Mortsel, Intersentia, 2006), pp. 3–47.

[2] See for such work, BOELE-WOELKI, K, "The Road Towards a European Family Law", (1997) 1:1 *EJCL* http://law.kub.nl/ejcl/11/art11-1.html, and also BOELE-WOELKI, K, "Comparative Research-Based Drafting of Principles of European Family Law" in FAURE, M, SMITS J, and SCHNEIDER, H (eds) *Towards a European Ius Commune in Legal Education and Research* (Intersentia Uitgevers Antwerpen–Groningen, 2002) pp. 171–201. Also see MARTINY, D, "The Harmonization of Family Law in the European Community; Pro and Contra", in ibid., pp. 191–201.

tity".[3] In the past, in a number of societies certain principles and beliefs have violated interests by relying solely on traditions with social legitimacy. However, the fact that we live in an era of "equality" and "freedom" seems to override these traditional values today, and comparative family lawyers are called on to help create a suitable receptive environment for a modern family law.[4] In our age many principles have universality and therefore transferability, while cosmopolitan pragmatism wins over culturalism.

As yet there is no uniform family law for Europe, however, there are efforts to create standardisation in some aspects of family law through European Law and Conventions related to respect for family life, the equal treatment of men and women, the equal treatment of legitimate and illegitimate children and the recognition of divorce, maintenance and custody judgments. There is lively comparative law research activity in this field. Most of these efforts are academic. Nonetheless, European norms enunciated through the European Convention on Human Rights in relation to Article 8 on the right to family life have also had a substantial impact on the legislation of several countries.

We know that attitudes in this field depend on political agendas. One such agenda is further integration. This can be one stance, "keeping apart" can be another. In fact, the possibilities are endless. One might be a utopian, a realist, a sceptic, a conservative, a nationalist, have strong religious bias, fear the different, feel superior or fear the superior; one might be a dedicated private international lawyer who prefers harmonising conflict rules rather than substance, a comparatist who belongs to the integrationist camp or new *ius commune* seekers and who stresses similarities and convergence, a so-called "post-modern" comparatist who feels that context and culture are vital and hence differences, diversity, identity and non-convergence, a young comparatist who is not necessarily post-modernist but needs to stress difference in order to be in current demand, an old comparatist who regards harmonisation of family law as a long yet extremely worthwhile project but who would advise painstaking scholarly research with kid gloves to be worn for conversion of the "others" dedicated to different causes for whatever reason, and a comparative family lawyer who feels that the time has come for her to be recognised as an indispensable academic serving the families in Europe who

---

[3]   See DE CRUZ, P, "Legal Transplants: Principles and Pragmatism in Comparative Family Law", Chapter 6 in HARDING, A and ÖRÜCÜ, E (eds), *Comparative Law in the 21ˢᵗ Century* (London, Kluwer Law International, 2002,) pp. 101–121.

[4]   See for example ANTOKOLSKAIA, MV "The Process of Modernisation of Family Law in Eastern and Western Europe: Differences in Timing, Resemblance in Substance", (2000) 4:2 *EJCL* http://kub.nl/ejcl/42/art42-1.html.

want Europe-wide solutions to their human rights and freedom of movement.[5] The Commission on European Family Law (CEFL) set up in 2001 in the hope of contributing towards the creation of a European family law, has members wearing all these colours.

1.1. THE EUROPEAN SCENE, THE COMMISSION ON EUROPEAN FAMILY LAW AND ITS WORK

1.1.1. The European Scene

Until recently, European integration focused on economics. There are however, important social implications of economic change such as labour market regulations and social welfare systems and these changes in turn have an impact in a significant way on the family. Initiatives for gender equality and against sexual discrimination in employment, have been actively followed by European institutions, however, there has been considerable variation in the ways these changes have been implemented across Europe.[6]

The overlap between work and family life has also been highlighted in the application of the European principle of equal treatment for men and women in employment and here it has at times been clear that the European Court of Justice feels constrained by its lack of jurisdiction to intervene in family matters.[7] While progress is made in the workplace, the barrier to the private family remains in place and consequently gender inequalities, particularly in the context of domestic caring roles, continue. The EU's lack of competence or reluctance to engage with family law may be leading to a European concept of the family which, far from being forward looking and modern, in fact lags behind that of many member states.[8]

Although the European Court of Justice treats aspects of family law under "freedom of movement", it cannot make specific rules for the family. In addition, it can be argued that issues can only be dealt with when imperative for the functioning of the common market, since the European Union as such has no competence

---

5   See for an analysis, ÖRÜCÜ, E, "A Family Law for Europe: Necessary, Feasible, Desirable?" in BOELE-WOELKI, K (ed), *Perspectives for the Unification and Harmonisation of Family Law in Europe*, (Intersentia: Antwerp, Oxford, New York, 2003), pp. 551–572.
6   See LLOYD, C, "The Transformation of Family Life and Sexual Politics" in GUIBERNAU, M (ed) *Governing European Diversity* (London, Sage Publications, 2001), p. 150.
7   See eg *Hofmann v Barmer Ersatzkasse* [1984] ECR 3047 where the ECJ, at para 24, refused to intervene in the "organisation of the family".
8   See *Grant v South West Trains Ltd* [1991] ECR 1-621; *D v Council* [2001] ECR 1-4319.

regarding unification of family and succession laws. It might be argued that, a specific European Family Law, at least for cross-border situations, is necessary. It is possible to find a legal basis for this in the Amsterdam Treaty, Article 65. This Article refers to measures in the area of judicial co-operation in civil matters that "have cross-border implications". In fact, hypothetically, each internal relationship can become a cross-border relationship and, therefore, to guarantee free movement of persons, the EU Commission must take appropriate steps. Though it may seem like a broad interpretation, it is feasible to envisage the EU being competent to take measures to harmonise or unify the substantive family law in Europe.[9]

As a result of lack of a cross-border family law in a Europe where many spouses and children have dual or even multiple citizenship and 5% of the population in the European Union are not citizens of the state in which they live and work, and in view of the ever increasing migration of peoples in Europe, it is now necessary to move towards further integration rather than fragmentation. It can be argued that if it is desirable to move towards a European civil society and to forge a European identity encompassing common values, the best way to achieve these aims could be via a harmonised family law.[10]

There will always be diversity of culture and moral views that use arguments such as "harmonisation destroys national identity", but these should not hinder the search for Europe-wide solutions, because European citizens need European solutions. Member states face pressing shared problems such as same-sex marriage, adoption by cohabiting couples, cross-border adoption, and acquisition and loss of nationality of minors and the rights of spouses, partners and children. They need shared solutions.

European norms, the European Convention on Human Rights and the European Courts already have considerable impact on national family laws. Yet, this is not enough. What is needed is the creation of Europe-wide Principles to run at the start parallel with, if not to replace, national legislation. Incremental harmonisation covering the whole field, while at first keeping culturally specific aspects aside, seems to be a workable beginning. Whatever the obstacles now, in the long term pragmatism and cosmopolitanism will prevail. At this stage work can only be academic and is bound to remain at the level of finding, analysing and comparing the rules and then formulating and presenting General Principles. This how-

---

[9]   See BOELE-WOELKI, K, "De competentie van de Europese Unie in familiezaken", *FJR* 2004, p. 289.
[10]   For a strong opposition to the need for such a project, however, see MCGLYNN, C, *Families and the European Union* (Cambridge, Cambridge University Press, 2006).

ever, must be regarded as the starting point, as Europeans need a European Family Law.[11]

1.1.2. Commission on European Family Law (CEFL) and its work

The CEFL was set up in September 2001 with a team of specialists from twenty-two jurisdictions,[12] now twenty-six, to carry out research in the field of comparative family law, the aim being to create a set of Principles of European Family Law in areas thought to be most suitable for harmonisation. Obviously the hope is that in time the Principles should function as a source of inspiration and a frame of reference for national, European and international legislators.

After considering the ultimate aim of Europeanisation of family law, arguments for and against unification and harmonisation of family law, the methodological aspects of such a harmonisation, the "better law" approach, the unification of Private International Law, divorce and maintenance, the related topics of human rights, the expansion of Europe, and the American experience, the Commission decided to concentrate first on divorce and maintenance as in those areas there was already growing convergence and the time for unifying substantive divorce law and maintenance seemed ripe. The Commission then moved on to the drafting and publication of Principles of European Family Law regarding divorce and maintenance between former spouses.[13] The Principles were published three years after the establishment of the Commission.[14]

It may be that in the field of convergence or integration the simplest option is to wait for spontaneous approximation, but this takes time. Free movement of decisions could also provide a practical path, but this is not enough. Instead, common principles could be distilled into the form of a Restatement through "common core research" accompanied by functional equivalence. This seems to be the most obvious approach for creating a harmonised family law. In addition, the "better

---

[11] For such an academic effort see SCHWENZER, I and DIMSEY, M, *Model Family Code From a Global Perspective* (Antwerpen, Intersentia, 2006).

[12] Austria, Belgium, Bulgaria, Czech Republic, Denmark, England and Wales, Finland, France, Germany, Greece, Hungary, Republic of Ireland, Italy, The Netherlands, Norway, Poland, Portugal, Russia, Scotland, Spain, Sweden, and Switzerland.

[13] For the working method of the CEFL see BOELE-WOELKI, K "The Working Method of the Commission on European Family Law", in BOELE-WOELKI, K (ed) *Common Core and Better Law in European Family Law*, European Family Law Series No. 10 (Antwerp, Intersentia, 2005), pp. 15–41.

[14] See BOELE-WOELKI, K, FERRAND, F, BEILFUSS, CG, JANTERA-JAREBORG, M, LOWE, N, MARTINY D and PINTENS, W, *Principles of European Family Law Regarding Divorce and Maintenance between Former Spouses*, European Family Law Series N: 7, (Intersentia: Antwerp, 2004). (Hereafter CEFL Principles, throughout the volume)

law" approach, that is the one that provides the most choice and not to be understood as the most permissive law, is a useful tool. The Commission opted for this distillation.

An Organising Committee of seven members and an Expert Group with twenty-two members, first studied the working methods of a number of academic groups engaged in other private law projects, but did not follow any of those methods. They used, what they themselves call, the "comparative research-based drafting of principles" as the process, having been inspired by the American Restatements. Their working method consisted of six steps: selecting family law fields most suitable for harmonisation, drafting a questionnaire employing the functional approach, drawing up national reports reflecting both the law in the books and law in action, collecting, integrating and disseminating the material,[15] drafting the Principles having chosen between the "common core" and "better law" approaches, and finally publishing the Principles. This methodological approach provided the Principles with a basis built on in-depth and comprehensive comparative research.

The CEFL hopes to create a source of inspiration to legislators who may be in the process of modernising their national family laws. In concert with this hope, "functional equivalence" was sought and both the "common core" and "better law" approaches were adopted. The drafters chose, "the best", "the more functional" and the "most efficient" rules, and their touchstone was the modernisation of the law. The overall justification lay both in facilitation of free movement of persons in Europe and in the shared notions of human rights. The question of legitimacy did not arise for the Commission as the work remains at the level of an academic activity. The view of the Commission was that Europeanisation of family law could be achieved through a didactic elaboration of common principles, these principles serving as a basis.

In divorce, for instance, the starting point is a rather loosely construed "common core" defining the lowest level of protection, hoping that the member states and the courts raise this level. This model is no threat to national cultures or national sovereignty. The three general trends in Europe in family law are liberty, equality and secularism and these are upheld in the Principles, but by providing for voluntary acceptance of the Principles, the Commission is respectful of the values and cultures of all European citizens.

---

[15]   See the two volumes: BOELE-WOELKI, K, BRAAT, B and SUMNER, I (eds), *European Family Law in Action Volume I: Grounds for Divorce, Volume II: Maintenance between Former Spouses*, European Family Law Series Nos. 2 and 3, (Intersentia: Antwerp, 2003). The integral reports can also be found on the CEFL website: www.law.uu.nl/priv.cefl

However, the drafters of the Principles go beyond the level of the shared European notion of human rights, preferring "increased choice" and opt for the "better law" approach whenever necessary by either selecting the "best rule" or creating one. The assessment of solutions offered through the answers provided by national reports, enabled the drafters to choose between "the best", the more "functional" and the more "efficient" rule. While drafting, the options to be decided upon were: there was a common core and this was selected as the best solution; there was a common core, but a better solution was selected; again, there was a common core, but the selection was left to national law; there was no common core and "a best solution" was selected, and finally there was no common core and the solution was left to national law.[16]

It must be stated here that though the "functional approach",[17] in any of its forms, is not the sole approach in comparative law research, it has recently gained a special place in "common core" studies in Europe. In the search for general Principles it is the most appropriate one. Without doubt, some will claim that many surrounding issues must be considered in determining the answers to any one of the questions. Though in European Family Law converging tendencies exist in the rise in divorce rates, increase in the age of first marriage, increase in cohabitation, decline in fertility rates, problems in substantive law of divorce, and formal equality between spouses, there are also significant differences due to different structures of administration of justice and the law of procedure; different family policies and family realities; different political and economic considerations and different value systems.

All the above may be true, but, history tells us that in Europe there are also common historical and religious roots in the area of family law.[18] Though diversity emerged after secularisation, secularisation is also a shared value. The ECHR expresses the European cultural identity. Social realities in Europe are basically similar. In addition, it seems that legal systems are heading in the same direction though with a different degree of alacrity and speed.

The drafters could have chosen to formulate new rules themselves instead of the "common core". Yet, "common core" is the better method to use since it makes justification simpler by restating what represents the majority. This was the method predominantly used by the CEFL in its work, supplemented by the func-

---

16   These options are assessed in Part four.
17   For discussion and analysis of functionalism, see ÖRÜCÜ, E, "Methodological Aspects of Comparative Law" VIII *European Journal of Law Reform* (2007), pp. 29–42. For the functional approach in Family Law see SCHWENZER, I, "Methodological Aspects of Harmonisation of Family Law" in BOELE-WOELKI (ed) *supra* note 5, pp. 143–158.
18   See for a recent assessment ANTOKOLSKAIA, *supra* note 1.

tional approach in gathering rules that achieve the same end. Obviously, the CEFL was aware at all times that similar legal concepts may hide functionally different results.

At times the drafters had to select either the "better law" or engineer one.[19] The crucial justification for the choice made appears in the comparative overviews referring to national reports and the comments which elucidate the provisions, both published together with the Principles.

The work of the CEFL goes a long way towards the goal of serving European families. These CEFL Principles are not merely restatements of family laws in Europe, but contributions to the establishment of a European Family Law. The work of the Commission must be taken seriously as it is providing the building blocks for a European "*acquis communautaire*'" in family values. The CEFL bravely ventured into this area believing that the time had come to talk of a "European Family Law".[20]

Put simply, the Commission used functionalism as the comparative law working methodology, and searched for "common core". In areas where "common core" was lacking, the "better law" approach was employed in the drawing up of Principles. The most important step of the project was the drafting of the questionnaire. The following "musts" were of paramount importance: There should be a sufficient number of questions and these should be formulated as independently of national legal systems as possible. The respondents should be given precise guidelines. The functional or problem-oriented approach should be used. The questionnaire should contain both conceptual and factual questions and be addressed to family law experts. The questionnaire and the national reports should be immediately published on the CEFL website.[21]

In this first project, the results of which we are juxtaposing to a number of chosen legal systems, there were 105 questions on the subject of divorce and maintenance, which culminated in twenty Principles dealing with 35 aspects of the subject.

---

[19]   See for an analysis of the "better law" approach, ANTOKOLSKAIA, MV, "'The Better Law' Approach and the Harmonisation of Family Law", in BOELE-WOELKI (ed) *supra* note 5, pp. 150–182.

[20]   For an assessment of the work of the CEFL see ÖRÜCÜ, E, "Viewing the Work in Progress of the Commission on European Family Law", 2005 *International Law FORUM du droit international* 7:220–228, (Koninklijke Brill N.V., Leiden, The Netherlands, 2005).

[21]   http://www2.law.uu.nl/priv/cefl.

2. THE GENERAL OUTLINE OF THE PRINCIPLES

The Principles were distilled from the analysis of the 105 questions posed to the twenty-two national reporters, following the methods already discussed. Not all the national systems played a role in the drawing up of the Principles, but neither was any one legal system the dominant model. In the formulation of the Principles the CEFL tried to adhere to a truly European perspective.

The Principles are not meant to be binding for obvious reasons as they are the product of academic and scientific work. Neither are they presented as "model law". Though directed towards the legislators, they are meant to provide a "frame of reference" and inspiration for reform. It is said that, "the Principles may serve two purposes: First, they could be considered as recommendations to the legislators and second, legislators could use them as a model for the applicable law."[22] They can be taken as a source of encouragement and intellectual stimulation for change.

There is a Preamble for both Parts of the Principles, and comments and comparative overviews follow each Principle. The working language is English and the publication is in English. However the Principles themselves are in three languages: English, French and German. No version is a translation. They have then been translated into Dutch, Spanish and Swedish. All five versions appear as annexes to the publication.

It may be useful to reproduce here the Preamble to indicate the vision underlying the Principles, they themselves, together with the questionnaires originally sent to the national reporters, being annexed to this volume for a better understanding of the individual chapters:

> Recognising that, notwithstanding the existing diversities of national family law systems, there is nevertheless a growing convergence of laws; Recognising that the free movement of persons within Europe is hindered by the remaining differences; Desiring to contribute to the harmonisation of family law in Europe and to facilitate further the free movement of persons within Europe; Desiring to balance the interests of spouses and society and to support actual gender equality, taking into account the best interests of children, The Commission on European Family Law recommends the following Principles:[23]

---

[22]   CEFL Principles, p. 3.
[23]   *Ibid*, p. 7.

Part I of the Principles deals with divorce and consists of ten articles. Cited as 1:1 to 1:10, these Principles cover permission of divorce; procedure by law and competent authority; types of divorce; mutual consent; reflection period; content and form of the agreement; determination of the consequences; factual separation; exceptional hardship to the petitioner; and determination of the consequences. Each one of these headings forms one Principle, some with sub sections.

Part II of the Principles deals with maintenance between former spouses also in ten articles laid out as 2:1 to 2:10. They cover relationship between maintenance and divorce; self-sufficiency; conditions for maintenance; determining claims for maintenance; method of maintenance provision; exceptional hardship to the debtor spouse; multiplicity of maintenance claims; limitation in time; termination of the maintenance obligation; and maintenance agreement. Again each of these headings forms one Principle, some having sub-sections.

3. THE AIM OF THIS RESEARCH

3.1. INCEPTION OF THE RESEARCH

Assuming that diversity in family law constitutes a serious obstacle to the free movement of people within the EU, we support harmonisation. However, in view of the enlargement of Europe a number of questions must be asked: Is there a European consensus on European standards in family law? If there is such consensus, should these standards have been in place before the further enlargement of Europe? Should not experiences emanating from Central and Eastern Europe become part of the European vision? Can the so-called "progressive North"[24] and the "conservative South" benefit from the emerging value statements of Central and Eastern Europe? What about Malta, which is already a member of the EU, and Turkey, a country aspiring to membership? Where global European solutions may seem more appropriate for issues concerning principles such as "equality", "freedom", "interest of the child", "free movement of persons" and property rights, should the principle of subsidiarity and value pluralism be respected?

Following the publication of the *Principles of European Family Law Regarding Divorce and Maintenance Between Former Spouses* by the CEFL, we considered it to be worthwhile to produce an edited volume, *Juxtaposing Legal Systems and The Principles of European Family Law: Divorce and Maintenance*. The aim is to assess the reality of some legal systems in view of the Principles, and the Principles in

---

[24] When "North" comes to mean also the Baltic States, the concept of progressiveness becomes dubious. See the contribution on Lithuania and compare it with that on Estonia.

view of the reality of these legal systems. Only by empirical testing in a number of legal systems could we demonstrate whether the Principles are acceptable and/or an improvement on existing laws.[25]

3.2 CHOICE OF SYSTEMS

In the choice of the systems, we decided to follow a logic, meaningful both for comparative law purposes and for inclusion of some legal systems not part of the original exercise. Thus for our purposes it was important first to re-test the Principles in a sample of legal systems already considered by the CEFL: France, one head of the civilian tradition; Scandinavia, a variation on the civilian theme;[26] England, the mother of the common law tradition, Scotland, a mixed jurisdiction that has gained popularity within the European Union as a model; and then, to test the Principles in the untested: Malta, a new EU member with a conservative background, Estonia and Lithuania, two new EU members with a socialist background; and Turkey, a country bridging two cultures and aspiring to membership of the EU.

Although some of these systems such as France, Denmark, Sweden, Norway, England and Scotland were among the twenty-two jurisdictions[27] covered by the questionnaire[28] leading to the drafting of the Principles, our chosen authors were not part of the team of experts responsible for drawing up the Principles and some were not even aware of the existence of the Principles. This, we thought, would give a healthy slant to our research. On the other hand, Estonia, Lithuania,[29] Malta and Turkey were not considered in the original exercise and are not among the twenty-two jurisdictions covered by the questionnaire.

---

[25] For instance, in a similar vein MV Antokolskaia undertakes a juxtaposition exercise. In her inaugural speech, she juxtaposed divorce laws in the Netherlands and the CEFL Principles. As an advocate of the "better law" approach, though she prefers the Principles on a number of counts, she would rather that Dutch law, which already embodies the "mutual consent" principle, went further. The Principles did not dare to go so far as to accept "divorce on demand", which Antokolskaia regards as the most modern and advanced option of our day, as seen in Sweden, Finland, Spain and indirectly in Russia. See ANTOKOLSKAIA, MV, "Nederlands echtscheidingsrecht en the CEFL Principles on Divorce", November 2006 *Tijdschrift voor Familie en Jeugdrecht*, pp. 262–269.

[26] In the contribution on Scandinavia four systems (Sweden, Denmark, Norway and Finland) are covered and sometimes Iceland is also considered.

[27] See for these CEFL *Principles* and *supra* note 15.

[28] See the questionnaire and the answers provided to the questions in *supra* n. 15. The questionnaire and the Principles are also attached as annexes to this volume.

[29] We cover two Baltic States since no Baltic State was considered while drafting the Principles. An additional reason is that, though family laws in Estonia and Lithuania were very similar while they were socialist republics, since independence in 1991, these laws have taken different directions.

The reader will also immediately notice that some contributions such as those on Estonia, Malta and Turkey are much longer than others and contain additional information on family law in those jurisdictions beyond the subjects covered by the Principles. There are legitimate reasons for these discrepancies. As these jurisdictions were not considered before the Principles were drafted, we thought it appropriate to give readers a brief history and relevant aspects of family laws of these jurisdictions. In the case of Malta, for instance, it is also important to note that there is no divorce; but, the grounds for separation correspond to the grounds for divorce seen in many other European jurisdictions. Divorces obtained abroad however, are regarded as valid. In Turkey the law in the books and the law in action present sometimes quite different pictures, and the principle of laicism has serious implications for marriage and divorce.

Again, and more important, it will be noted that many contributions cover matrimonial property arrangements and distribution of matrimonial property after divorce as our authors see a close connection between matrimonial property and maintenance provisions. This lack of consideration by the Principles, though be it for good reasons,[30] will be critically assessed in the final section of this volume.[31]

The overall aim of each contribution is to set out the situation in divorce and maintenance in that legal system at present and see whether the Principles could be introduced with ease into the existing framework of national family law. This might involve not only structural and substantive, but also sociological and political analysis.

3.3. ASSESSMENT OF LEGAL SYSTEMS AND CEFL PRINCIPLES

The purpose of this study is not to question whether family law in Europe should be going through a harmonisation process. Through the efforts of the Council of Europe, harmonisation has been taking place for the last two decades and as Katharina Boele-Woelki says, "the train has left the station".[32] The question is: Are the Principles as drafted, appropriate and sufficient to achieve this harmonisation?

---

30 See the explanation given in CEFL Principles, pp. 69–72.
31 Note that the Model Family Code, a later academic attempt to codify family law, does cater for these subjects under financial relief (Principles 1.19–1.39) See SCHWENZER and DIMSEY, *supra* note 11.
32 BOELE-WOELKI, "Comparative Research-Based Drafting of Principles of European Family Law" *supra* note 2, p. 183.

The final part of this research has two aims. The first is to juxtapose the legal systems we have selected against the Principles. Accepting the Principles as ideals, the national systems are assessed in order to identify whether they could accommodate the Principles and what their shortfalls are. Here there would be a chance to suggest improvements in those national laws.[33] The second aim is to take the opposite view, that is, to regard the provisions of the selected legal systems as ideal for those societies in relation to their social, economic and moral contexts, and assess the Principles in view of the reality of these legal systems. Here there would be a chance to be critical of the Principles and make suggestions for improvements, where possible.[34]

4. CONCLUDING REMARKS

It must always be remembered that there is a strong interdependency of rules in the field of family law, all aspects of which add together and make up a whole. Therefore it is not enough to remain at the level of divorce and maintenance—this first project—or the later projects of the CEFL on parental responsibility and matrimonial property. What will be needed, in the not too distant future, is standardisation of the whole of family law for Europe.[35] The future work of the CEFL remains indispensable for the achievement of this. Indeed the CEFL does have other ongoing projects. The second project, started in 2004, is the distillation, creation and publication of Principles on Parental Responsibilities. This field of work is linked to the first project, as both fields have been modernised in national systems in recent years and EU instruments and Conventions have played a significant role in these matters regarding cross-border relationships. In family law, the principle of the "rights of the child" is increasing in importance and reform is needed to clarify and reinforce the legal status of the child in the member states. To this end, again twenty-two family law experts in Europe were asked to prepare national reports and at an early stage common solutions were found in the great majority of aspects.[36] These Principles have now been formulated and will be published in 2007.[37]

---

[33]   See Part four, first section.
[34]   See Part four, second section.
[35]   The Model Family Code is an attempt in this direction. See SCHWENZER and DIMSEY, *supra* note 11.
[36]   See BOELE-WOELKI, K, BRAAT, B and CURRY-SUMMER, I (eds) *European Family Law in Action*, Volume III: Parental Responsibilities, European Family Law Series No. 9 (Intersentia, 2005).
[37]   Thirty-nine Principles have been classified into eight chapters. See: BOELE-WOELKI, K, FERRAND, F, Gonzalez Beilfuss, C, JANTERA-JAREBORG, M, LOWE, N, MATINY, D and PINTENS, W, *Principles of European Family Law Regarding Parental Responsibilities*, European Family Law Series No. 16 (Intersentia, 2007).

CEFL's Organising Committee decided in December 2006, that the third field to be covered should be matrimonial property. Within the EU, recent years have witnessed important developments in this field such as the *Green Paper on Conflict of Laws in Matters Concerning Matrimonial Property Regimes, Including the Question of Jurisdiction and Mutual Recognition*[38] published by the European Commission in July 2006. The establishment of a European matrimonial property regime may be the final outcome. To this end, the CEFL decided that there was a growing need to justify the drafting of the next set of Principles in this field.

Once it is assumed that a single family law policy is needed in Europe, feelings of fairness, justice and security, equality and, more pressing, convenience and expediency demand that several issues of family law such as marriage, matrimonial regime, divorce, legal separation and annulment, maintenance claims, filiation, succession, custody, parental responsibility and access rights should all be resolved at the European level and even be directly applicable in all member states. In this context it could be argued that since the quest is for certainty at a European level, this advances a general family law agenda.

With increasing Europeanisation and at a time when solutions to Europe's pressing problems are urgently sought, consideration of these issues by the CEFL is most timely. The creation of an "area of freedom, security and justice" in matters with cross-border implications—a goal of the European Union—can best be served by work such as this.

However, one could ask whether freedom of movement should be regarded as the only vehicle for protecting family life rather than EU citizenship and human rights? Is family law not to be regarded as part of economic law? Should harmonisation extend to substantive law or stay at the level of procedure? Who has the remit of and the competence for harmonisation: researchers and academics, legislators, judges? Should harmonisation and unification be achieved through general principles, restatement, competition of rules, directives, regulations, a code, through top-down or through bottom-up approaches? Should any such development be applicable to cross-border family ties only? Is there respect for diverse family forms in the present family laws? Some of these questions will be addressed in the final part of this study.

---

[38]   COM (2006) 400 final.

PART ONE
RE-TESTING THE TESTED:
THE SAME AND THE DIFFERENT

FRANCE AND THE PRINCIPLES OF EUROPEAN FAMILY LAW REGARDING DIVORCE AND MAINTENANCE BETWEEN FORMER SPOUSES

Joëlle Godard and Gaël Henaff

1. INTRODUCTION

Since its introduction in France at the time of the Revolution, divorce has undergone many changes in response to various social pressures. Under the *Ancien Régime* marriage was regarded as a sacrament governed by Canon Law. Only nullity of marriage and separation were allowed. The French Revolution secularised marriage and on the basis of individual liberty, introduced divorce even on mutual consent and incompatibility of temperament. The *Code Napoléon*, in a spirit of compromise and moderation, curtailed the grounds for divorce. Divorce was abolished in 1816, at the *Restauration*, being incompatible with Catholicism, which was recognised as the official religion of the State. Separation was the only matrimonial remedy. Divorce became possible again in 1884 (*loi Naquet*) but only on the ground of fault (*faute*) and it was not until 1975 that there was a major reform of divorce law. The Act of 11 July 1975 re-introduced the possibility of divorce by mutual consent. In 1976, there were about 60,000 decrees of divorce. Eight years later, in 1984, they increased to over 100,000 and reached 130,676 in 2002.

Nearly 30 years after the 1975 reform, the law of divorce went through another major change with the law adopted on 26 May 2004, which came into effect in January 2005. It aims to make the conditions for divorce more flexible without upsetting the fundamental principles laid down in 1975. The spouses are more involved in dealing with their separation and are encouraged by the court to state at any time during the procedure that they have reached an agreement. To facilitate this agreement, financial consequences are dissociated from the apportionment of blame but the fault-based divorce remains. There is growing recognition of the freedom of the spouses to terminate their marriage and they are encouraged to find a solution themselves as to the consequences of divorce.

This new reform gives us an opportunity to assess if French Law is now in conformity with the Principles drawn by the Commission on European Family Law (CEFL) in 2004, and to appraise if they could be accommodated in the existing framework of family law.

2. DIVORCE

2.1. GENERAL PRINCIPLES

Principle 1:1 Permission of divorce

After the reform of May 2004, there remain 4 grounds for divorce: divorce by mutual consent; by acceptance of the breakdown of marriage; by irretrievable breakdown of the marital relationship; and divorce on grounds of fault.

The 2004 reform recognises the right to divorce by making it less acrimonious. Bringing some peace was one of the leitmotivs the 2004 reform was striving to achieve, as well as *dédramatisation*.

The petition for divorce, which must be presented by a lawyer and is addressed to the court, only mentions that the petitioner is asking for divorce and requests that the spouses be called to a conciliation hearing. The aim of this hearing is no longer an attempt to reconcile the spouses, but to reach agreement on the principle of divorce and on its consequences. A further target is to try to lead the couple to an agreed divorce.

The rules of petition for divorce by mutual consent remain unchanged: divorce can be requested jointly by the spouses when they agree on the principle of the breakdown of the marriage and its consequences by submitting a proposal of agreement on the consequences of the divorce to the *juge aux affaires familiales* (family affairs judge). The real change is in the procedure: it lies in the fact that the process is shortened as the second meeting before the judge is no longer necessary.

The 6-month period laid down by the former Article 230 of the C. Civ. has been removed. Spouses can now divorce the day after their marriage. No duration of the marriage is required in France. This is in conformity with Principle 1:1 (2).

Principle 1:2 Procedure by law and competent authority

A divorce in France must be obtained through a judicial process commonly involving the parties' appearance before a court. Divorce cannot be obtained by an administrative process. The preliminary works of the 2004 reform had considered the possibility of a divorce given by an administrative authority in the simplest of cases (consensual divorce and absence of patrimony and/or of children) but this route, which is not very protective of the spouses' interests, was abandoned (see Principle 1:2 (2)).

The fundamental divorce principles are laid out in the Civil Code, the most recent reform being the Act of 4 March 2002. The *décrets d'application* provide detailed rules on the procedure for the implementation of the law so they should also be included in the notion of "law" mentioned in Principle 1:2(1).

The divorce must be pronounced by a court, either the *juge aux affaires familiales* in the procedure of divorce by consent, or the *Tribunal de Grande Instance* in other cases. Court appearance is normally required and representation by a lawyer is compulsory although where divorce is by consent, only one lawyer is necessary. The court cannot grant a divorce based on the papers alone. Some might think that the process is quasi-administrative in practice as a judge effectively rubber-stamps a consensual agreement. The expeditious character of this procedure has been criticised because the judge does not have any opportunity to investigate and it will be difficult for him/her to appreciate the situation. This weakness in the system has been negatively commented on by the Doyen Carbonnier: "the increasing pressure of the number of cases constrains the [*juge aux affaires familiales*] to a less and less thorough examination."[1]

French law is in conformity with Principle 1:2(2) as the competent authority is designated by the State, but there is no choice between judicial and administrative process. This option was considered by the preliminary works of the 2004 reform but was not retained.

Principle 1:3 Types of divorce

Whereas the Principle 1:3 considers only two types of divorce (mutual consent and without consent of the spouses), the French reform of 2004 maintains 4 types of divorce (see 2.1. above). Divorce on grounds of fault remains unchanged, although during parliamentary discussions its suppression has been considered.

---

1   *Traité de droit civil* (2003) chap. 21, p. 570.

One can however group these four types of divorce into two categories corresponding to those stated in Principle 1:3: those which rest on an agreement of the spouses on the divorce itself (divorce by mutual consent and divorce by acceptance of the breakdown of the marriage), and those which do not suppose any particular agreement of a spouse on the divorce itself (divorce for fault and divorce for irretrievable breakdown of the marital relationship). Even then the spouses are encouraged to find an agreement.

2.2. DIVORCE BY MUTUAL CONSENT

Principle 1:4 Mutual consent

The law in France distinguishes between two types of divorce based on an agreement of the spouses on the principle of divorce (Principle 1:4 (2)). On the one hand, there is divorce by mutual consent (C. Civ. article 230) where the spouses agree on the breakdown of the marriage and its effects by submitting an agreement (convention) regulating the consequences of the divorce for the approval of the judge. On the other hand, there is the accepted divorce (C. Civ. Articles 233 and 234) by which the spouses agree on the principle of the breakdown of the marriage with the judge ruling on its consequences. However, French law reserves the designation of "divorce by mutual consent" for the sole case of divorce based on an agreement of the spouses on the principle and its consequences. These two types of divorce correspond to the contents of Principle 1: 4. The spouses, depending on the type of divorce, can make a single or common request (divorce by mutual consent; C. Proc. Civ. Article 1089), just as one of the spouses can file a request approved by the other.

No period of factual separation is required in this ground for divorce as in Principle 1:4 (1).

Principle 1:5 Reflection period

Prior to the reform of May 2004, for divorce by mutual consent a period of minimum 3 months and maximum 9 months for consideration (C. Civ. anc. article 231) was required, between the initial demand for divorce and the reiterated request to which was to be annexed a plan of the regulation of the consequences of the divorce. The Delnatte report (no: 1513) submitted to the National Assembly in the name of the "Commission des lois" in April 2004 reveals that the number of reconciliations at that stage was 0.1.[2]

---

[2]   http://www.assemblee-nationale.fr/12/rapports/r1513.asp.

Since 2004, and to speed up the procedure, no period of reflection is henceforth necessary for divorce by mutual consent, which can be pronounced within a very short time.

Principle 1: 5 on the period of reflection does not have an equivalent in French law. The Principle is relatively complex because its existence depends on several factors which can overlap: the presence of a child of less than 16 years, the disagreement of the spouses on the consequences of the divorce, and the factual separation of more than 6 months. This complexity was desired to encourage agreement between the spouses rather than to favour a hypothetical reconciliation.

One can say that the French reform moves away from the technique advocated by Principle 1:5; it is not very probable that the legislator would reconsider this point since the procedure of divorce has been accelerated considerably. According to the Ministry for Justice, the average duration of a procedure of divorce by mutual consent today is 3.5 months for cases introduced under the Law of May 26, 2004, compared to 9.5 months in 2004. However the French legislation is in conformity with the spirit of Principle 1:5, because the French legislator encourages agreements between the spouses; it is indeed the purpose of the phase of reconciliation planned for all cases of divorce (C. Civ. Article 252).

In the case of divorce initiated by one party and accepted by the other, there is no longer a mandatory minimum period of reflection, but the judge has the possibility of suspending the attempt at conciliation by allowing time for reflection. He can even suspend the procedure at any time to renew this attempt at conciliation within a delay of six months maximum (C.Civ Article 252–2).

Principle 1:6 Content and form of the agreement

In order to simplify the process, the parties' proposal regulating the financial arrangements for their separation and the consequences of divorce relating to the children must be annexed, in writing, to their petition for divorce. Having acquired "the certainty that the will of each spouse is real, and that their consent is free and well understood" (C. Civ., Article 232), the *juge aux affaires familiales* can ratify (*homologuer*) the parties' agreement and grant a decree of divorce, unless he finds that the agreement does not sufficiently protect the interests of the children or one of the spouses, or if the rights and obligations of the spouses are inequitably determined (C. Civ., Article 278 al. 2). In such a case, which is rare, the court can ask for a new agreement to be presented within 6 months. At the end of this period or in the event of refusal to ratify or homologate the agreement, the divorce petition will be null and void. It is possible to appeal this decision.

Principle 1:7 Determination of the consequences

The law of 4th March 2002 sets the principle of the joint exercise of parental authority as a right of the parents of the child (article 372 al. 1), whether they are married or not. The parents can have their agreement on the exercise of parental authority homologated if it complies with the interests of the child. The judge can suggest measures of family mediation.

The usual residence of the child has to be set with one of the parents, or exceptionally with a third person. Nevertheless, the alternate residence is mentioned in the Civil Code (C. Civ., Articles 373-2-9), and the place of residence can be alternated between the parents.

The spouse with whom the children do not usually live always has a right of visit and of lodging (the terms are set by the parents, or in case of lack of agreement, by the judge), except for serious grounds. The same spouse also always has a duty of support and education, which may take the form of a maintenance allowance (*pension alimentaire*) to be paid to the other spouse. This allowance remains liable to modifications depending on the income of the parents, and sometimes on the income of the grown-up child.

Spouses who reach a complete agreement can at any time of the procedure, and whatever the rules applicable, deposit an agreement that definitely settles the consequences of their divorce, enclosing the necessary documents for the compensatory benefit.

compensatory benefit—(article 279-1)—the new possibility for the parties to determine the compensatory benefit in the agreement is very important, as it allows them to set it freely, even if it goes against rules on duration, on conditions of life income, on mode of revision (possibility to increase it for instance), on term setting (new marriage, retirement, common law marriage...);

liquidation of matrimonial regime (article 265-2): the possibility to settle an agreement (convention) of liquidation is extended to all matrimonial regimes, including separation. The spouses, or one of them, can ask the judge to rule on one specific difficulty, which may then allow the liquidation of the regime.

Spouses are then called before the court with the assistance of their lawyers, and the decree of divorce is pronounced during the audience.

All these agreements are homologated by the judge after verification that the interests of each one of the spouses and of the children are sufficiently protected (C. Civ. article 232). This is in conformity with Principles 1:7 (1) and (2)

2.3. DIVORCE WITHOUT THE CONSENT OF ONE OF THE SPOUSES

Principle 1:8 Factual separation

Under French law there are two cases of divorce without consent of the spouses: divorce on grounds of fault and divorce for irretrievable breakdown of the relationship. In all cases of divorce, except for divorce for irretrievable breakdown of the relationship, no minimum period of separation is required by the law contrary to the statement of Principle 1:8.

Only divorce for irretrievable breakdown of marital relationship necessitates a minimum period of separation. This divorce can be initiated when the spouses have been separated for 2 years instead of 6 in the former procedure. This kind of divorce can be petitioned by one of the spouses when the marital bond is definitively altered (C. Civ., Article 237). It is longer than the year of factual separation mentioned in Principle 1:8 but too short for those who criticise this ground for divorce. Divorce for irretrievable breakdown raises strong criticism in France because it is initiated by unilateral will. As in the former procedure of divorce for *rupture de la vie commune* (failure to live as a couple), it is petitioned by the spouse who caused the rupture without any possibility for the other spouse to oppose the petition. The exceptional hardship clause (*clause de dureté*) which allowed the judge to dismiss the petition (former C. Civ., Article 240) has disappeared. Moreover, there no longer exists the obligation for a spouse who petitions for divorce on these grounds to "bear all the expenditures thereof", notably the duty of assistance after the divorce decree.

The issue of separation still raises discussions about the determination of the time limit and the meaning of separation; the breakdown of marital life shall not be simply based on material separation but also on affective grounds.

Principle 1:9 Exceptional hardship to the petitioner

A minimum period of separation is required only in cases of divorce for irretrievable breakdown of the marital relationship. The breakdown of the relationship is presumed when the spouses have lived separately for a minimum of 2 years (art. 238). As previously mentioned, the *rupture de la vie commune* (failure to live as a couple) was a minimum of 6 years before the 2004 Act.

In cases of exceptional hardship, the petitioner can start proceedings and ask the court at the preliminary hearing to regulate the separation and to be allowed to live elsewhere than at the marital home. These provisional measures are valid for 30 months. When the two-year period expires, the spouse requesting the divorce can raise the action for irretrievable breakdown of marriage.

A dispensation of the two-year period is possible when one of the spouses starts divorce proceedings on the ground of fault and the other spouse introduces a counter claim based on irretrievable breakdown of the marital relationship. If the petitioner's action is dismissed—for example the fault cannot be proved—the judge is obliged to grant a divorce on irretrievable breakdown of the marital relationship even if the spouses have not been separated for two years. This is the only exception to the requirement of separation for two years in the case of divorce for irretrievable breakdown of the marital relationship.

If living together is made intolerable by actions constituting "a serious and repeated violation of the duties and obligations of marriage" (art. 242), the petitioner can also raise an action based on fault. No separation period is required.

The 2004 Act abolished Article 243 C. Civ. which allowed one of the spouses to petition for divorce, on the ground of fault, when the other was found guilty of a serious criminal offence.

Principle 1:10 Determination of the consequences

The *juge aux affaires familiales* seeks to conciliate the spouses. This attempt at conciliation is compulsory and may be renewed during the proceedings. The judge must talk in person with each of the spouses separately before bringing them together and then call their lawyers to be present and participate in the talk (C. Civ. Article 252(1)). The aim of the conciliation procedure in the new law seems to be to encourage the spouses to regulate amicably the consequences of divorce rather than to resume their life as a married couple and to abandon the divorce proceedings. At this stage, the court may order provisional measures, taking into account the possible agreement of the spouses (C. Civ. Article 254).

Divorce consequences

Under the 1975 Act, it was only in the case of divorce by mutual consent that the spouses were allowed to deal with the consequences of the dissolution of their marriage (except for questions relating to parental authority, which are now independent from divorce). Now, this possibility is not only extended to all kinds of divorce but is encouraged by the legislator: "During the proceedings, the spouses may submit for the approval of the judge agreements settling all or part of the consequences of the divorce" (C. Civ. Article 268).

Where the spouses cannot reach an agreement, the *juge aux affaires familiales* will give an order regulating the position on an interim basis. The interim order is valid until the judgment granting the divorce, subject to a maximum period of thirty months. The judge can suggest a family mediator (Article 255).

General aspects of parental responsibilities

Since the Act of 4 March 2002, provisions concerning children of parents who are separated are not covered under divorce law but under parental authority (C. Civ., Article 286): "The consequences of divorce for the children shall be settled in accordance with the provisions of Chapter I of Title IX of this Book" (parental authority). Common joint parental responsibility is the statutory rule, before and after divorce: "The father and mother shall exercise parental authority in common" (Article 372) and "Separation of the parents has no influence on the rules of devolution of the exercise of parental authority" (Article 373–2).

The parents can draft an agreement organising "the terms of exercise of parental authority and establish their contributions to the support and education of the child" and submit it to the *juge aux affaires familiales*. "The judge shall approve the agreement unless he observes that it does not sufficiently protect the welfare of the child or that the consent of the parents was not freely given" (C. Civ., Article 373–2–7).

In case of disagreement, the *juge aux affaires familiales* can, in order to decide the terms of exercise of parental authority, take into consideration previous agreements entered into earlier by the parents (Article 373–2–11 §1), feelings expressed by the child (Article 388–1), capacity of each parent to assume his or her duties, and social enquiries reports, among other criteria. The judge will decide which solution is in the child's best interests.

Contact

According to C. Civ., Article 373–2–9 "the residence of a child may be fixed alternately at the domicile of each of the parents or at the domicile of one of them". Before the Act of 4 March 2002, there was no mention in the civil code of "alternating residence" but it was prescribed by some judges.

In exceptional cases, for example when one of the parents is deprived of the exercise of parental authority, "the judge can entrust the child to a third person, chosen preferably within his relatives" (C Civ., Article 373–3).

In most cases, the residence of the child is fixed with one of the parents, usually the mother. The other parent has a right of access and of lodging. The terms of exercise of these rights must be specified.

In case of consensual divorce, the terms are set by the parents. In case of non-consensual divorce, if the parents cannot find an agreement, the *juge aux affaires familiales* determines the residence and contact arrangements according to the best interests of the child.

Generally, the judge determines that the right of access and lodging is free but in the absence of an agreement, this right can be exercised one week-end out of two and half of the school holidays. However, the Civil Code does not envisage any sanction for the parent who would not exercise his or her right of access and lodging.

Child maintenance

Parents, married or not, have the obligation of feeding, supporting and educating their children (C. Civ., Article 203) and each one of the parents has to contribute in proportion to his or her means, to those of the other parent and to the needs of the child (C. Civ., Article 371–2.). The duty of maintenance does not end with the child reaching the age of majority.

Validity of agreements affecting children

Even in the case of non-consensual divorce, the spouses are encouraged to reach an agreement at any time during the procedure. If they reach an agreement as to the consequences of their separation, they will draft an agreement which will be presented to the judge for its homologation.

With the 2004 Act, French law is now in conformity with Principle 1:7 and Principle 1:7 (1) in the case of consensual divorce, and Principle 1:10 in the case of non-consensual divorce: any agreement between the spouses with respect to the children should be taken into account by the competent authority insofar as it is consistent with the best interests of the child.

3. MAINTENANCE BETWEEN FORMER SPOUSES

3.1. GENERAL PRINCIPLES

Compensatory benefits were introduced by the 1975 Act "to compensate, as far as possible, for the disparity that breakdown of the marriage creates in the respective lifestyles" (C Civ., Article 270). In principle, the *prestation compensatoire* was supposed to be paid as a capital sum but the court developed the practice of ordering monthly payments.

The laws of June 30, 2000 and May 26, 2004 reaffirm that compensatory benefit should take the form of a capital payment which may be payment of a sum of money or surrender of property in kind (movable or immovable). Where the maintenance creditor is unable to comply, the court will impose a scheme for payment or transfer which may not extend beyond 8 years (C. Civ., Article 275). In very exceptional circumstances, when the maintenance debtor is unable to meet to his/her own needs by reason of age or state of health, the compensatory benefit can take the form of a life annuity in the form of a monthly payment (*rente viagère*) (C. Civ., Article 276) and this life annuity can be supplemented by the payment of a sum of money.

Payment of a lump sum is the rule and periodical payment is the exception. The judge can allow the combination of various capital sum payments, or of a capital sum payment with an allowance.

Principle 2:1 Relationship between maintenance and divorce

The divorce Bill 2004 had intended to abolish fault as a ground for divorce but this ground was retained in the final version adopted by Parliament. However, with the 2004 Act the financial consequences of divorce are dissociated from the apportionment of blame.

Now, the consequences of divorce due to fault are the same as for other non-consensual divorces. A spouse divorced due to fault will not automatically be deprived of a compensatory payment. It is hoped that this will encourage spouses to negotiate and reach an agreement at an early stage.

Regardless of the type of divorce, the spouses can draft an agreement concerning maintenance and submit it to the *juge aux affaires familiales* at any time in the proceedings (article 268). The spouses need to agree on the amount and the methods of payment. If the agreement protects sufficiently the interests of each spouse and the welfare of the children, the agreement will be ratified by the judge.

If the spouses cannot reach a suitable agreement the judge will determine the compensatory benefits and, as already mentioned, the financial consequences of a divorce are dissociated from the apportionment of blame so fault on the part of the creditor spouse cannot exclude his or her maintenance.

However, fault can still have an impact as compensation can be granted to one spouse who faces consequences of a particular seriousness either when he or she was defendant in a divorce granted for irretrievable breakdown of the marital relationship, or where the divorce was granted against his or her spouse and the blame lies wholly with the latter (C. Civ., Article 266). It seems that article 266 aims to compensate moral wrong (*préjudice moral*) as the *prestation compensatoire* compensates "the disparity that breakdown of the marriage creates in the respective lifestyles" (C. Civ., Article 170).

It is also possible to claim compensation on the basis of C. Civ. Article 1382 (general rule on liability) when a spouse can prove the other spouse's fault.

With the 2004 Act the ground of divorce for *rupture de la vie commune*[3] (failure to live as a couple) has been abolished, so there is no longer a special duty of one spouse to the other financially (*devoir de secours*).

As fault should not affect maintenance claims, all maintenance between former spouses is now subject to the same rules regardless of the type of divorce and *prestation compensatoire* is now the sole form of financial relief.

Principle 2:2 Self sufficiency

The purpose of maintenance is to provide economic support to the dependent former spouse and according to the Principle 2:2 the rule should be self-sufficiency, but a maintenance obligation after divorce can exist between former spouses (Principle 2:3).

According to C. Civ., Article 270, divorce puts an end to the duty of support between spouses and this regardless of the type of divorce. However, the same article states that "one of the spouses may be compelled to pay the other a benefit intended to compensate, as far as possible, for the disparity that the breakdown of

---

[3]   Where one of the spouses became mentally ill without hope of cure or where the spouses had been separated for more than 6 years.

the marriage creates in the respective ways of living". So the *"prestation compensatoire"* (compensatory benefit) is to compensate for any economic imbalance between the parties caused by the divorce.

To promote the independence of spouses following their divorce and in order to obtain a "clean break", the *prestation compensatoire* should take, if possible, the form of capital payment. It is even an obligation in theory (see below).

3.2. CONDITIONS FOR THE ATTRIBUTION OF MAINTENANCE

Principle 2:3 Conditions for maintenance

A compensatory benefit must be fixed according to the needs of the spouse to whom it is paid and to the means of the other, taking into account the situation at the time of divorce and of its evolution in the foreseeable future (Article 271). This article is in conformity with Principle 2:3 on conditions for maintenance.

Principle 2:4 Determining claims for maintenance

In determining the needs and means of the parties, according to C. Civ. Article 271 the court will have regard, in particular, to the ages and states of health of the spouses, to the duration of the marriage and to the time already devoted or that will require to be devoted to the education of the children. The court will also be required to take into consideration the professional qualifications of the spouses and the fact, if relevant, that one of them had to give up a career to devote time to the education of the children or to support the other spouse's career, to the detriment of his own. The court is required to consider any award by reference to the position which will apply (by taking account of matters such as the property that the respective spouses will own) after the liquidation of the matrimonial regime, but must also take into account other benefits of a foreseeable nature, such as rights arising under succession and any retirement pension that will be payable.

Most of the defined criteria in C. Civ. Article 271 are included in the list provided by Principle 2:4. The *prestation compensatoire* aims to "compensate the disparity that breakdown of marriage creates in the respective lifestyles" so the "standard of living during the marriage", even though not mentioned in C. Civ., Article 271, is a factor in determining maintenance.

The only criterion not mentioned in C. Civ. Article 271 is "any new marriage or long-term relationship". A new marriage or long-term relationship can improve or diminish the economic situation of the spouses. As the factors enumerated in C. Civ. Article 271 are not an exhaustive list of circumstances it can be assumed that this criterion can be taken into consideration by the judge in determining the needs and means of the parties (see Principle 2:7). Indirectly, by focusing on the needs of one spouse and the means of the other, C. Civ. Article 271 integrates remarriage and cohabitation the moment they influence, whether by increasing or decreasing, the means of the debtors/creditors. There is much case-law on this question, especially on the review of the compensatory benefit.[4]

There is no standardised maintenance calculation and no detailed guidance for the courts to calculate maintenance. The assessment of maintenance is left to the judge and the amount of maintenance after divorce seems to vary from court to court.

Principle 2:5 Method of maintenance provision

The compensatory benefit must take the form of capital payment (C. Civ. Article 270 §2) which may be payment of a sum of money or surrender of property in kind (movable or immovable). Where the spouse who is required to pay or contribute the capital is unable to comply, the judge will impose a scheme for payment or transfer, which may not extend beyond 8 years (Article 275). There is no time-limit if divorce is by mutual consent.

In exceptional circumstances, the compensatory benefits can be made by way of periodical payments where the age or state of health of the creditor spouse does not allow him or her to meet his or her needs (C. Civ. Article 276). When the benefit is determined by the spouses' agreement for divorce by mutual consent, just as for the other cases of divorce, an agreement on this ground is always possible; it can deviate from a payment in capital without any particular justification. The judge can however refuse to homologate the agreement if it inequitably fixes the rights and obligations of the spouses (C. Civ. Article 278 §2).

Principle 2:6 Exceptional hardship to the debtor spouse

Before the 2004 Act, a spouse against whom the divorce judgment had exclusively been entered could not claim any compensation but the judge could grant him/her some compensation if the marriage had been of long duration and if the

---

4   Civ. 1st, 28 June 2005, no. 02–16556: Bull. 2005 I no. 286 p. 237; 17 September 2003, no. 01–16249, unpublished; Civ. 2nd July 1997, no. 96–10274: Bull. 1997 II no. 211 p. 124.

"guilty spouse" had contributed to the other spouse's professional standing (repealed C. Civ., Article 280–1). With the 2004 Act, the financial consequences are dissociated from the apportionment of blame: where divorce is granted on the basis of the exclusive fault of one of the spouses, that spouse does not automatically lose his or her entitlement to any compensatory benefit.

However, in such a case, the judge can decide to refuse any pecuniary compensation if it appears contrary to equity, considering the particular circumstances of the breakdown (C. Civ. Article 270).

Subsequently, the judge cannot limit or terminate maintenance because of the creditor spouse's conduct.

3.3. SPECIFIC ISSUES

Principle 2:7 Multiplicity of maintenance claims

There is no explicit rule on priority in case of multiplicity of maintenance claims in French law.

When calculating the compensatory benefit, the judge (or the spouses by agreement) must take account of the needs of the spouse to whom it is paid and the means of the other. He therefore needs to consider the totality of the family expenses. Amongst these is the obligation of maintenance and education of the children[5], but also the obligation to contribute to the payments in case of a possible remarriage. Principle 2: 7 only considered the situation where the debtor spouse increases his/her payments. However, one can equally consider that the creditor spouse could be responsible for the education and the upkeep/maintenance of his/her children. Finally, one can suppose that in certain cases, a remarriage will increase the standard of life and the means of the debtor spouse.

Principle 2:8 Limitation in time

As a rule, compensatory benefits take the form of a capital sum payment but where this is not possible, the court will impose a scheme for payment or transfer, which may not extend beyond 8 years (C. Civ. Article 275). When the maintenance debtor is unable to meet his own needs, by reason of age or state of health, the compensatory benefit can take the form of life annuity in the form of a monthly payment (*rente viagère*) (C. Civ. Article 276). This is exceptional.

---

[5]   Cass. 1st civ, 25 January 2005: No. 2005–026645.

Principle 2:9 Termination of the maintenance obligation

As the *prestation compensatoire* is supposed to take the form of a capital sum payment, the full amount has to be paid even if the creditor spouse remarries or establishes a long-term relationship. When deciding upon the *prestation compensatoire*, the judge cannot include conditions that will end the debtor's obligation, such as remarriage. On the contrary, when the *prestation compensatoire* is part of a divorce agreement, the spouses are free to decide that it is for a set period of time and can end upon a certain event mentioned in the agreement (such as remarriage etc.) (C. Civ, Article 278).

Before 2004, on the death of a debtor spouse his/her heirs had to pay the *pension alimentaire* (article 284 in case of divorce for *rupture de la vie commune*) or the *prestation compensatoire* if it was paid as a life annuity (C. Civ., Article 276–2).

The 2004 Act puts an end to this principle as C. Civ. Article 280 now stipulates: "On the death of a debtor spouse, payment of a compensatory benefit, whatever its form may be, must be set apart from the succession. Payment must be borne by all the heirs, who may not be liable for it personally, within the limit of the assets of the succession, and in case they are insufficient, by all the specific legatees, in proportion to their portion of inheritance... Where a compensatory benefit was fixed in the form of capital to be paid on the terms set out in Article 275, the balance of this index-linked capital falls due immediately. Where it was fixed in the form of an annuity, capital falling due immediately must be substituted ..."

The debtor spouse's heir is no longer personally responsible for the payment of the compensatory benefit but the benefit is deducted from the succession. When the succession asset proves to be insufficient, payment will also be supported by all the particular legatees, in proportion to their income. The compensatory benefit is only due within the limits of the succession assets. If the compensatory benefit takes the form of an annuity, it is due until the death of the beneficiary; if it is in the form of capital, it is in principle a claim that is transmitted like all others to the heirs.

Principle 2:10 Maintenance agreement

Under the law of 1975, an agreement on maintenance was only possible in the case of a divorce by mutual consent (C. Civ., Article 230). Since the 2004 Act, such agreement is compulsory in the case of a divorce by mutual consent (C. Civ., Article 278) but is also possible in all other types of divorce and is encouraged at any stage of the proceedings. According to C. Civ., Article 268: "During the proceedings, the spouses may submit to the approval of the judge agreements settling all or part of the consequences of the divorce."

When the agreements can be made

Agreements about maintenance are not allowed before and during the marriage and can only be agreed during the divorce proceedings. The position has recently been confirmed by the Supreme Court[6] and might be justified because an agreement which the spouses have entered into many years in advance can be dangerous and a spouse who, for example, renounces his/her future rights to maintenance should only do so if he/she is fully informed about the financial situation resulting from divorce.

Content of the agreement

The spouses can usually agree on the amount of the maintenance and on the way it will be paid. The spouses can determine freely the compensatory benefit in their agreement, even if it goes against the rules on duration, on conditions of life income, on mode of revision (possibility to increase it for instance) on term-setting (new marriage, retirement, common law marriage…). However, the judge can refuse to ratify (*homologuer*) the parties' agreement "where it fixes unfairly the rights and obligations of the spouses" (C. Civ., Article 278 §2).

4.   GENERAL CONCLUSION

The legislation in France was already close to the Principles recommended by the Commission on European Family Law; the reform of May 2004 served to bring it closer still: reduction of the minimum required duration of the marriage in order to divorce, favouring agreements between spouses on the consequences of divorce, decreasing of the period of factual separation in order to ask for a divorce without consent of the spouse, independence of the allocation of compensatory benefits and of the type of divorce requested.

However, there still exist certain points of divergence, among which one can underline the absence of a required period of reflection before divorce, regardless of any prior agreement between the spouses on the consequences of the divorce or the presence of a child. One of the most important characteristics to remain is the existence of the four different types of divorce in French law, especially divorce on grounds of fault which has no equivalent in the Principles set out by the Commis-

---

6   Cass. 1st civ., 3 Feb 2004, Bull. Civ. I, no. 30.

sion. Excluding divorce on grounds of fault, both divorce by mutual consent and divorce by acceptance of the principle of the breakdown of the marriage can be classed under the category of consensual divorce, one based on the principle and the consequences, the other primarily on the principle. Divorce for irretrievable breakdown of the marital relationship remains comparable, except for the duration of required separation, to divorce without consent of the other spouse.

The legislator had in 2001 considered eliminating divorce on grounds of fault, but the various reports on the reform of family law, presented by Mrs. Irène Théry[7] and Françoise Dekeuwer-Défossez,[8] had stressed the importance of maintaining the sanction of fault and of retaining the obligations and duties of marriage that it entails. This is the case in particular of marital violence, which will most probably be the only important case of divorce for fault.

Nevertheless, it is not unlikely that in the long term, this ground of divorce will disappear. Indeed, it has lost much of its specificity since the attribution of a compensatory benefit no longer depends on the apportionment of fault. It has also lost some of its attraction since the reform: according to statistics from the Ministry of Justice, 36.7% of the divorce procedures in 2004 were on grounds of fault, with the number dropping to 29.2% in 2005. At the same time, divorce by mutual consent increased from 49.6% to 59.9%.[9]

---

7   THERY, I (dir.) *Couple, filiation et parenté aujourd'hui : le droit face aux mutation de la famille et de la vie privée*, (1999, Ministère de la justice et ministère de l'emploie de la solidarité, la documentation française).

8   DEKEUWER-DEFOSSEZ, F (dir.) *Rénover le droit de la famille : propositions pour un droit adapté aux réalités et aux aspirations de notre temps*, (1999, Ministère de la justice, la documentation française).

9   JOAN 18 Juill. 2006, p. 7629.

DIVORCE SYSTEM AND MAINTENANCE OF FORMER SPOUSES IN SCANDINAVIAN COUNTRIES

Urpo Kangas

1. THE MYTH OF JOINT SCANDINAVIA AND THE MYTH OF THE JOINT LEGISLATION IN NORDIC COUNTRIES

The concept of Scandinavia was originally, and still is, a geographical one. The peninsula of Scandinavia covers the area where Norway and Sweden are located. Scandinavia, as a political concept, first gained prominence during the 19th century. The extension of the political concept of Scandinavia was and is much wider than its geographical counterpart. The political concept of Scandinavia encapsulates an expression of joint aims and goals of this political movement. The essence of Scandinavianism is integrated in the idea of there being a joint Nordic culture of all Nordic countries.

The most active group among the earliest supporters of Scandinavianism consisted of lawyers. By the end of the 19th century they had already organised a series of meetings and this tradition still carries on. At their meetings these lawyers discussed joint legal problems facing all Nordic countries. Concrete proposals were also drafted regarding joint legislation. During the 1930s Denmark, Norway, Sweden and Finland had many committees, which tried to work out a solution to the "Scandinavian legislation" question. In this respect the project was successful. As a result the Nordic countries got quite similar legislation in the area of marriage, inheritance, insurance and contract law. The main part of this legislation is still in force in all five countries. This co-operation was limited only to the area of civil law, and never extended to cover the area of public law.

The effort to harmonise the Nordic legislation is understandable if the historical reasons and the close political connections between the Nordic countries are taken into account. For example, the fundamental premise of the Finnish civil law originally rested upon the Swedish counterpart due to the fact that Finland was a part of (the state of) Sweden until 1809. Swedish legal tradition retained its prominence even while Finland was a part of Russia from 1809 to 1917. Much in the same way Danish legal tradition was actually at the same time Norwegian legal tradition, because Norway was, for a long time, a part of Denmark. The co-operation between Nordic countries has also been possible for linguistic reasons, because the Nordic languages (Danish, Swedish, and Norwegian) all originate from the same language group.

Taken at face value, the unity of Nordic legislation seems apparent. However, a closer inspection provides an alternative account. In fact, the legal institutions seem to be similar in different Nordic countries only if they are analysed from a distance. Spouses for instance, can in every country get a divorce, make a will or sign a marriage settlement. However, the micro structure of these institutions differs from one Nordic country to another. The similarity of the civil law system in Scandinavia is merely an illusion rather than a reality in a broad sense. Hence, the issue at stake concerns the similarity of only some special laws in Nordic countries. It is noteworthy to emphasise that the similarity concerns some special laws only and should not be taken as an indicator that the legal systems function according to the same principles in all legislative matters.

My task in this article is to compare the divorce regulations and the maintenance of the former spouse in these five respective Nordic countries. The purpose is to evaluate whether it is possible to adopt the CEFL (Commission on European Family Law) Principles regarding divorce and maintenance in Nordic countries. The comparative part of this chapter acts as an analytical tool and the evaluation of the question at hand uses that as a reference point. The manner in which this study proceeds follows the order of the CEFL Principles.

2. THE COMPULSORY END OF JOINT FAMILY LIFE DURING AND AFTER MARRIAGE

The CEFL Principles of European Family Law do not contain any enactments concerning the compulsory end of joint family life without necessary connection to the divorce process. Finland is the only Nordic country where an institution dealing with problems arising from this particular situation is in force. The history of this institution is closely connected to the history of the regulation of divorce. According to the Finnish Marriage Act, since coming into force in 1988, one of the spouses has had the right to make a petition to the court as part of the divorce process demanding an immediate leaving order to the other spouse. If the petition is considered legitimate by the court, the other party to the marriage must, by necessity, leave the common home. The idea and goal of this institution was to offer protection to the weaker party in the case of family violence.

In connection with the reform of the divorce system the future of the old institution became of interest. Because the planned and later accepted divorce system was a non-fault divorce system, the legislator considered it necessary to have a remedy to protect the weaker party in the family crisis. The selected remedy in this case was the compulsory end of joint family life during and after marriage. The following is a description of the contents of this system.

Upon either the joint petition of the spouses or the petition of one of the spouses, a court of law may decide that the spouse who is in greater need of a residence shall have the right to continue residing in the common home, order the other spouse to vacate the common home and give the spouse in need the right to use movables that belong to the other spouse. Petition for the compulsory end of joint family life is possible during the marriage prior to the petition on divorce or in connection to the divorce process. The decision of the court shall be immediately enforceable even if it is not yet final or otherwise ordered in the decision. The decision shall be in force until further notice, but it shall lapse after two years from the date of the decision.

In connection with the case concerning the end of joint family life, the spouse may request a court order confirming maintenance and the custody of a child or visiting rights, as well as any other order relating to the case concerning the end of family life.

3. GENERAL PRINCIPLES OF DIVORCE

3.1. PERMISSION OF DIVORCE

The starting and the leading point of the divorce Principles of the CEFL is the permission of divorce. According to Principle 1:1.1 the law should permit divorce. This principle is easy to accept. Divorce itself has not posed any problems in the Nordic countries since the 16th century. Divorce has been permitted in all Nordic countries for many centuries, but in the past the number of divorce grounds was limited to adultery and some other, similar fault based reasons.

According to Principle 1:1.2 no duration of marriage should be required as the condition of divorce. A right to divorce is independent of the duration of marriage in every Nordic country. For instance, in Finland the rate of divorce is approximately 13 000 per year and of those, about 100 marriages have lasted for less than one year. This is a clear example of the importance of obtaining a right to get a divorce immediately in cases where the marriage has failed. Perceived from the society's point of view there is no function in forcing people in failed marriages to find some other solution to their problems than permitting them to divorce. The door to freedom must be open in these kinds of cases.

The right to get a divorce after a very short marriage is justified especially in Sweden and in Finland due to the fact that the institution of annulment of the marriage is not in force any more. The only way to terminate the marriage *inter vivos* is a divorce in these countries. In the Nordic perspective this is an exception as the institution of annulment is still in force in Denmark and Iceland. In Norway if a marriage has been solemnised despite the fact that one or both parties lacked legal capacity, proceedings to have the marriage declared null and void may be brought within six months after the solemnisation.

The right to give a petition for divorce immediately after the solemnisation of marriage and the right to get divorce immediately after the rapid divorce process are two different things. Even though a spouse can make a petition immediately after the solemnisation, it is not at all clear that she or he will get divorce in a short time after the petition has been submitted. In Sweden if the spouses agree that their marriage should be dissolved, they shall be entitled to divorce without a reconsideration period only in the case where neither of them is living on a permanent basis with a child of his or her own who is less than 16 years old. If they have such a child, divorce is possible only after an appropriate reconsideration period has been completed. The length of that period is six months. After the termination of that period, a decree of divorce shall be granted if either of the spouses then submits a separate application for such a decree.

In Finland the basic divorce case is always where the spouses have the right to a divorce after the period of consideration has been completed. Immediately after the six-month minimum period of consideration, the spouses shall be granted divorce upon their joint request or upon the request of one of the spouses. The request must be made within one year from the beginning of the period of consideration. However, if the spouses have lived separately continuously for the past two years, the spouses shall have the right to divorce without the otherwise mandatory period of consideration. This is so with respect to Finland, Sweden, Denmark and Norway.

Nevertheless, the divorce system in Scandinavia is not coherent and similar in all realms in these five countries. In Norway, Iceland and Denmark the divorce systems consist of two elements: decision on separation and decision on divorce. The institution of "separation" differs from the institution of "period of consideration" in the following manner: "separation" ceases to have legal effect, if the spouses continue or resume cohabitation. During the "period of consideration" spouses may live together and still make a petition for divorce.

In Norway and in Denmark each of the spouses may demand a divorce when they have been separated for at least one year. If they both have reached a consensus on divorce, in Denmark the spouses can make a joint petition for divorce after six months of separation,

If the meaning of Principle 1:1.2 (no duration of the marriage should be required) is that a divorce system cannot include any delaying mechanism after the petition for divorce has been made, only the Swedish legislation is in balance with Principle 1:1.2. Furthermore, this requirement would be fulfilled only in cases where the spouses have made a joint petition and do not have children under the age of sixteen. But, if the meaning of the Principle is only to prohibit a solution where the possibility to get a divorce is limited to those cases where the marriage has lasted some definitive time before the petition is allowed, all the Nordic countries can accept Principle 1 without any reservations.

3.2. PROCEDURE BY LAW AND COMPETENT AUTHORITY

The second of the CEFL Principles (1:2) is a very general one. According to the first part of the Principle, divorce procedure should be determined by law. The only meaning of this Principle is to emphasise that a divorce process is a secular matter. Nevertheless, it could be possible (without its coming into a conflict with the second Principle) to allow in the legislation a solution where the right to give a divorce belongs, e.g. to a Sharia court in cases where both spouses are Islamic. According to me the formulation of the Principle 1:2 has failed. From the Scandinavian point of view, however, it is easy to accept a principle according to which the right to make a decision regarding divorce belongs always to the state authority. This is the state of affairs in all Nordic countries.

The divorce process is always a matter of court procedure in Finland and Sweden. The competent court in both countries is the local district court. In Norway separation and divorce are granted by County Governor whether or not the parties are in agreement. However, the decision shall be made by a court if the question is divorce on grounds of abuse or is some other atypical divorce case. In Denmark, if the spouses are unanimous they can submit a petition for divorce as an administrative procedure at the state county office.

The content of the procedural rules in divorce matters in Nordic countries varies from one country to another. Despite this variation, it is possible to accept the original idea behind CEFL Principle 1:2 even though the formulation of the Principle could have been better than it is.

3.3. TYPES OF DIVORCE

According to CEFL Principle 1:3, law should permit divorce by mutual consent as well as divorce without the consent of one of the spouses. In all Nordic countries this principle is easy to accept. In both Finland and in Sweden one of the spouses alone may submit a petition for divorce. If the petition has been filed by one spouse only, the court shall grant the other spouse an opportunity to be heard. From a legal point of view the possibility to be heard is a mere formality. If a spouse does not take up this possibility, it will not stand in the way of making a decision in a case at hand. In short, the law permits two types of divorce in all Nordic countries: divorce by joint petition and divorce without mutual consent.

According to the comment on the Principles, neither fault nor irretrievable breakdown of marriage are grounds for divorce under the Principles. However, it is noteworthy that this is not the logical consequence of CEFL Principle 1:3. Divorce without consent of one spouse can be based also on fault grounds. For example, in Norway a spouse may demand divorce if the other spouse has intentionally attempted to kill him or her or their children or wilfully exposed them to severe maltreatment. The same applies if that spouse has behaved in a manner that is likely to arouse grave fear of such behaviour.

3.4. DIVORCE BY MUTUAL CONSENT

CEFL Principle 1:4 consists of many sub principles. The main Principle is nevertheless the first 1:4.1: Divorce should be permitted based upon the spouses' mutual consent. Sub Principles 1:4.2 and 1:4.3 express the refinement of the mutual consent. According to Principle 1:4.2, mutual consent is to be understood as an agreement between the spouses that their marriage should be dissolved. This agreement may be expressed according to Principle 1:4.3 by a joint application of the spouses or by an application by one spouse with the acceptance of the other spouse.

In terms of all Nordic countries the divorce legislation is quite liberal. The legislation is based upon a commonly agreed premise allowing one spouse to make an effective petition for a divorce alone. Thus, in comparison to the CEFL Principles, such as that of treating the whole idea of mutual consent as an expression of an irretrievable breakdown of marriage seems very strange from the Scandinavian point of view. Despite the minor fractions in perceptions concerning the right to divorce, the recommendations of the CEFL Principles are nevertheless acceptable from the Nordic point of view.

According to CEFL Principle 1:4.1, the divorce legislation should not require any period of factual separation as a condition for divorce by mutual consent. The concept of factual separation can be understood in at least two different ways. Firstly, it can be understood as a condition of a period under which the spouses *must* live apart *before* they are allowed to apply for divorce. This meaning seems to have been in the minds of those who formulated the Principles. In this sense it is possible to accept CEFL Principle 1:4.1 in all Nordic countries.

The particular time during which the spouses live apart from one another voluntarily, can gain legal relevance in those cases when the time spent living apart is not long enough. If the spouses have lived apart for at least two years, either of them shall be entitled to divorce without a preceding reconsideration time. This rule has been accepted in Finland, Sweden, Norway and Denmark. Regarding the three first aforementioned countries the reasons behind the spouses' decision to live apart are not of relevance. A normal situation is that one of the spouses has worked abroad. In Denmark and Iceland it is mandatory for the spouses to present evidence proving that the reason for the factual separation arises from a disagreement between spouses. From the Scandinavian point of view some kind of two-year rule should also be included in the leading principles of divorce in Europe.

Secondly, Principle 1:4.1 can also be understood as a condition of a certain period of time *after* the preliminary court decision, during which the spouses must live apart before they can make a final request for divorce. In Norway, Denmark and Iceland for example, the spouses can demand a separation from the first phase of divorce. After the separation decision, one of the spouses must leave the joint home and move to live elsewhere. If the spouses continue living together or resume cohabitation, separation ceases to have legal effect. The institution of separation differs in this point radically from the institution of consideration. In Finland and in Sweden spouses can continue living together during the period of consideration. The length of that period, as was mentioned earlier, is six months. The final decision on divorce is possible only after the period of consideration. Only in Sweden can the spouses get divorce by mutual consent immediately without a period of consideration and only on the condition that they do not have children younger than sixteen years of age.

The Swedish and Finnish legislation fulfils the criteria of Principle 1:4.1 according to which no period of factual separation should be required. Instead of an obligatory period of factual separation, a six-month delay of divorce has been accepted in those countries. That kind of reconsideration period can form a guarantee against too hasty divorce petitions.

The CEFL Principles 1:5 and 1:6 belong closely together. The question is: should the criteria set for divorce differ depending on whether the spouses have no children, opposed to a situation where the spouses have got children. According to the CEFL Principles the answer is: yes. If the spouses have no children under the age of sixteen and they have agreed upon all the consequences of the divorce, no period of reflection shall be required. And in a case where the spouses have children, the length of the period of reflection can vary from three months up to six months. Only in cases where the spouses have agreed upon a) their parental responsibility, b) child maintenance, c) the division or reallocation of property and d) spousal maintenance in a written document, the period of reflection could be three months.

From the Scandinavian point of view these kinds of restrictions and compulsions are unnecessary elements of a divorce system. Although noble at the level of ideas, in practice these kinds of restrictions can rarely prevent divorce taking place in the first instance.

If Principles 1:5 and 1:6 are adopted, it seems to me that there are too many elements mixed up in the divorce process that ought to be kept separate. For example, according to the Icelandic law parents' disagreement about custody and support payments for children shall not prevent a divorce or a legal separation being granted upon a claim from either of them, provided other conditions are fulfilled. In terms of Finland, in a case regarding a divorce or end of cohabitation, the court shall, upon its own initiative, consider how the custody and visiting rights of the child/ren of the spouses should be arranged in the best interests of the child/ren.

3.5. DIVORCE WITHOUT THE CONSENT OF ONE OF THE SPOUSES

According to CEFL Principle 1.8, divorce should be permitted without consent of one of the spouses if they have been factually separated for one year. From the Scandinavian point of view, divorce must always be possible without the consent of one of the spouses, but the possibilities should be wider than those in Principle 1:8.

In Finland, the spouses have the right to divorce without a period of consideration, if they have separated and lived apart from each other for the past two years without interruption. In this case divorce is possible without the consent of one of the spouses. In Sweden and Norway, the spouses have the same right to get divorced, if they have lived apart for at least two years. The reasons for the separation are irrelevant and either of the spouses can file a petition of divorce independently and without the consent of the other.

In Iceland and Denmark, if the spouses have discontinued their cohabitation by reason of their discord, each may claim divorce when they have lived separately for the last two years.

The regulation of divorce without the consent of one of the spouses in Scandinavia is not coherent in all Scandinavian countries. In Sweden and in Finland, one of the spouses can submit a petition for the dissolution of the marriage. The period of consideration shall start to run when the petition of one spouse is served upon the other spouse. After a six-month minimum period of consideration, the spouses shall be granted divorce upon the request of one of the spouses or upon their joint request. The spouses can live together during the period of consideration both in Sweden and in Finland. This type of divorce without the consent of one of the spouses should be included in the CEFL Principles.

In Norway, Denmark and Iceland the divorce process is divided into two phases. In the first phase one of the spouses must request legal separation. During the time of separation (which is six months) one of the spouses must move away from the joint home, because the effects of legal separation shall terminate if the spouses continue their cohabitation. In Norway, Denmark and Iceland each spouse shall be entitled to divorce when one year has elapsed from the date a permit for legal separation was issued or judgment pronounced.

3.6. EXCEPTIONAL HARDSHIP TO THE PETITIONER

In Sweden and in Finland the divorce systems can be described as pure non-fault systems. There are no extra grounds for a divorce when one of the spouses is "guilty" in the divorce. In Sweden and in Finland the divorce system is built on the principle of divorce on demand.

In Norway, in Iceland and in Denmark however, the divorce systems are some kind of combination of non-fault divorce system and fault divorce system. In Iceland one of the spouses may claim divorce in a case where a spouse either commits adultery or evinces conduct analogous thereto. The same shall apply if it is established that one spouse has committed physical assault or a sexual offence directed against the other spouse or a child residing at their home, provided the act was committed wilfully and, in the case of physical assault, resulted in an injury or damage to the health of the victim. Action shall be brought or claim submitted within six months from the time that a spouse became aware of such offence or conduct and within two years from the time of its commission.

In Norway a spouse may demand a divorce if the other spouse has intentionally attempted to kill him or her or their children or wilfully exposed them to severe maltreatment. The same applies if the spouse has behaved in a manner that is likely to arouse grave fear of such behaviour. A demand for divorce must in these kinds of cases be submitted within six months after the spouse learned of the act, and not later than two years after it took place. Similar rules are in force in Denmark.

3.7. DETERMINATION OF THE CONSEQUENCES

According to CEFL Principle 1:10.1, where necessary, the competent authority should determine (a) parental responsibility, including residence and contact arrangements for the children, and (b) child maintenance. Any admissible agreement of the spouses should be taken into account insofar as it is consistent with the best interests of the child.

In Nordic countries the spouses have a right to agree about the custody and the child's maintenance in connection to divorce matters. For instance, in Finland the parents may agree 1) that they have joint custody of the child; 2) that the child is to reside with one of them, if they are not living together; 3) that one of them has sole custody of the child and 4) that the child has the right to maintain contact and meet with the parent with whom he/she no longer resides, in the manner agreed upon by the parents. An agreement on child custody and right of access shall be made in writing and submitted for confirmation to the social welfare board in the municipality where the child has his/her residence. When considering whether to approve the agreement, the social welfare board shall take the best interests and the wishes of the child into account. An agreement confirmed by the social welfare board shall be valid and enforceable similar to a final court decision. In a similar way the parents can make an agreement on maintenance of a child. In most divorce cases the parents make an agreement on the custody of a child, an agreement on the contact rights of a child and an agreement on maintenance before they (or one of them) submit a petition for divorce. In the divorce process they only present the agreement to the court.

Without going into the technical differences of this legislation, it is possible to say that the principles of custody and maintenance are very similar in all Scandinavian countries.

The second part of CEFL Principle 1:10.1 states that the competent authority may determine the economic consequences for the spouses, taking into account any admissible agreement made between them. This principle is very important, because the property of the former spouses is often the only source of economic security after the divorce. Most of the Scandinavian matrimonial property systems are built according to the principle of deferred community of property. After the divorce, the matrimonial property should effectively be split in two halves. In all Nordic countries the starting point of the division is the autonomy of the parties to make an agreement of the division. In Sweden and in Finland, if the spouses are unable to make a contract the court shall appoint, on petition, a suitable person as the distributor of matrimonial property. The distributor has the competence to make a division of the matrimonial property after divorce. A spouse who wishes to contest a distribution carried out by a distributor shall bring an action against the other spouse within six months of the distribution.

4. MAINTENANCE BETWEEN SPOUSES

4.1. MAINTENANCE DURING THE MARRIAGE

The CEFL Principles do not mention maintenance during marriage. This has, nevertheless, been an important starting point to the whole question. During the marriage each spouse shall, according to his or her abilities, participate in the common household expenses of the family and maintenance. The maintenance of the spouses includes, according to the Finnish Marriage Act for example, fulfilling the common needs of the spouses as well as the personal needs of each spouse. The duty to participate in the common household expenses and the maintenance of the spouses is obligatory and the spouses cannot make an agreement during the marriage that they do not have any maintenance duties to each other.

The consequence of this duty is very important in many respects. One such example is when one of the spouses must leave the common home to go to an old-age home. In that case this spouse still has a duty to participate in the maintenance of the common household as well as of the spouse who lives in the joint home of the spouses and vice versa. A balance must be found between the right of the spouse to get maintenance from the other spouse who is living in the old-age home and between the size of his/her payment for the care he/she is receiving at the old-age home.

In all Scandinavian countries the spouses have a joint responsibility for the maintenance of the family. In Iceland maintenance shall include all reasonable necessities for keeping the matrimonial home and fulfilling other common needs, the upbringing and education of children, and the personal needs of each of the spouses. Maintenance contributions of a spouse shall be made in the form of monetary payments, domestic work or other support of the family. The contributions shall be shared between the spouses according to their capabilities and conditions. The same kind of rule is in force in Norway, Denmark and Sweden.

4.2. MAINTENANCE BETWEEN FORMER SPOUSES

There is a systematic connection between the matrimonial property system and the maintenance law. If the matrimonial property system shall give economic security to the spouses after the divorce by dividing the net value of the matrimonial property into two halves, the spouses are on equal terms as owners after the divorce. They have the same economic possibilities to safeguard their independent lives after the divorce has taken place, and in all Nordic countries the matrimonial system guarantees a part of the matrimonial property to the spouses after divorce. This is the main rule. The second rule is the following: After divorce has been granted one spouse shall not be ordered to pay alimony to the other, except in very exceptional circumstances.

According to CEFL Principle 2:1, maintenance between former spouses should be subject to the same rules regardless of the type of divorce. This is so in all Nordic countries.

CEFL Principle 2:2 states that each spouse should provide his or her own support after divorce. According to Norwegian law the mutual obligations of spouses cease to exist upon separation and divorce. But, if the ability and opportunity of a spouse to ensure adequate support have been reduced as a result of caring for children of the marriage or of the distribution of joint tasks during the cohabitation, the other spouse may be ordered to pay maintenance.

4.3. CONDITIONS FOR THE ATTRIBUTION OF MAINTENANCE

Maintenance after divorce should be dependent upon the creditor spouse having insufficient resources to meet his or her needs and the debtor spouse's ability to satisfy those needs. This CEFL Principle 2:2 consists of two sub principles: the "need" principle and the "ability" principle.

For example, according to Finnish law when the spouses are granted a divorce and one spouse is deemed to be in need of maintenance, the court may order the other spouse to pay him or her the maintenance deemed reasonable in view of his or her ability and other circumstances.

In Sweden, on the other hand, the main rule is that each spouse shall be responsible for his or her own support after divorce. If a contribution to the maintenance of either spouse is needed for a transitional period, a spouse shall be entitled to receive maintenance payments from the other spouse on the basis of what is reasonable in view of the latter's ability and other circumstances

In Norway maintenance shall be assessed based on the need for maintenance of the person who is entitled to receive it and on the ability of the person liable to pay maintenance to make such a contribution. In Iceland the solution must accord with the earning ability of the claimant and the financial capabilities of the other spouse. In Denmark the situation is the same.

CEFL Principle 2:2 and the content of the legislation of Nordic countries seem to be in balance. Hence, Principle 2:2 is easy to accept as a starting point for European legislation.

4.4. DETERMINING CLAIMS FOR MAINTENANCE

Perhaps the most difficult problem in the whole of a maintenance system is to quantify the just amount of maintenance in a particular case. It is an exhaustive task to answer this question with respect to one legal culture, let alone in relation to the totality of European legal cultures. The principles of need and ability give only a rough guideline in determining claims for maintenance.

CEFL Principle 2:4 consists of six criteria, which should be taken into account in decision making for maintenance. These criteria are (1) the spouses' employment ability, age and health, (2) the care of children, (3) the division of duties during the marriage; (4) the duration of marriage: (5) the standard of living during the marriage and (6) any new marriage or long-term relationship.

In Sweden the main rule after a divorce is that each spouse shall be responsible for his or her own support. This starting point already implies that the amount of alimony cannot be very high in a single case. The amount of alimony must always be reasonable in view of the ability of the debtor spouse and other circumstances. In practice this means that the typical amount of alimony (and only for the short period of transition after divorce) fluctuates between 220–870 euros per month in Sweden. The decision in maintenance cases is typically an "all things considered" decision. However, when assessing the right of a spouse to get maintenance, his or her right to acquire pension insurance must be taken into account.

In Finland the situation is similar to that of Sweden. According to Finnish law the amount of alimony must be reasonable in view of spouses' ability and other circumstances. In practice the amount of alimony is lower than in Sweden and the whole maintenance system plays only an extremely marginal role in divorce cases. For instance, during the past ten years the Supreme Court has given less than 10 decisions in maintenance cases. Only in two of those cases was the former spouse entitled to maintenance. In KKO 1993:78, it was ruled that the former spouse was entitled to maintenance for a transition period of 4 years and 5 months after the divorce and the amount of alimony was set at 200 euros per month. In KKO 1992:33, the Supreme Court decided that the length of the transition period was two years whilst the amount of the alimony was set at 679 euros per month.

In Norway the former spouse has the right to maintenance only if his/her ability and opportunity to ensure adequate support has been reduced as a result of caring for children of the marriage or of the distribution of joint tasks during cohabitation. The amount of the maintenance shall be assessed on the basis of the need principle and the ability to pay principle. The main rule is that the right for maintenance is limited. Maintenance shall be ordered for a limited period not exceeding three years. Only if the marriage has lasted for a long time or if there are other special reasons, maintenance may be ordered for a longer period or without any time limit. The amount of the alimony is directly dependent upon the financial ability of the other spouse. In Rt.1992 s. 1098, the court found that the yearly income of a man in question exceeded 44,000 euros. The income of the former wife, who had lived at home during the marriage, was a little bit more than 7000 euros. Thus, she was granted the right for maintenance without any time limit at a rate of 540 euros per month.

In Iceland the amount of alimony after divorce is rendered with regard to the earning ability of the claimant and the financial capabilities of the other spouse. Any other relevant facts shall be taken into account, including the duration of the marriage and any need of the claimant for education or rehabilitation, if applicable.

In Denmark the right of the former spouse to maintenance depends on his or her need and the ability of the other spouse. According to the law the length of marriage is an important factor in determining the right for maintenance. If the spouses have high enough incomes, the former spouse has no right for maintenance even if the income of the other spouse is twice as high and even if the marriage has lasted a long time before it terminated in divorce. Some instructions on the maximum and minimum alimony to the former spouse have also been outlined by the administrative practice. For example, the former spouse cannot get alimony if his or her income is higher than 26,700–32,000 euros per year. According to the minimum rule, the former spouse has the right to alimony if his or her monthly income is lower than 2,200 euros per month.

In Finland obligation to pay maintenance lapses if the spouse to whom maintenance is granted remarries. The same rule is in force in Norway, Denmark and Iceland. Even though there is not a similar rule in Sweden, the right of the former spouse to get maintenance is almost always limited to a short transition period.

4.5. METHOD OF MAINTENANCE PROVISION

According to CEFL Principle 2:5.1, maintenance should be provided at regular intervals and in advance. This is the state of affairs in all Nordic countries. But in theory a competent authority may order a lump sum payment upon the request of either or both spouses, taking into account the circumstances of the case. The lump sum payment is possible according to Finnish, Swedish, and Norwegian law. As far as I am aware this possibility is not used in court praxis.

4.6. EXCEPTIONAL HARDSHIP TO THE DEBTOR SPOUSE

This CEFL Principle 2:6 is formally not relevant in a divorce system, if the system is a pure non-fault system as in Sweden and Finland. But it can be of relevance in a divorce system that still retains elements characteristic to the fault divorce system. This is the situation in Denmark, Norway and Iceland, where the exceptional hardship to one spouse still forms an independent ground for divorce. In practice, the exceptional hardship, such as domestic violence, shall be taken into account also in pure non-fault systems in maintenance cases. This is possible, because the criteria for maintenance is so open that it allows one to hide behind these covert arguments in decision making.

4.7. SPECIFIC ISSUES

4.7.1. Multiplicity of maintenance claims

According to CEFL Principle 2:7, in determining the ability of the debtor spouse to satisfy the needs of the creditor spouse, the competent authority should (a) give priority to any maintenance claim of a minor child of the debtor spouse and (b) take into account any obligation of the creditor spouse to maintain a new spouse. Even though there is no special rule about the priority of the maintenance of a minor child as against the maintenance of the former spouse, in the case law of all Nordic countries this priority has been accepted. And because a judgment concerning maintenance may be adjusted by the court if there are reasons to do so in view of the circumstances having changed, the obligation of the debtor spouse to maintain a new spouse is one factor which can possibly be taken into account in decision making. This is the state of affairs in all five Nordic countries.

4.7.2. Limitation in time

CEFL Principle 2:8 states that the competent authority should grant maintenance for a limited period, but may exceptionally do so without a time limit. This principle seems to be very similar to the Norwegian solution. In Norway, according to the special rule, maintenance shall be ordered for a limited period not exceeding three years. If the marriage has lasted for a long time, or if there are other special reasons, maintenance may be ordered for a longer period or without any time limit.

In all other Nordic countries the situation is the same. The maintenance provided for the former spouse after divorce is an exception to the main rule, according to which the mutual obligations of spouses (including the duty to participate in the common household of the family and the maintenance of the spouses) cease to exist upon divorce. If the need for maintenance is established, the right to acquire it is conditional. The competent authority may restrict the right to get alimony to a certain period.

4.7.3. Termination of the maintenance obligation

CEFL Principle 2:9 defines the circumstances when the obligation to pay alimony to a former spouse ceases. The first criterion is the remarriage or long-term relationship of the creditor spouse. In Finland, Norway, Denmark and Iceland obligation to pay maintenance shall lapse if the spouse to whom the maintenance is granted remarries or lives in registered partnership. There is no special rule in the Swedish legislation in case of a remarriage, but the right to maintenance in Sweden is limited to three years after the date on which the payment originally became due.

In the Scandinavian countries informal long-term relationship does not automatically end the maintenance obligation, but it can be a sign of the changed circumstances. A judgment or agreement concerning maintenance may be adjusted by the court if there are reasons to do so in view of the circumstances having changed.

According to CEFL Principle 2:9.3, the maintenance obligation should cease upon the death of either the creditor or the debtor spouse. This is an important principle, which is not implemented directly in legislation either in Finland, Sweden or Norway. In Iceland and Denmark the duty to pay alimony shall cease upon the death of either of the former spouses.

4.7.4. Maintenance agreement

The last CEFL Principle 2:10, concerns the possibility of the spouses to make an agreement concerning maintenance after divorce. The agreement should be in writing and it may concern the extent, performance, duration and termination of the maintenance obligation and the possible renouncement of the claim to maintenance. In order to be certain that the agreement is just, the competent authority should at least scrutinise the validity of the maintenance agreement.

All the Scandinavian countries accept an agreement concerning maintenance after divorce. In Sweden such an agreement may be adjusted by the court if there are reasons to do so, such as those brought about by a change in the circumstances. A maintenance agreement may also be adjusted by the court if the agreement is unreasonable when perceived either in view of the circumstances which existed when it came into being or in view of the overall circumstances. In Finland the spouses may also conclude a mutual contract on maintenance. According to the law such a contract shall be concluded in writing and it shall be presented for confirmation to the Municipal Board of Social Welfare. Before confirming the contract, the Board of Social Welfare shall consider whether the contract is deemed reasonable in view of the spouses' need for maintenance, the ability of a spouse to pay maintenance and other relevant circumstances. A confirmed contract shall be enforced like a final court decision. A maintenance agreement concluded by the spouses may be changed if it is deemed to be unreasonable. The situation is the same in Denmark.

In Norway and Iceland the spouses may enter into an agreement regarding maintenance. If spouses have agreed between themselves to pay alimony or agreed on the amount thereof, their agreement may be changed by a judgement if its continued implementation would clearly be unreasonable owing to changed circumstances.

5. CONCLUSION

Even though there is not a coherent legal system in Scandinavia, the CEFL Principles of European Family Law regarding Divorce and Maintenance between Former Spouses could be adopted with ease into the existing framework in all Scandinavian countries. The question of reception of these Principles is political rather than practical, moral or technical.

Sources of laws:

The Marriage Act of Denmark (originally from 1922)
The Marriage Code of Sweden (from 1987)
The Marriage Act of Finland, (originally from 1930, remarkable changes 1987)
The Marriage Act of Norway (from 1991)
The Marriage Act of Iceland (from 1993)

ENGLAND AND WALES JUXTAPOSED TO THE EUROPEAN PRINCIPLES OF FAMILY LAW

REBECCA PROBERT

1. INTRODUCTION

In evaluating the possibility of adopting *The Principles of European Family Law Regarding Divorce and Maintenance Between Former Spouses* into the law of England and Wales, two connected but distinct issues need to be considered. First, is there anything in the *Principles* that would constitute a radical breach with the current law as a matter of either policy or practice? Secondly, would incorporation of the *Principles* be feasible from a political point of view? The answer to the first is not conclusive as to the answer that would be given to the second: what is desirable as a matter of legal logic may not be feasible as an issue of political reform. The following discussion will identify those aspects of the *Principles* that might be particularly problematic from a political point of view, but will focus mainly on the first issue.

2. REFORMING DIVORCE LAW

Divorce reform in England and Wales has never been straightforward. It was one of the few Protestant countries not to make provision for divorce after the Reformation, and it was not until 1857 that it became possible to obtain a divorce from a court.[1] In modern times, the main opposition to divorce reform has come from outside Parliament.[2] It is to be regretted that the fact that the proposals for reform are inspired by the desire to harmonise family law within Europe is likely in itself to generate opposition from certain sections of the press. An issue that presents the opportunity for both moral posturing and the demonstration of anti-European sentiments is likely to be seized upon with glee in the tabloid press. Such

---

[1] See STONE, L, *Road to Divorce* (Oxford: OUP, 1990).
[2] Note in particular the furore generated by the (unimplemented) Family Law Act 1996.

opposition will be taken for granted in the following discussion, which will consider whether any substantial objections could be made to the proposals.

2.1. THE PRINCIPLE THAT THE LAW SHOULD PERMIT DIVORCE AND THAT NO DURATION OF THE MARRIAGE SHOULD BE REQUIRED

That the law should permit divorce is now uncontroversial, since it is no longer feasible to believe that marriages can be saved in any real sense by restricting divorce.

That the law should permit a couple to divorce immediately after the wedding is, on the face of it, inconsistent with the law as it now stands, which requires that a minimum period of one year should elapse between the celebration of the marriage and a petition for divorce. However, it is less clear whether the one-year bar is fundamental to the law of divorce in England and Wales.

The first point to note is that the current one-year absolute bar on petitioning for divorce is a relatively recent innovation in the divorce law of this jurisdiction. When divorce was first introduced in 1857 there was no such limitation.[3] In fact, eighty years were to elapse before a time bar was introduced by the Matrimonial Causes Act 1937. The intention behind the introduction of the time bar was to encourage couples to work at their marriage (and also to bolster the claim of the Bill's proponents that the reform would support marriages).[4] The restriction on petitioning for divorce within the first three years of marriage was, however, not an absolute one: High Court judges had a discretion to allow earlier petitions to be presented in cases of "exceptional hardship suffered by the petitioner or exceptional depravity on the part of the respondent."[5]

It was rational to have no bars on petitioning for divorce when the law drew a sharp distinction between the "innocent" and the "guilty" spouse, since by definition the innocent spouse should not be expected to remain with the guilty partner. It could be argued that it is equally rational to have a time bar when the ground for divorce is that the marriage has broken down irretrievably, on the basis that those actions that would previously have been regarded as grave matri-

---

[3]   Indeed, even the two-stage process of decree *nisi* and decree absolute was not introduced until 1860: see s. 7 of An Act to amend the Procedures and Powers of the Court for Divorce and Matrimonial Causes 1860, which provided that a decree *nisi* could not be made absolute for three months.

[4]   See HERBERT, AP, *The Ayes Have It* (1937), p. 65.

[5]   Matrimonial Causes Act 1937, s. 1.

monial faults are in fact issues that may be resolved with appropriate support. Yet the 1937 reform was not dictated by this consideration, since divorce remained largely fault-based until 1969 (the only exception being that divorce was available on the ground of a spouse's incurable insanity). Moreover, when the Law Commission considered the issue in the 1980s it noted that "[g]iven that the sole ground for divorce is the irretrievable breakdown of marriage it is difficult to deny the theoretical inconsistency between that ground and the restriction on petitioning in the early years of marriage."[6]

Despite this theoretical inconsistency, the Law Commission remained convinced that "some restriction on the availability of divorce in the early years of marriage should be retained."[7] As a result of its recommendations the three-year discretionary bar was changed to a one-year absolute bar by the Matrimonial and Family Proceedings Act 1984. Do the justifications offered for this view have any relevance over two decades later? It is clear that the Commission regarded the issue as one of social policy rather than legal theory. It noted the subtle effect of the law in shaping "an attitude of mind"[8]—although the evidence that many people were ignorant of the restriction before seeking a divorce might suggest that this was not a particularly powerful argument.[9] It also referred back to the views it had expressed in 1966 that the restriction "is a useful safeguard against irresponsible or trial marriages and a valuable external buttress to the stability of marriages during the difficult early years."[10] But the profile of newly-weds has changed since 1966, and even since 1982. In 1966 the mean age of brides marrying for the first time was 22.5, and by 1982 it had only risen to 23.3.[11] By contrast, in 2003 it was 28.9: it is no longer plausible to suggest that young couples are rushing into marriage. Moreover, the "difficult early years" will, for most, have been spent cohabiting. Pre-marital cohabitation was rare in the 1960s—fewer than five per cent of first-time brides reported cohabiting with their future husbands—and tended to be for a fairly short period.[12] By contrast, the vast majority of modern marriages are preceded by a lengthy period of cohabitation.[13] Such demographic changes mean that it is unlikely that the one-year bar performs the function it once did.

---

6   LAW COMMISSION, *Family Law: Time Restrictions on Presentations of Divorce and Nullity Petitions* (London: HMSO, 1982), Law Com No. 116, para. 2.16.

7   *Ibid*, para. 2.9.

8   *Ibid*, para. 2.14.

9   *Ibid*, para. 2.15.

10   *Ibid*, para. 2.14, quoting *The Field of Choice* (1966) Law Com No. 6 Cmnd. 3123, para 19.

11   Birth Statistics 1837–1983, Historical Series FM1 No. 13, table 1.6.

12   HASKEY, J "Cohabitation in Great Britain: past, present and future trends—and attitudes" (2001) 103 *Population Trends* 4, p. 10.

13   *Ibid*, p. 12.

In addition, there are a number of arguments in favour of dispensing with the current bar. First, it should be noted that even in 1982 there was "a considerable body of opinion which saw no case for retaining a restriction."[14] Secondly, the current bar does not serve any practical purpose in that it is only a bar on petitioning for divorce, rather than a bar on separating from one's spouse. There is nothing to prevent a couple from separating immediately after the ceremony. Other remedies are available during the first year of marriage: not only the protective measures that are available to any couples,[15] but also judicial separation.[16] Nor is there any requirement that the parties should use the one-year period to undertake marriage counselling or make other attempts to save their marriage. Finally, it does not appear that the bar is particularly effective in encouraging couples to work at their marriage in its early years. Of the 153,490 marriages dissolved by divorce in 2003, 3,288 had lasted less than two years.[17] It is interesting to compare this with the position in Scotland, which has no bar on divorce in the first year of marriage. Here, of the 11,227 divorces in 2004, a mere eight involved marriages that had lasted for less than one year, and only 68 had lasted less than two years. To reduce this into percentages, a mere 0.6 per cent of marriages in Scotland lasted less than two years, despite the lack of any bar on divorce in the early years, while 2 per cent of marriages in England and Wales lasted less than two years, despite the one-year bar.

There is one argument in favour of such a bar that was not canvassed by the Law Commission in 1982 and which is itself the product of changing social conditions, namely the problem of sham marriages entered into for immigration purposes. However, since the marriage must last for at least two years before the immigrant spouse is granted indefinite leave to remain,[18] the one-year bar clearly serves no additional purpose in this context.

In short, the current one-year bar is inconsistent with the ground for divorce and was designed in the light of social conditions that have now changed out of all recognition. It is highly unlikely that any minimum duration would have been introduced had it not been for A. P. Herbert's proclaimed view that divorce should be available "in the genuine hard cases, without making it too easy for the merely irresponsible or foolish."[19] This was implicitly acknowledged by the Law Commission when it pointed out that the key issue was not the message sent by a law of which the vast majority of the population was ignorant, but rather the message

---

[14] See *supra* note 6 at para. 2.9.
[15] E.g. non-molestation orders under the Family Law Act 1996, s. 42.
[16] Matrimonial Causes Act s. 17.
[17] *Marriage, Divorce and Adoption Statistics*, Series FM2 2003, table 4.9.
[18] *MacDonald's Immigration Law and Practice* (London: Butterworths, 2005), para. 11.69.
[19] See *supra* note 4 at p. 65.

sent by a *change* in the law.[20] Despite the political difficulties in changing the law, it seems clear that the approach proposed in the *Principles* would have little effect in practice.

2.2. THE PRINCIPLE THAT DIVORCE SHOULD BE GRANTED BY A COMPETENT BODY

The proposal that divorce should be granted by a competent body, either judicial or administrative, is unproblematic, since it is clearly consistent with the current procedure. Indeed, it appears from the review that other jurisdictions are considerably more demanding in usually requiring the parties' appearance before a court. The misleadingly named "special procedure" used by over 99 per cent of divorcing couples is judicial in form but administrative in nature, since the parties are not required to attend court and the judge only has the information supplied by the parties when deciding whether or not to grant a divorce. As Wilson J. noted in *Bhaiji v Chauhan*,[21] the continued use of the term "special" in this context "well illuminates the time-warp in which the law and practice governing the dissolution of marriage have become caught."[22]

At present divorces can only be granted by the High Court or certain county courts, but there are proposals to create a unified Family Court whereby those courts would share jurisdiction with the family proceedings courts (i.e. those magistrates' courts that have a family jurisdiction),[23] and the assumption would be that cases would "start at the lowest possible level."[24] While the *Principles* themselves do not require England and Wales to move to an administrative procedure, it is suggested that such a reform would be desirable, and could usefully be included in any package of reforms designed to give effect to them.[25] The fact that no specific grounds for divorce would need to be satisfied under the scheme proposed is a further argument for making divorce an administrative process.

---

20 See *supra* note 6 at para. 2.15.
21 [2003] 2 F.L.R. 48.
22 At para 5.
23 DCA, *A Single Civil Court? The Scope for unifying the civil and family jurisdictions of the High Court, the county courts and the Family Proceedings Courts*, (CP 06/05).
24 DCA, *Focusing judicial resources appropriately: The Right Judge for the Right Case* (CP25/05), p. 26.
25 As proposed by CRETNEY, S, "Private Ordering and Divorce - How Far Can We Go?" [2003] *Family Law* 399.

2.3. THE PRINCIPLE THAT THE LAW SHOULD PERMIT DIVORCE BY MUTUAL CONSENT WITHOUT ANY PERIOD OF SEPARATION

At first sight this would appear to be a radical departure from the current law of England and Wales, which only allows divorce by mutual consent where the parties have been separated for two years.[26] Indeed, English law was for long suspicious of any hint of agreement between the parties: prior to 1963 any agreement between the parties would have been termed collusion and—if discovered—would have led to a divorce being refused. When the possibility of divorcing by consent after two years' separation was introduced in 1969 it was expected that this would become the most popular ground for divorce, and that it would enable divorce to become a more civilised procedure. In practice, the practical difficulties raised by this provision—the necessity either of moving into alternative accommodation or leading separate lives under the same roof—means that it has never matched the popularity of the fault-based grounds for divorce.

It is true that in recent years an increasing number of petitions have been based on this ground—34 per cent in 2004, in contrast to 24 per cent in 1991—but it is clear that it is still only used by a minority of petitioners. This is likely, however, to be due more to the necessity of waiting for two years before petitioning for divorce rather than to a desire to allocate blame. It might also be argued that under the current law spouses who are in accord in their desire to divorce, if in nothing else, may choose for one of them to base a petition on fabricated faults,[27] since the opportunities for the court to investigate the truth of the allegations in the petition is extremely limited. For obvious reasons it is impossible to ascertain how many of the petitions apparently based on the fault of one spouse conceal an essentially consensual divorce, but the available evidence does not suggest that it is the majority. Research by Walker found that only 38.3 per cent of respondents in her study wanted a divorce—and in some of these cases no doubt a new relationship was both the fact cited in the petition and the reason for the respondent's desire for a divorce.[28]

Two factors mitigate the differences between the current law and the system proposed in the *Principles*: first, the fact that a period of separation would be required in certain circumstances,[29] and, secondly, the possibility that the proposed sys-

---

[26] Matrimonial Causes Act 1973, s. 1(2)(d).
[27] See e.g. DAVIS, G and MURCH, M, *Grounds for Divorce* (Oxford: Clarendon Press, 1988), p. 83.
[28] WALKER, J, *Picking up the Pieces: Marriage and Divorce Two Years After Information Provision* (DCA 2004).
[29] Principle 1.5.

tem would in fact be a better way of achieving the objectives of the current law. After all, the principle of divorce by mutual consent was accepted in 1969 in the hope that divorce would become a more civilised process, but it would appear that the current requirement of two years' separation is frustrating this aim. Moreover, since 1969 there has been a distinct shift towards emphasising the importance of agreement and co-operation within other areas of family law, not just in relation to the agreement of the division of assets on relationship breakdown but also in the context of the arrangements to be made for the children. All the indications are that divorce by mutual consent would be welcomed by both the general public and legal professionals. Ninety per cent of respondents to the Law Commission's public opinion survey in the late 1980s felt that immediate divorce by mutual consent was acceptable.[30] Similarly, a more recent study of policy-makers noted that "it was marked how the vast majority of study participants strongly favoured the introduction of a non-fault framework."[31]

There would be objections to divorce by mutual consent being the *only* option for the legal termination of a marriage, since this would give rise to the risk that the spouse who is more desirous of obtaining a divorce—perhaps to be able to formalise a new relationship, perhaps to obtain freedom from a violent spouse— would have to pay for the other's consent by accepting a lesser degree of provision on divorce. However, such objections do not apply with the same force to the possibility of divorce being accelerated by mutual consent.

The ability of spouses to agree that their marriage is at an end does not necessarily indicate that they will also be able to agree on the arrangements to be made for themselves and any children. It is perhaps fortunate that there is no suggestion that such matters should be resolved before the divorce is granted, else the process of obtaining a divorce might take rather longer than at present.[32] The matters on which divorcing spouses are to be required to reach agreement include parental responsibility, the residence and contact arrangements for the children, maintenance (both for the children and the spouse, as appropriate) and the division or reallocation of property. Under English law parental responsibility would not be an issue, as both spouses would automatically have parental responsibility for their children and would continue to have parental responsibility after the divorce. Parents are encouraged to agree upon the residence and contact arrangements for their children, and the majority are able to do so without litigating. Divorcing couples are also entitled to agree on the level of child and spousal maintenance to

---

30 Law Commission, *Family Law: The Ground for Divorce* (Law Com. No. 192, 1990), para. 3.13.
31 HASSON, E, "Wedded to 'fault': the legal regulation of divorce and relationship breakdown" (2006) Legal Studies 267, at p. 272.
32 Note the concerns expressed by the Law Commission in 1990, *supra* note 30, at para. 5.56.

be paid, but are not entitled to agree that *no* maintenance will be paid. Any such agreement may be disregarded by the Child Support Agency or the courts. The *Principles* are, however, sufficiently flexible to accommodate the approach of England and Wales in this regard, since although agreement is encouraged, whether or not such agreements are binding on the matters is left to national authorities to decide.[33]

As with the removal of the one-year bar, to allow divorce by mutual consent without any delay might be seen as facilitating the speedy termination of marriages entered into solely for immigration purposes that have served their function. The reality of the current system, however, is that couples who have conspired to flout the immigration laws are unlikely to be concerned about colluding to present a case for divorce and obtaining a speedy divorce on manufactured fault grounds. The special procedure offers little opportunity for the genuineness of the petitioner's claim to be tested. It is true that divorces were denied to a number of couples in *Bhaiji v Chauhan*[34]—the suspicions of court staff having been aroused by a number of identically-worded claims of unreasonable behaviour—but this case is likely to be the exception rather than the rule. In any case, it would be preferable for the law to focus on preventing sham marriages rather than denying a divorce in such cases.

On balance, the shortening of the necessary period of separation, while on the face of it a departure from the current law, would perhaps be a better way of achieving the aims that underpinned the 1969 reforms. Were the period of separation to be shorter, the incentive to secure freedom by alleging fault on the part of the respondent would be lessened, and this would reduce one potent cause of acrimony in the current divorce process.

2.4. THE PRINCIPLE THAT THE LAW SHOULD PERMIT UNILATERAL DIVORCE AFTER A PERIOD OF SEPARATION, SAVE WHERE DELAY WOULD CAUSE EXCEPTIONAL HARDSHIP TO THE PETITIONER

At present, unilateral no-fault divorce is only available after the parties have been separated for five years.[35] The fact that the period of separation required is so lengthy is no doubt due to the fact that this option was introduced in 1969 and constituted a significant break with the previous fault-based approach. It conse-

---

[33] See p. 40.
[34] [2003] 2 F.L.R. 48.
[35] MCA, s. 1(2)(e).

quently behoved the legislature to exercise caution, although even the demanding requirement of five years' separation did not prevent opponents of the bill dubbing it a "Casanova's charter." While this ground proved popular in the immediate aftermath of the Act's coming into force, as long-separated spouses took the opportunity to divorce, this back-log of cases was soon cleared. Almost forty years on it is clear that relatively little use has been made of this option, no doubt because of the length of the required separation. Add to this the evidence that allegations of fault may increase conflict between the spouses and there is a strong argument for reducing the required period of separation to increase the use that is made of this more neutral option. Indeed, there is a precedent in English law for the possibility of divorce after one year's separation being accepted, in the Family Law Act 1996. While the Act was never implemented, this was not on account of the central principle that divorce should be available after a period of time.

The fact that one party may be the victim of domestic violence or other extreme behaviour might suggest that there would be a need to shorten any period of separation still further and allow an immediate divorce in such cases. Yet the availability of immediate divorce on the basis that delay would cause exceptional hardship seems at odds with the removal of fault from the process in other respects. The statement in the *Principles* that "fault is not necessary"[36]—since what matters is the effect on the petitioner—should not obscure the fact that such an option is guaranteed to lead to allegations of spousal fault. The points made by the Law Commission in 1982, in considering the then rule that a petition for divorce could not be brought in the first three years of marriage save in cases of exceptional hardship on the part of the petitioner or exceptional depravity on the part of the respondent, are also relevant. It pointed out that "it seems that the making of the allegations thought to be necessary to ensure that leave is given often causes considerable bitterness, distress and humiliation even to the extent of jeopardising any reasonable settlement between the parties about financial provision and arrangements for custody of and access to children."[37] It should be noted that under the current law of England and Wales, it is not in fact the case that an immediate divorce is available on the basis that the respondent has behaved in such a way that the petitioner cannot reasonably be expected to live with him or her:[38] as with all of the five facts upon which a petition can be based, at least one year must have elapsed from the celebration of the marriage before a petition for divorce can be presented to the court.

---

[36] At p. 58.
[37] Law Commission, *supra* note 6, at para. 2.5.
[38] C.f. the suggestion in the *Principles,* p. 58.

The proposal that the period might be shortened in cases of exceptional hardship would be difficult to reconcile with the underlying philosophy that has governed divorce law in England and Wales for the last forty years, namely that if a marriage has irretrievably broken down it should be dissolved with the minimum bitterness, distress and humiliation.[39] It should also be noted that the fact that a spouse is prevented from seeking a divorce would not leave him or her unprotected: other legal remedies may be available, short of terminating the legal tie.[40] It might be preferable to rely on these other remedies to provide protection, rather than allowing the divorce to be accelerated.

In line with the general thrust of the *Principles*, there is no suggestion that a divorce may be *denied* on the basis of hardship to the respondent. In English law, by contrast, if a petition if based on five years' separation there is the possibility that a divorce will be denied to the petitioner if the respondent would suffer grave financial or other hardship as a result of the divorce and it would be wrong in all the circumstances to dissolve the marriage.[41] This defence was introduced to reassure those concerned about innocent spouses being divorced against their will. In practice, it has proved of limited effect: the hardship in question must be the result of the divorce, rather than of the breakdown of the marriage and consequent separation of the parties, and the allocation of assets on divorce may compensate for the loss of any pension rights that were contingent on spousal status. There is only one reported case in which the court exercised its discretion to deny a divorce, and this occurred over 30 years ago.[42] The removal of any such defence would reflect both the greater powers of the courts to reallocate assets and the reality of divorce law in practice.

Finally, in relation to the consequences of a divorce being granted, it should be noted that the *Principles* are somewhat more demanding than the current law in stipulating that agreement between the spouses should be taken into account "insofar as it is consistent with the best interests of the child."[43] Under the current system there is relatively little scrutiny of consent orders.

Although the grounds for divorce are likely to attract considerable comment and opposition, in reality, since a divorce is obtainable sooner or later, it is the *conse-*

---

[39] Law Commission, *Reform of the Grounds of Divorce—The Field of Choice* (1966).
[40] Thus for example a spouse who was the victim of domestic violence could seek a non-molestation order prohibiting a recurrence of the violent behaviour, as well as an occupation order requiring the other to leave the matrimonial home, under the Family Law Act 1996.
[41] Matrimonial Causes Act 1973, s. 5.
[42] *Julian v Julian* (1972) 116 S.J. 763.
[43] Principle 1.10.

quences of divorce that are now of more practical importance, and to which we shall now turn.[44]

3. MAINTENANCE BETWEEN FORMER SPOUSES

England and Wales are relatively unusual among the jurisdictions surveyed in treating periodical payments as part of the package of orders that can be made on divorce rather than separating the issue of property division from the issue of maintenance. In recent years there has been a move towards equal division of the assets where this is fair to both spouses,[45] and this has had an effect on the use of periodical payments, since ongoing payments by one spouse may be needed to leave the parties in a position of broad equality.[46] The recent decision of the House of Lords in *Miller v Miller; McFarlane v McFarlane*[47] has introduced a new dimension, namely the application of compensatory principles in order to address any economic disadvantage suffered by one spouse as a result of the marriage. On the facts of *McFarlane*, such compensation had to be achieved by way of periodical payments, since the capital assets of the parties were not sufficient for this purpose. Lord Nicholls emphasised that periodical payments were not limited to payments needed for maintenance, and that different principles applied to periodical payments intended to compensate a spouse and those intended as post-divorce support. It is thus rather difficult, and somewhat artificial, to disentangle the provision of maintenance from the broader context of financial provision on divorce generally. Accordingly, while the following discussion will focus on maintenance in the traditional sense of ongoing payments intended to meet the needs of the recipient, the wider role of periodical payments should be borne in mind, and any potential conflict with the *Principles* noted.

Another potential problem in considering whether the *Principles* could be incorporated into English law arises out of the extremely discretionary nature of the current law. This means that while points of convergence may be found between the exercise currently carried out by the courts under the Matrimonial Causes Act 1973 and the *Principles*—particularly since judges are currently required to have regard to all the circumstances of the case—it is the overall effect of the provisions that needs to be considered.

---

44   See CRETNEY, S, "Breaking the Shackles of Culture and Religion in the Field of Divorce?" in K. BOELE-WOELKI (ed) *Common Core and Better Law in European Family Law*, Intersentia, Antwerp 2005.

45   *White v White* [2000] 2 F.L.R. 981; *Lambert v Lambert* [2002] EWCA Civ 1685.

46   The number of orders made for periodical payments increased sharply in the wake of *White v White* [2000] 2 F.L.R. 981 but has since fallen back again.

47   [2006] UKHL 24.

3.1. THE PRINCIPLE THAT MAINTENANCE IS NOT DEPENDENT ON THE TYPE OF DIVORCE

This principle reflects the current law of England and Wales, since the fact that forms the basis for the court's inference that the marriage has irretrievably broken down has no influence on the way in which assets are divided. Whether it would be possible or desirable to excise considerations of fault completely is considered further below.

3.2. THE IDEAL OF SELF-SUFFICIENCY

The law of England and Wales contains a number of provisions designed to promote a clean break between the parties. The court must, for example, consider whether it would be appropriate to exercise its powers in a way that ensures "that the financial obligations of each party towards the other will be terminated as soon after the grant of the decree as the court considers just and reasonable."[48] As Baroness Hale noted in *Miller; McFarlane*:

> Periodical payments are a continuing source of stress for both parties. They are also insecure. With the best will in the world, the paying party may fall on hard times and be unable to keep them up. Nor is the best will in the world always evident between formerly married people. It is also the logical consequence of the retreat from the principle of the life-long obligation. Independent finances and self-sufficiency are the aims.[49]

Yet, despite such explicit statutory and judicial endorsements of the desirability of self-sufficiency, the courts have made it clear that this is not the main objective of the courts when dividing assets on divorce.[50] Moreover, the House of Lords in *Miller; McFarlane* suggested that a clean break was not appropriate if periodical payments were intended as compensation rather than as maintenance. While in practice relatively few orders for periodical payments are made, the judiciary favour the retention of a wide discretion in order to deal with deserving cases.

---

[48] MCA s. 25A(1).
[49] At para. 133.
[50] *Clutton v Clutton* [1991] 1 F.L.R. 242.

3.3. NEEDS-BASED MAINTENANCE

It goes without saying that an order for maintenance can only be made if one spouse has the resources to make payments to the other. More problematic is the suggestion that maintenance "should be dependent upon the creditor spouse having insufficient resources to meet his or her needs."[51] As noted above, periodical payments are not used merely for the purposes of maintenance. It would in theory be possible to draw a distinction between periodical payments intended to meet the needs of one of the parties and those granted with the purpose of compensating the recipient or leaving the parties on an equal footing, but this would be a somewhat artificial exercise and would complicate the existing discretionary scheme.

3.4. FACTORS TO BE TAKEN INTO ACCOUNT

The factors listed in principle 2.4 are not dissimilar to those set out in s. 25(2) of the Matrimonial Causes Act 1973. The latter explicitly requires courts to have regard to the duration of the marriage and the standard of living enjoyed by the parties during it,[52] while responsibility for the care of children and the division of duties during the marriage are factors taken into account when assessing the contribution that each party has made to the welfare of the family.[53] Indeed, the House of Lords in *Miller; McFarlane* drew on the same language of "compensation" when discussing the appropriate provision to be made for a wife who had given up her career to care for the children of the marriage. Employment ability, age and health are also listed in s. 25,[54] while any new relationship would be a relevant factor in evaluating the parties' needs and responsibilities.[55] In any case, neither list is exhaustive, leaving it open for other relevant factors to be taken into account as the case requires. Moreover, the meaning of each of these relatively broad factors is to be determined by national law, although the option of meeting only those needs arising out of the relationship itself is clearly regarded with disfavour in the Principles,[56] while it received judicial endorsement in the judgment of Baroness Hale in *Miller; McFarlane*.

---

[51] Principle 2.3.
[52] Matrimonial Causes Act s.25(2)(d) and (c) respectively.
[53] *Ibid*, s.25(2)(f).
[54] *Ibid*, s.25(2)(a), (d) and (e) respectively.
[55] *Ibid*, s.25(2)(b).
[56] See p. 93.

3.5. THE MODE OF PROVIDING MAINTENANCE

English law already contains a number of provisions designed to enforce the regular payment of periodical payments, so the stipulation that maintenance should be provided regularly and in advance could be incorporated without difficulty. The possibility of providing one spouse with a lump sum would not in itself be problematic, since the English courts have a wide range of powers at their disposal in deciding how the assets should be divided upon divorce. Under the current system, of course, such an award would not necessarily be conceptualised as maintenance, but might instead be directed at awarding compensation or ensuring equality.

3.6. CIRCUMSTANCES IN WHICH MAINTENANCE SHOULD BE DENIED

The fact that fault is to be—at least for the most part—irrelevant to the maintenance awarded is consistent with the approach adopted by English law over the last thirty years. As Lord Denning MR noted in the early 1970s, in *Wachtel v Wachtel*:[57]

> There will no doubt be a residue of cases where the conduct of one of the parties is ...
> "both obvious and gross", so much so that to order one party to support another whose
> conduct falls into this category is repugnant to anyone's sense of justice... But, short
> of cases falling into this category, the court should not reduce its order for financial
> provision merely because of what was formerly regarded as guilt or blame.

While there is evidence that divorcing parties may want fault to be reflected in the provision made on divorce—and even that perceptions of fault may be an element in the provision agreed between the parties themselves[58]—the courts have for the most part followed the approach set out in *Wachtel*. A recent judicial attempt to reintroduce considerations of fault into the process was firmly rejected by the House of Lords in *Miller; McFarlane*. As Lord Nicholls pointed out, "in most cases misconduct is not relevant to the bases on which financial ancillary relief is ordered today. Where, exceptionally, the position is otherwise, so that it would be inequitable to disregard one party's conduct, the statute permits that conduct is to be taken into account."[59] The terminology of "exceptional hardship" would give

---

[57] [1973] Fam. 72.
[58] See e.g. WRIGHT, K, "The divorce process: a view from the other side of the desk" (2006) 18(1) *Child and Family Law Quarterly* 93, at p. 101.
[59] At para. 65.

sufficient scope for the more extreme cases—including financial misconduct—to be taken into account, as at present.[60]

3.7. MULTIPLICITY OF MAINTENANCE CLAIMS

The requirement that "priority" should be given to the maintenance claim of a child of the paying spouse is in accordance with the current practice in this jurisdiction, even if the statutory direction is rather weaker than that contained in the *Principles*. While s. 25(1) of the Matrimonial Causes Act 1973 merely states that "first consideration" is to be given to the welfare of any minor child of the family, and even though the courts have emphasised that "first" does not mean "paramount",[61] in practice the courts have made it their priority to ensure that any children and their primary carer have first call on any resources.[62]

This, however, assumes that the child in question is living with the spouse in receipt of maintenance. There is a difference between the concept of the "child of the family" under the Matrimonial Causes Act—who might not be the biological child of the debtor spouse but will at least have been treated by both spouses as a child of the family—and the "child of the debtor spouse" in the *Principles*—who will necessarily be the biological child of the debtor but may not have shared a home with the creditor spouse at any stage. The interests of the latter are not the "first consideration" for the courts of England and Wales. In practice, however, the obligations of a spouse under either the Child Support Act or a private agreement would be taken into account as part of that spouse's obligations and responsibilities.[63]

The same is true of any new spouse of the debtor spouse, and the *Principles* reflect the flexible approach that is taken to new obligations of this kind. There is a broader debate as to whether obligations to a new spouse are a factor that may justify a departure from equality in dividing the capital assets,[64] but this would not affect the issue of maintenance. Nor do the *Principles* prevent practical obligations to other dependants—for example a new cohabitant—being taken into account as a matter of national law.

---

60   See e.g. *Evans v Evans* [1989] 1 F.L.R. 351; *Clark v Clark* [1999] 2 F.L.R. 498; *Le Foe v Le Foe and Woolwich plc* [2001] 2 F.L.R. 970.
61   *Suter v Suter* [1987] 2 F.L.R. 232.
62   See e.g. *B v B (Financial Provision: Welfare of Child and Conduct)* [2002] 1 F.L.R. 555.
63   Matrimonial Causes Act 1973 s. 25(2)(b).
64   Contrast *S v S (Financial Provision: Departing from Equality)* [2001] 2 F.L.R. 246, with *H-J v H-J* [2002] 1 F.L.R. 415.

3.8. TIME-LIMITED

Under the current law, if periodical payments are ordered, then the court must consider whether it would be appropriate to specify a term,[65] and it may also direct that no application should be made in the future to increase that term.[66] Despite the statutory direction to consider whether a clean break would be appropriate, English law is more generous than the *Principles*, in that it does not require that the circumstances should be "exceptional" before maintenance without limit is ordered. Indeed, the middle-aged wife who has not been in paid employment for a number of years is an all-too-familiar figure in the law reports.[67] Self-sufficiency may be a vain hope in such cases. It might be preferable if the *Principles* were to state that maintenance should only be provided without limitation in "compelling" circumstances, which would ensure consistency with the current approach of the English courts.

3.9. CIRCUMSTANCES IN WHICH MAINTENANCE SHOULD CEASE

The suggestion in the *Principles* that maintenance should cease upon the marriage or long-term relationship of the recipient, or the death of either party, is largely consistent with the current law. At present periodical payments will terminate if the recipient remarries or enters into a civil partnership.[68] By contrast, the treatment of informal long-term relationships is left to the discretion of the court: under the current law the courts may decide that on the facts of the particular case payments of maintenance to a person who has formed a new relationship should cease, but there is no absolute rule to this effect.[69] As Thorpe L.J. noted in *Fleming v Fleming*, cohabitation is not to be equated to marriage for these purposes.[70] It is clear that this approach is influenced by the consideration that the new cohabiting relationship would not give either party rights against the other's assets. If the *Principles* were to be incorporated, there would no doubt be considerable debate as to what exactly constitutes a "long-term relationship", this point being left to the national courts to decide. There is an obvious risk that a relationship deemed by the legal authorities to be "long-term" may

---

[65]   MCA s. 25A(2).

[66]   MCA s. 28(1A).

[67]   See e.g. *Flavell v Flavell* [1997] 1 F.L.R. 353.

[68]   Matrimonial Causes Act 1973 s. 28(1)(a).

[69]   Although it is apparently common "for orders for periodical payments to specify that the order will terminate in the event of the recipient cohabiting for more than six months with a third party": Law Com No. 179, para. 6.273.

[70]   [2003] EWCA Civ, para. 9.

prove in practice to be short-lived. This is less of a problem for those jurisdictions which confer rights on cohabiting couples, but at present the courts in England and Wales do not have the power either to reallocate property or to order maintenance for an ex-cohabitant.[71] However, if the Law Commission's recent consultation paper on the rights of cohabiting couples should lead in due course to legislation conferring rights on such couples, it might be thought reasonable that a new relationship would have the effect of terminating the obligations of a former partner.[72]

3.10. MAINTENANCE AGREEMENTS

At present, divorcing spouses are allowed—and even encouraged—to make their own arrangements regarding their finances upon separation. While spouses cannot agree to oust the jurisdiction of the court,[73] the courts start from the position that a solemn and freely negotiated bargain should be adhered to unless there is a clear and compelling reason to do otherwise.[74] While there is no formal requirement that a separation agreement be contained in writing, it is unlikely that the courts would regard an unwritten agreement as carrying the same weight (quite apart from the obvious problems of proof).

A large number of such agreements are enshrined as orders of the court, if the parties request the court to make a consent order. This process does entail some limited scrutiny of the terms of the agreement. However, there is no requirement that the parties should bring any agreement they have reached before the court, and it would appear that a significant proportion of divorcing spouses choose not to do so in practice. In 2005, the courts made only 10,946 property adjustment orders, 9,470 lump sum orders and 4,721 orders for periodical payments.[75] When this is contrasted with the 142,393 divorces granted that year, it will be obvious that a substantial number of couples are eschewing avoiding the judicial system. Given the current emphasis not only on agreement but also upon diverting divorcing couples away from the courts altogether, any suggestion that the courts should

---

[71] Although provision for a child of the relationship may include an element for the child's carer.

[72] This point was specifically canvassed by the Law Commission in its consultation paper: see *Cohabitation: The Financial Consequence of Relationship Breakdown: A Consultation Paper* (2006), Law Com No. 179, para. 6.280.

[73] Matrimonial Causes Act 1973, s. 34.

[74] See e.g. *Edgar v Edgar* [1980] 1 W.L.R. 1410; *G v G (Financial Provision: Separation Agreement)* [2000] 2 F.L.R. 18.

[75] *Judicial Statistics 2005*, tables 5.6 and 5.7.

take on a greater role in relation to couples who are happy to make their own arrangements is unlikely to find favour with the legal establishment.

Rather different issues arise in relation to pre-nuptial contracts, which do not carry the same weight as an agreement made upon separation. While such contracts may be taken into account as part of all the circumstances of a case, their significance will depend very much on the facts of each individual case.[76] However, assuming that the scope of the proposed judicial scrutiny of the validity of such an agreement would be wide enough to allow for the agreement to be disregarded if it were to be unfair to either party, this would not pose a problem for the incorporation of the *Principles*.

4. CONCLUSION

It is perhaps somewhat paradoxical that those *Principles* relating to the grant of a divorce might in fact be easier to incorporate into English law than those relating to awarding maintenance, even though at first sight the English law of divorce would appear to take a very different approach, while the law relating to financial provision is notorious for its discretion. The reason for this is that the *Principles* may provide a better way of achieving the underlying objectives of the current divorce law—since it is widely agreed that the current law is unsatisfactory in a number of respects. In many respects the approach outlined in the Principles would not only be clearer than the current law but also more appropriate for a society in which divorce has become commonplace. By contrast, the very flexibility of the current system of financial provision means that it is more difficult to identify any such underlying aims, and to focus on the points of convergence may give a misleading impression of the overall approach of the courts. Overall, while parallels may be found between the *Principles* and the discretion of the courts as currently exercised, it is doubtful whether the courts would welcome the more structured approach set out in the former. In the recent case of *Miller; McFarlane*, the flexibility of the current system was approved by the House of Lords. In particular, Lord Hope of Craighead, having examined the more prescriptive system that operates in Scotland, noted the unfairness that could result from the application of over-rigid principles.

Even if the *Principles* would offer a better way of regulating the divorce process, the task of incorporation would not be an easy one, given the political problems posed by reform of divorce law generally. The real problem is likely to be one of

---

[76]   Contrast *K v K (Ancillary Relief: Prenuptial Agreement)* [2003] 1 F.L.R. 120, with *J v V (Disclosure: Offshore Corporations)* [2003] EWHC 3110 (Fam).

presentation. Over 30 years ago Rheinstein referred to the "democratic compromise" that had been adopted in the field of divorce law, and gently mocked the concerns of academic lawyers:

> The conservatives are made happy by the strictness of the law on the books. Those who are liberal to the extent of seeking freedom of remarriage for themselves are satisfied by the ease with which their desire is accommodated in practice....The only ones who feel troubled are those occasional academics who view with alarm the hypocrisy of the system, the light-hearted way in which perjuries are committed and condoned, and who fear for the integrity of the law and the respect in which the law and its priests should be held by the public.[77]

Yet the current law does raise a number of problems for the parties themselves, since the evidence suggests that the current system—in particular the need to establish fault in order to obtain a speedy divorce—exacerbate the bitterness between spouses in a way that the scheme set out in the *Principles* might not.[78]

Any discussion of marriage must today include reference to the new institution of civil partnership. However, the existence of civil partnerships would not necessarily pose an obstacle to the implementation of the *Principles*. While the *Principles* do not deal with the legal treatment of same-sex registered relationships, there would be nothing to prevent the legislature in England and Wales from reforming the basis on which a civil partnership may be dissolved in order to ensure that it remains as similar to marriage as possible, as is current policy.

The task of identifying or formulating common principles for different countries is rendered more difficult by the fact that issues such as divorce and maintenance are not self-contained topics but are connected to other aspects of the legal system. For example, as already noted, the cessation of maintenance upon the termination of a long-term relationship may be fair if the subsequent relationship itself gives rise to obligations but less so if it does not. More broadly, the ability of each spouse to achieve self-sufficiency may depend on broader structural factors such as family-friendly employment polices and the system of state benefits. Changing one aspects of domestic law may lead to inconsistency between different areas of domestic law. It may also lead to different outcomes in different jurisdictions.

The final point is a related one. Common law is one thing, common application quite another. The *Principles* allow considerable latitude to individual countries

---

[77] RHEINSTEIN, *Marriage Stability, Divorce and the Law* (Chicago: University of Chicago Press, 1972), ch 10.

[78] See e.g. WRIGHT, K, "The divorce process: a view from the other side of the desk" (2006) 18(1) *Child and Family Law Quarterly* 93, at p. 101.

in the way in which the scheme outlined will operate in practice. Each jurisdiction will approach the common principles in its own way: legal culture may be less susceptible to change than the law on the statute books. This means that the same set of facts may be treated differently in different countries. It is one thing to say that the *Principles* are not inconsistent with the current law. It is more difficult to predict whether in the long run they will lead to a consistent approach to the common issues of divorce and maintenance.

COMMON PRINCIPLES AND PURPOSES? SCOTS LAW AND THE COMMISSION ON EUROPEAN FAMILY LAW

Jane Mair

Scots family law has undergone considerable change and modernisation during the last 40 years as a result of which the rules have been to a large extent codified in a series of Acts. Much of this reform has been the product of the work of the Scottish Law Commission which has sought to simplify and clarify the provisions and processes and to create a system of family law which suits modern families and their ways of living. Recently this process of reform has been continued by the Scottish Executive which undertook a full and lengthy period of consultation prior to the latest reforms in the Family Law (Scotland) Act 2006. To what extent therefore do the Principles of European Family Law Regarding Divorce and Maintenance Between Former Spouses fit within Scots family law and how well do they match the concerns of the lawmakers that "reform needs to keep abreast of change"[1] and the expectations of individuals who "depend on family law at stressful and difficult times in their lives"?[2]

1. DIVORCE IN SCOTS LAW: AN INTRODUCTION

The key date for divorce in Scots law was the Reformation of 1560: prior to that time the law on marriage was governed by the church through canon law and divorce was not permitted. Scots law did however permit separation a mensa et thoro, for example in the case of cruelty, and declarator of nullity on a wide range of grounds including lack of consent and being within the prohibited degrees of relationship.[3] From the time of the Reformation, however, "Scotland no longer held marriage to be a sacrament, and divorce was countenanced on the grounds

---

1   SCOTTISH EXECUTIVE, *Family Matters: Improving Family Law in Scotland* (2004) p. 7, available at www.scotland.gov.uk/Publications/2004/04/19220/35694.
2   *Ibid*, p. 6.
3   HAY, W, *Lectures on* Marriage, pp. 61–71.

of adultery"[4] with the addition in 1573 of desertion as a ground for divorce.[5] Adultery was seen as a matrimonial offence going to the heart of marriage and as such divorce was available for the innocent party and resulted in the guilty party being "pronounced legally dead in relation to his or her former spouse".[6] Divorce for desertion reflected the legal obligation of marriage for the spouses to adhere. These continued as the only two grounds for divorce until the Divorce (Scotland) Act 1938 which added cruelty, incurable insanity, sodomy and bestiality. While the introduction of cruelty, sodomy and bestiality continued the philosophy of the earlier grounds which tied the availability of divorce to the notion of fault on the part of either spouse, the acceptance of incurable insanity as a basis for divorce can be regarded as the first sign of recognition in Scots law of non-fault divorce.[7]

Significant modern reform of the law relating to divorce came about as a result of the Divorce (Scotland) Act 1976 which introduced "irretrievable breakdown" as the sole ground for divorce.[8] This move outwardly created a new no-fault divorce system in Scots law but this was contradicted by the further provisions to the effect that irretrievable breakdown can only be established in one of five cases.[9] These methods of establishing irretrievable breakdown—which are often loosely referred to as the grounds for divorce—are a combination of fault and no-fault provisions reflecting the old idea of matrimonial offence but also recognising the more modern movement towards separation and consent as an indication of relationship breakdown. According to section 1 of the 1976 Act, irretrievable breakdown could be established in the event of adultery, desertion, intolerable conduct, non-cohabitation for a period of two years together with the consent of the defender or non-cohabitation for five years. Recently there has been further modification of this framework as a result of the Family Law (Scotland) Act 2006 which has abolished desertion as a distinct way of establishing irretrievable breakdown and has reduced the required periods of non-cohabitation.

In 2004 the Divorce (Scotland) Act 1976 was amended as a result of the Gender Recognition Act 2004 and consequently there are now two grounds for divorce. Irretrievable breakdown continues unchanged in section 1(1)(a) but a separate ground for divorce has been added in section 1(1)(b) where, since the date of the

---

4   LENEMAN, L, *Alienated Affections: The Scottish Experience of Divorce and Separation 1684–1830* (1998), p. 6.

5   For an excellent discussion of early divorce in Scotland see LENEMAN, L, *supra* at note 4.

6   LENEMAN, L, *supra* note 4, p. 6.

7   SeeCLIVE, E, *Husband and Wife* (1997), para. 20.002.

8   s.1(1)(a).

9   s.1(2)(a)-(e).

marriage, either party to the marriage has obtained an interim gender recognition certificate.

2. THE CEFL PRINCIPLES: DIVORCE

2.1. GENERAL PRINCIPLES

Principle 1:1 Permission of divorce

In seeking to devise common principles for divorce in Europe, the starting point, that divorce should be legally permitted and that it should be available regardless of the duration of the marriage, is easily met by Scots law. As set out above, divorce has been available since the Reformation, at first on the sole ground of adultery and gradually on a wider range of grounds. In its early development, Scots law offered relatively liberal access to divorce. In comparison to England, for example, where early divorce was first possible only by private Act of Parliament and not introduced by statute until 1857,[10] divorce was available in Scotland much earlier to a broader range of people.[11] Significantly, there was no legal distinction between men and women, with divorce for adultery being available to both husband and wife.

Divorce should be available regardless of the duration of the marriage and in principle this also fits with Scots law.[12] In particular there has been no requirement of a minimum duration of the marriage before divorce can be sought or granted. In practice, however, divorce is available where the marriage is shown to have broken down irretrievably and two of the methods of showing such breakdown depend on periods of non-cohabitation.[13] There has been a very steady trend towards these grounds being the most common for divorce, with 82% of all divorces granted in 2004 being on the basis of non-cohabitation.[14] In 1981 the average duration of marriage at the time of divorce was nine years which rose by 2004 to 14 years. A small number of divorces however are granted each year in relation to marriages which have lasted for less than one year. Non-cohabitation is now quite clearly the most common method of establishing irretrievable breakdown of marriage necessary to obtain divorce. As a result of amendments in the

---

[10]   Matrimonial Causes Act 1857.
[11]   For some examples of English couples seeking divorce in Scotland see LENEMAN, L, *supra* note 4, chapter 11.
[12]   Principle 1:1(2).
[13]   Divorce (Scotland) Act 1976 s.1(2)(d) and (e).
[14]   *Registrar General's Annual Review of Demographic Trends: Scotland's Population 2004*, chapter 1, available at www.gro-scotland.gov.uk/files/2004-rg-review.pdf.

Family Law (Scotland) Act 2006, a period of one year's non cohabitation is required where the defender consents to the granting of the decree of divorce and two year's regardless of consent. If couples choose to seek divorce on the basis of a period of non-cohabitation there is therefore in practice a minimum requirement for the duration of the marriage.

Principle 1:2 Procedure by law and competent authority

Under the pre-Reformation canon law, divorce was not legally permitted and since its introduction it has been a judicial process. As it is an important matter of status, actions for divorce were originally only competent in the Court of Session but, in 1983, jurisdiction to deal with divorce was extended to the sheriff courts. Divorce procedure has also been considerably simplified leading to the use of affidavits and in some situations the simplified or do-it-yourself procedure. In Scotland, divorce is only currently available through a judicial body, either the local sheriff courts or the Court of Session in Edinburgh. Although decree of divorce may only be granted by a court it is no longer necessary in many cases for the parties to appear in court. There has been significant change in divorce procedure and as a result for many couples the process has become much more administrative in nature despite the fact that the formal decree is granted by a judicial body.

There are currently three forms of procedure for divorce action: ordinary, affidavit and simplified (Do-it yourself) procedures. In all procedures, the ground of the action must be established by evidence with the standard of proof being "on balance of probability".[15] In ordinary procedure, the summons or initial writ in which the pursuer seeks a divorce is served on the defender who then has a period of 21 days[16] within which to respond. If the defender intends to defend the action, he or she will lodge defences with the court whereas in the case of an undefended action, the procedure will usually switch to affidavit. Where the process continues as a defended divorce the outcome will be the granting by the court of either a decree of divorce or a decree of absolvitor where the defence is successful. In 1978, the divorce process was significantly changed by the introduction of affidavit evidence thus removing the need for personal court appearance.[17] Affidavit evidence is used in undefended divorce actions and has greatly altered the divorce process. The process begins in the same way as for the Ordinary procedure but where no defences are entered sworn affidavits of the pursuer and at least one other witness are submitted to the court together with a minute from counsel or

---

[15]   Divorce (Scotland) Act 1976, s.1(6).
[16]   42 if living outside Europe.
[17]   Act of Sederunt (Rules of Court Amendment No. 1) (Consistorial Causes) 1978.

the pursuer's solicitor. Decree of divorce will then be granted by the court without the need for any of the parties to appear personally in court. This process obviously involves much less cost and for the parties at least makes the granting of divorce seem less judicial in its nature. The third procedure, the simplest and least expensive, was introduced as a result of the Divorce Jurisdiction, Court Fees and Legal Aid (Scotland) Act 1983, and is known as the simplified or do-it-yourself (D-I-Y) procedure.[18]

Whereas the Marriage (Scotland) Act 1977 provides for both civil and religious marriage in Scotland, there is only one form of secular divorce. This separation of church and law has been eroded, if only to a minimal degree, by the recent introduction into the Divorce (Scotland) Act 1976 of section 3A which provides for postponement of decree of divorce where a religious impediment to remarriage exists.[19]Either party to a marriage may seek postponement of the decree of divorce, notwithstanding that irretrievable breakdown of the marriage has been established, on the basis that he or she is not free to enter into a religious marriage, because of the rules of that religion on divorce, according to which the other party has the power to remove the obstacle to the remarriage. This provision is most obviously directed to the situation of those of Jewish faith for whom "[f]reedom to re-marry within the Jewish faith is acquired not by court order but by "Get", which is a process of mutual consent to terminate marriage".[20]

2.2. TYPES OF DIVORCE

Principle 1:4 introduces the framework of the proposed CEFL Principles to the effect that there should be provision for two types of divorce: divorce by mutual consent[21] and divorce without consent.[22] This is not a division which currently operates in Scots law where a more commonly made distinction is between fault and non-fault divorce. At present Scots law could be said to provide for divorce both by mutual consent and without consent, as proposed by the CEFL Principles, but only where the parties are able to satisfy the requirements of section 1(2) of the 1976 Act which in practice requires either "a marital offence"—adultery or unreasonable conduct—or a period of non-cohabitation. While there has been an

---

[18]   Evidence in Divorce Actions (Scotland) Order 1989, S.I. 1989 No. 582.
[19]   Inserted by Family Law (Scotland) Act 2006 s.15.
[20]   NORRIE, K, *The Family Law (Scotland) Act 2006: Text and Commentary* (2006) p. 33.
[21]   BOELE-WOELKI, K, FERRAND, F, BEILFUSS, CG, JANTERA-JAREBORG, M, LOWE, N, MARTINY D and PINTENS, W, *Principles of European Family Law Regarding Divorce and Maintenance between Former Spouses*, European Family Law Series N: 7, (2004), chapter II, principles 1:4–1:7.
[22]   *Ibid*, chapter III, principles 1:8–1:10.

attempt in recent reforms to simplify the grounds for divorce the current position remains a compromise between the principal ground of irretrievable breakdown and the list of specific "grounds" which are the only means of establishing irretrievable breakdown.

2.2.1. Divorce by mutual consent

The Principles propose a clear distinction between two types of divorce: divorce by mutual consent and divorce without consent. While they state that divorce should be available in both situations, the process and consequences will be slightly different. Scots law, while it provides in some circumstances for divorce both with and without consent, has not approached the questions in this way. Scots law currently only provides for divorce by mutual consent where the consent follows a period of non-cohabitation.[23] This has become the most used route to divorce in Scotland [24]and the period of non-cohabitation required has recently been reduced from two years to one year.[25] The defender must then consent to the granting of the decree of divorce although this consent may be withheld for any or no reason.

Unlike Principle 1:4, which places emphasis on the concept of mutual consent to dissolution of the relationship, Scots law only requires action to be taken by one spouse, the pursuer, and for the other spouse, the defender, to consent to the final decree of divorce. In the past, couples who agreed to be divorced but who did not want to wait for the period of non-cohabitation, might have acted together to present an action for divorce based on a false case of adultery or unreasonable conduct. Such actions, however, involved the risk that decree might be refused on the grounds of collusion. Evidence of collusion between the parties gave rise to a bar to divorce. Collusion as a bar to divorce has now been abolished by means of the Family Law (Scotland) Act 2006[26]and while this should not be interpreted as acceptance or encouragement of fabrication of a false case it does clear the way for co-operation between the parties in the presentation of an action for divorce.

2.2.2. Reflection period and agreements

While allowing for divorce by mutual consent with no requisite period of separation, Principle 1:5 introduces a period of reflection. This is a good way of accom-

---

[23]   Divorce (Scotland) Act 1976, s.1(2)(d).
[24]   In 2004, 54% of all divorces were on the basis of two years' non-cohabitation with consent: *Regsitrar General's Annual Review of Demographic Trends: Scotland's Population 2004* available at www.gro-scotland.gov.uk/files/2004-rg-review.pdf.
[25]   Divorce (Scotland) Act 1976, s.1(2)(d), as amended by Family Law (Scotland) Act 2006 s.11.
[26]   Family Law (Scotland) Act 2006 s.14.

modating the desire to have a clear principle of divorce on mutual consent with the concerns often expressed to the effect that some couples may rush into divorce without trying to make their relationship work. At present, Scots law does not meet Principle 1:4 for divorce by mutual consent as it requires a period of separation. This separation may have come about for a variety of reasons and need not follow on from a decision of the parties to bring their relationship to an end: it therefore does not necessarily fulfil the purpose of reflection.

Principle 1:5 expressly encourages the parties to reach agreements as to their children, if any, and the other consequences of divorce. Reaching an agreement on these matters will shorten the period of reflection required which, in turn may encourage couples to consider the consequences prior to reaching a decision to divorce. While the principle does not specifically require any attempts at reconciliation during this period of reflection, it importantly facilitates such attempts by providing that there is no need for the parties to live separately during the period of reflection. Scots law, in respect of section 1(2)(d) and (e) of the Divorce (Scotland) Act 1976 makes the establishment of irretrievable breakdown dependent on continuous periods of non-cohabitation. While a couple may remain in the same house, they must not be living together as husband and wife. There is some limited provision for resumed periods of cohabitation in that section 2(4) provides that no account shall be taken of periods not exceeding six months in total although this time will not count towards the overall period of non-cohabitation. There is further provision in section 2(1) where the court considers that there is a reasonable prospect of reconciliation. In that situation the court can continue the action for as long as considered appropriate in order to allow the couple to attempt reconciliation and in that situation there is no limit on the cumulative periods of resumed cohabitation.

2.2.3. Divorce without consent

Divorce without consent is currently available under Scots law in three situations: where the pursuer seeks divorce on the grounds of the defender's adultery,[27] where the defender has behaved in such a way that the pursuer cannot reasonably be expected to continue to cohabit[28] and on the basis of a period of non-cohabitation.[29] While it is possible to obtain divorce without consent, the provisions do not match with those proposed in CEFL Principles 1:8–1:9. Scots law allows divorce without consent either on the basis of fault or following a two year period of separation.. There are, however, signs of progress towards the clear and simple

---

[27]   Divorce (Scotland) Act 1976 s.1(2)(a).
[28]   Divorce (Scotland) Act 1976 s.1(2)(b).
[29]   Divorce (Scotland) Act 1976 s.1(2)(e).

CEFL Principle to the effect that divorce without consent should be available if "they have been factually separated for one year". In the Family Law (Scotland) Act 2006, one of the fault grounds, desertion, was abolished and the non-cohabitation period for non-consensual divorce was reduced significantly from 5 years to 2 years. In these reforms there is evidence of willingness to move towards simpler and quicker forms of divorce although some of the views expressed in the process of consultation which preceded the legislation showed continuing reluctance to accept this principle.[30]

Although it might be argued that Scots law should aim to comply with Principle 1:8 by reducing the period of separation, it is less obvious that it would be beneficial to accept the need for some mental element in establishing non-cohabitation as suggested in the Commentary. Scots law defines cohabitation in section 13(2) of the Divorce (Scotland) Act 1976 as "in fact living together as husband and wife" and non-cohabitation is taken to be the absence of this factual situation. There is no mention in the Act of any need for intention to end the marriage and non-cohabitation is regarded as the simple fact of not living together as husband and wife. It has been argued "that to require a mental element in non-cohabitation would... give rise to difficulties".[31] Although it might be argued that Scots law should aim to comply with Principle 1:8 by reducing the period of separation, it is less obvious that it would be beneficial to accept the need for some mental element in establishing non-cohabitation as suggested in the Commentary.[32]

2.2.4. Exceptional hardship to the petitioner

In Principle 1:9, it is provided that non-consensual divorce should be available without a period of separation where there is exceptional hardship to the petitioner. It is possible under Scots law for a pursuer to seek divorce immediately, and without consent, on the grounds of the defender's adultery[33] or unreasonable or intolerable conduct.[34] While these provisions allow Scots law to meet Principle 1:9, it would seem that it goes further. Arguably, divorces can be granted in situations which do not involve "exceptional hardship" as defined in the Commentary. These provisions are used in many cases as a means of securing a quicker divorce due to the absence of any requirement of a separation period although it is hoped that one of the benefits of reducing the non-cohabitation periods required

---

[30] See *Improving Family Law in Scotland: Analysis of Written Consultation Responses* (2004), available at www.scotland.gov.uk/Publications/2004/10/20057/44653.

[31] CLIVE, E, *The Law of Husband and Wife in Scotland* (1997), para. 21.073.

[32] *CEFL Principles, supra* note 21 at p. 56.

[33] Divorce (Scotland) Act 1976 s.1(2)(a).

[34] Divorce (Scotland) act s.1(2)(b).

to establish irretrievable breakdown will be a reduction in the use of fault-based grounds as a means of obtaining a quick divorce.

2.2.5. Agreements

Where divorce is with mutual consent, the CEFL Principles make clear links between the reflection period and agreement as to the consequences of divorce. In terms of Principle 1:6 agreement is required as to parental responsibility, including residence and contact arrangements where necessary, child maintenance, property settlement and spousal maintenance. Arrangements concerning children will ultimately be determined by the competent authority, although any agreement reached by the spouses will be taken into account. Agreements as to property and maintenance of ex-spouses will be open to scrutiny by the relevant authority.[35] It is made clear in the Commentary on this Principle that what is intended is partial harmonisation with the interpretation of key concepts in the Principle being left to national law. In particular it will be for national law to decide on the legal status of such an agreement. The real attraction of Principle 1:6 is that it shows consistency in the legal approach to divorce. The couple may decide by mutual consent to divorce but they must also accept joint responsibility for this decision, reflect, at least for a time, on the consequences and, if possible, reach their own agreement on these consequences.

In the case of a married couple, both husband and wife will normally have parental rights and responsibilities in respect of their children.[36] In the situation where a couple are divorcing and there is dispute over residence and contact in respect of children who are not the biological children of one of the parties, either party could apply to the court for parental responsibilities and rights under section 11 of the 1995 Act as a person "who claims an interest".[37] The court has power under section 11 to regulate parental responsibilities and rights including the making of residence[38] and contact[39] orders. Applications may be made to the court at any time but frequently arise in the context of divorce proceedings. In making any decision, the court is guided by three principles: the welfare of the child, the requirement that the child be allowed to express his or her own views and that they be taken into consideration and the presumption of non-intervention. It is this third principle which encourages parents to reach agreement. It is provided in section 11(7)(a) that the court should not make an order "unless it considers

---

[35]   Principle 1:7.
[36]   Children (Scotland) Act 1995 s.1.
[37]   *Ibid*, s.11(3)(i).
[38]   *Ibid*, s.11(2)(c).
[39]   *Ibid*, s.11(2)(d).

that it would be better for the child that the order be made than that none should be made at all." It is therefore open to the parties to reach their own agreement as to the children following divorce and where they do so, even if an application is subsequently made to the court in respect of parental responsibilities and rights, the court will follow the principle of non-intervention.

2.3. SCOTS LAW AND THE CEFL PRINCIPLES: SOME CONCLUSIONS

The Divorce (Scotland) Act 1976 represented a significant reform of divorce in Scotland with the replacement of a list of fault based grounds for divorce with a single apparently no-fault ground of irretrievable breakdown. Since then, the superficial simplicity of this system has been questioned on the basis of the pre-scribed methods of establishing irretrievable breakdown. It has been further dis-rupted by the addition of an extra ground necessitated by changes elsewhere in family law and the no-fault nature of divorce in Scotland has been challenged by continued reliance on fault as a means of securing a quick divorce. Despite these weaknesses in the legislation, the pattern of reform over the last 30 years has been relatively minor modification of the 1976 Act framework. In 1989 the Scottish Law Commission proposed reform of the divorce law in their Report on Reform of the Ground for Divorce[40] and these proposals again formed the basis for con-sultation by the Scottish Executive in 2004 which ultimately resulted in the reforms of the Family Law (Scotland) Act 2006. Much family law reform in Scot-land in recent years has followed considerable public consultation and there has been a clear attempt to match the law to public opinion and expectation. In its report in 1989, the Scottish Law Commission indicated that they might have been in favour of some more radical restructuring of the grounds for divorce but ulti-mately put forward only relatively minor modifications of the existing legal framework "in the light of comments received" and on the basis of "what was likely to prove acceptable to informed opinion at the time." When these proposals were taken up again, 14 years later, the process of consultation undertaken by the Scottish Executive, suggested little change in public opinion. Of those who responded to the proposals that the periods of non-cohabitation[41] needed to establish irretrievable breakdown be reduced, 73% of those representing organi-sations were in favour as opposed to 90% of individuals who were opposed. One of the most common reasons given for opposing the reduction was that it would limit the time which was available for couples to "rethink and seek reconcilia-

---

[40] Scot. Law. Com. No. 116 (1989).
[41] In s.1(2)(d) and (e) of Divorce (Scotland) Act 1976.

tion",[42] whereas for those in favour, a significant benefit was that the shorter periods of non-cohabitation would lessen bitter divorces and allow "the separation to focus on future needs, not conflict".[43] This focus on time to reflect fits well with the linkage of separation and reflection in the CEFL proposals. In Scots law, the period of non-cohabitation operates as a means of confirming that the relationship has irretrievably broken down and where attempts are made to reduce the required duration it is perhaps not surprising that there should be some resistance on the basis that it amounts to easier divorce with consequent fears of weaker marriage.

There is much to recommend the CEFL Principles on divorce, which provide a clear and simple framework for divorce. Recent reforms have focused on minor modification of the 1976 structure which despite the introduction of irretrievable breakdown still clings to the distinction between fault and no-fault grounds for divorce. With the lessening of the periods of non-cohabitation required to establish irretrievable breakdown, it is anticipated that the importance of adultery and intolerable conduct will continue to diminish leaving in effect a simple distinction between divorce with[44] or without consent:[45] a position much closer to the European Principles than perhaps at first glance appears.

3. MAINTENANCE – FINANCIAL PROVISION IN SCOTS LAW; AN INTRODUCTION

In Part II of the Principles, which deal with maintenance between former spouses, there is a fundamental difference between the proposed European framework and that which operates in Scots law. In 1985, with the introduction of a new system of financial provision on divorce by means of the Family Law (Scotland) Act; Scots family law signalled a clear preference for a one-off division of assets on divorce over any continuing economic dependency between former spouses.

---

[42]   See *Improving Family Law in Scotland: Analysis of Written Consultation Responses* 2004, at p. 24, available at www.scotland.gov.uk/Publications/2004/10/20057/44653.

[43]   *Ibid* at p. 25.

[44]   Divorce (Scotland) Act 1976 s.1(2)(d).

[45]   Divorce (Scotland) Act 1976 s.1(2)(e).

3.1. SPOUSAL ALIMENT AND SEPARATION OF PROPERTY

Husbands and wives, according to Scots law, owe each other an obligation of aliment[46] which exists throughout the relationship of marriage. It is a duty to provide reasonable maintenance and an action for aliment may be raised in the Court of Session or the sheriff court,[47] either on its own or together with other actions.[48] An action for aliment may be raised even where the couple continue to cohabit although the defender will have a defence where it can be shown that he or she is currently fulfilling the obligation by maintaining the spouse in their household. In making an award of aliment, the court should have regard to the needs, resources and earning capacities of the parties together with the overall circumstances of the case.[49] No account should be taken of the conduct of either of the parties unless it would be manifestly inequitable to ignore it.[50] Although an obligation of aliment only exists between spouses and between parents and children, the court may take into account the fact that the defender is supporting a dependant in his or her household regardless of whether or not he or she owes a duty of aliment to that person. Similarly the fact that the spouse seeking aliment is in fact receiving support from a person with whom he or she is now living may also be taken into account by the court in deciding on the appropriate level of aliment.[51]

This obligation of aliment is one of the few legal consequences of marriage in Scots law which operates a system of separate property. Marriage in itself has no effect on the property or ownership rights of either spouse[52] and therefore there is considerable legal support for the notion of the spouses as quite separate and independent persons. There is no automatic joint ownership of the matrimonial home although a non-entitled spouse is provided with occupancy rights during the existence of marriage[53] and there is a limited presumption of equal ownership of household assets although this does not extend to money.[54] It is against this background of separate ownership that the courts may be asked to order financial provision on divorce. In particular it is recognised that where there has been de facto sharing of resources during marriage there may be considerable unfairness on divorce or where the spouses have adopted a breadwinner/home-

---

46   1985 Act s.1(1)(a) and (b).
47   1985 Act s. 2(1).
48   eg an action for separation and aliment or divorce and aliment.
49   1985 Act s.4(1).
50   1985 Act s.4(3)(b).
51   1985 Act s.4(3)(b).
52   1985 Act s.24.
53   Matrimonial Homes (Family Protection) (Scotland) Act 1981 s.1.
54   Family Law (Scotland) Act 1985 s.25.

maker division of roles, the spouse who has stayed at home may have accumulated little income or property during the marriage and thus be at a considerable disadvantage on divorce. Within the statutory framework of financial provision on divorce, there is consideration of the effect of communal living during marriage on the spouses' financial positions but otherwise, both during marriage and after financial settlement, Scots law is strongly wedded to the ideal of the separate and independent individual.

3.2. FINANCIAL PROVISION ON DIVORCE

In common with many other jurisdictions, Scots law originally distinguished between the innocent and guilty spouse in respect of post-divorce financial settlement and at common law the guilty party was in effect treated as having died. Prior to 1964, financial provision could only be made in respect of the innocent spouse, who received a fixed capital award, according to the rules of intestate succession. An innocent wife would be entitled to *jus relictae* and a liferent of one third of her husband's heritable property whereas an innocent husband had the right of courtesy; the liferent of his wife's heritable property. Under this system, provision for the innocent spouse was based only on the capital assets of the guilty party at the point of divorce, with no entitlement to continuing maintenance from income. An exception existed in respect of divorce for incurable insanity where a capital sum payment or periodical allowance could be made by the court in terms of section 2(2) of the Divorce (Scotland) Act 1938.

Abolition of this system was recommended by both the Mackintosh Committee[55] and the Morton Committee[56], which resulted in new provisions being introduced by the Succession (Scotland) Act 1964. The common law system of fixed legal rights was replaced with powers being given to the court to award either a capital sum or periodical allowance, or both, on divorce.[57] In making such orders, the court had significant discretion, with the 1964 Act giving little guidance as to the purpose or extent of such awards. The right to apply for financial provision on divorce continued only to be available to the innocent spouse. Further amendment followed in the Divorce (Scotland) Act 1976 which left the underlying system of discretionary judicial award unchanged but extended the right to seek such an order of capital sum or periodical allowance to either spouse. This removed the distinction between guilty and innocent party which fitted well

---

[55] Report of the Departmental Committee on the law of Succession in Scotland (1950) Cmnd. 8144.
[56] Report of the Royal Commission on Marriage and Divorce 1951–1955 Cmnd. 9678.
[57] Succession (Scotland) Act 1964 s.26.

with the introduction by the same Act of irretrievable breakdown as the sole ground of divorce and the apparent move in Scots law towards no-fault divorce.

In 1985, a much more significant reform of the law was brought about by the Family Law (Scotland) Act which set out a new scheme for the distribution of matrimonial property on divorce, strongly favouring the notion of "a clean break" while treating continuing obligations of maintenance as the least desirable option. The legislation was adopted following extensive research and consultation by the Scottish Law Commission[58] and in the new framework there were key aims of seeking to achieve a clean break on divorce while acknowledging that the practicability of this may be affected by the nature of the marriage; recognising the economic advantages and disadvantages which may be experienced by each spouse within the course of a marriage relationship and providing clear guidance to the courts as to how to make financial provision. This increased clarity and certainty it was hoped would, in turn, encourage couples to negotiate their own settlements without need for judicial involvement.

3.3. THE 1985 ACT: ORDERS AND PRINCIPLES

The 1985 Act enables either party to apply to the court for financial provision[59] and section 8 sets out the range of orders which may be sought: capital sum payment, transfer of property, periodical allowance, pension sharing or payment and incidental orders. The court may make one or more of these orders where it is justified in terms of the section 9 principles, and reasonable with regard to the resources of the parties.[60] One of the principal criticisms of the previous system was that it gave great discretion to the courts, with little guidance as to how settlements should be made and in consequence with little certainty for the parties and their advisers as to how their assets might be divided or what provision might be made for their future. A key aim of the 1985 Act was therefore to create a much clearer framework to inform decisions about the financial consequences of divorce and the result was five principles which are set out in section 9.

---

[58]   SCOTTISH LAW COMMISSION, Consultative Memorandum on *Aliment and Financial Provision* (Scot. Law. Com. No. 22, 1976); Report on *Aliment and Financial Provision* (Scot. Law. Com. No. 67, 1981); MANNERS and RAUTA, *Family Property in Scotland* (1981).
[59]   Family Law (Scotland) Act 1985, s.8(1).
[60]   *Ibid*, s.8(2).

Principle 1 Fair sharing of matrimonial property

Scots law operates a system of separate property during marriage but the effect of the principle in section 9(1)(a) is to introduce a form of deferred community. The first principle is that "the net value of the matrimonial property should be shared fairly between the parties to the marriage". For this purpose, matrimonial property is made up of any assets acquired by either spouse during the marriage together with any matrimonial home, including furniture and fittings, acquired prior to the marriage but for the purpose of being used as a matrimonial home.[61] Such property must be acquired before the relevant date which is the earlier of either the date when the couple cease to cohabit or the date when the divorce action is served.[62] Matrimonial property is subject to an important exception in respect of any property acquired by reason of gift or inheritance from a third party although it is only the initial gift or inheritance which is exempt. Such property is to be shared fairly which is presumed to mean in equal shares[63] except where there are special circumstances[64] which justify sharing in some other proportions.

Principle 2 Economic advantage or disadvantage

The second principle set out in section 9 provides for the court to take account of any economic advantage derived by either party from the contributions of the other and of any economic disadvantage suffered in the interests of the other party or of the family.[65] Such advantages or disadvantages can have occurred either before or during the marriage and they include gains or losses "in capital, in income and in earning capacity".[66] Contributions similarly may have been made before or during the marriage, including in particular any contribution "made by looking after the family home or caring for the family."[67] In applying this principle however the court should also take into account the extent to which any advantages or disadvantages have already been balanced during the marriage

---

61 *Ibid*, s.10(4).
62 *Ibid*, s.10(3).
63 *Ibid*, s.10(1).
64 *Ibid*, s.10(6): special circumstances include the terms of any agreement between the parties as to ownership or division of matrimonial property; source of funds or assets used (excluding those derived from income or efforts of the parties during marriage) to acquire matrimonial property; destruction, dissipation or alienation of property; nature or use of any matrimonial property; liability for expenses in relation to transfer of property in connection with the divorce proceedings.
65 *Ibid*, s.9(1)(b).
66 *Ibid*, s.10(2).
67 *Ibid*, s.10(2).

or will be addressed by the sharing of matrimonial property under the first principle.[68]

Principle 3 Childcare

The third principle is that there should be fair sharing, after the divorce, of the economic burden of caring for any child of the marriage under 16. [69] Further guidance is provided for the court in applying this principle by means of a list of factors to be taken into consideration: arrangements of aliment of the child, expenditure or loss of earning capacity as a result of caring for the child; age and health of the child; educational, financial and other circumstances of the child; availability and cost of suitable child care facilities and the needs and resources of the parties.[70]

Principle 4 Readjustment

An important criticism of the previous system of financial provision was that where periodical allowance was awarded, there was no means of restricting the duration of the award, and in the new framework of the 1985 Act one of the principal aims was to move away from reliance on lifelong support from an ex-spouse. In keeping with the clean break principle, there was a strong preference for a one-off financial settlement, ideally achieved through property sharing, with the parties being left in a position whereby they could be self sufficient. The fourth principle recognises that this is not always immediately achievable and that at least there may need to be a period of economic readjustment.[71] Under this principle, where one person has been dependent to a substantial extent on the other during the marriage, reasonable financial provision may be awarded over a period of not more than three years in order to enable that person to adjust to the loss of that financial support on divorce. In making any such award the court must take into account all of the circumstances of the case and the needs and resources of both parties with particular consideration of the age, health and earning capacity of the party seeking the award, the duration and extent of their dependence prior to divorce and their intention to undertake any course of education or training.[72]

---

[68]   *Ibid*, s.11(2).
[69]   *Ibid*, s.9(1)(c).
[70]   *Ibid*, s.11(3).
[71]   *Ibid*, s.9(1)(d).
[72]   *Ibid*, s.11(4).

Principle 5 Serious financial hardship

The final principle in section 9 is designed to relieve serious financial hardship of one party as a result of the divorce.[73] In considering the making of any order under this principle, the court should consider the age, health and earning capacity of the parties, the duration of the marriage, the standard of living of the parties during the marriage together with their overall needs and resources and the circumstances of the case.[74] Unlike in the previous principle, there is here no limit on the period for which such financial provision may be made. Section 9(1)(e) provides for reasonable support over a reasonable period.

3.4. MAINTENANCE AND FINANCIAL PROVISION: COMMON PURPOSES?

To analyse the extent to which the European Principles fit within the Scots law of post-divorce maintenance is difficult as the starting point of the Scottish system is that maintenance should only be used to a very limited degree within any financial settlement: it is the last resort. In the introduction to the Principles, it is recognised[75] that in some jurisdictions a distinction is not made between maintenance and the division of property and it is also explained that, at this stage, no Principles have been drafted by the CEFL in respect of the division of property. Detailed analysis of the maintenance principles vis a vis the Scottish system is therefore not possible as like cannot be compared with like. From the standpoint of Scots law, it would have been preferable to see the Principles set within the context of an overall framework for division of property on divorce. The CEFL Principles, while beginning with a statement in support of self-sufficiency, operate by looking forward to make provision for future support where needed. The Scottish system holds to the view that the consequences of marriage should, where possible, terminate with the legal ending of the relationship itself: any economic adjustment or provision should concentrate on looking back.

General Principles: Principles 2:1 and 2:2

In the 1985 Family Law (Scotland) Act, the Scottish Law Commission set out to introduce a principled system of financial provision on divorce which had clear and considered objectives. In the Report which preceded the legislation, the Commission sought to articulate the possible purposes of financial provision on

---

[73] s.9(1)(e).
[74] s.11(5).
[75] *CEFL Principles, supra* note 21 at p. 70.

divorce,[76] beginning with a review of the possible justification for any legal involvement in the property and financial affairs of divorcing couples. Their starting point was to consider whether there was any need or justification for judicial intervention in property and finance following divorce. They recognised that, "while it would be theoretically possible to make no provision at all" and that it is useful to "assume that the parties should be economically independent after divorce",[77] in many cases to make no provision for adjustment of finances on divorce would lead to injustice. Having concluded that a right to ask the court to make some settlement should exist, not surprisingly they were of the view that the court should be able to make financial provision on the application of either party. The CEFL similarly prefaces the specific principles on maintenance with the general statement[78] that "each spouse should provide for his or her own support after divorce" and that maintenance principles should apply regardless of the type of divorce.

Principle 2:3

Having started from the principle of self sufficiency, however, the CEFL proceeds to provide for a system of post-divorce maintenance "dependent upon the creditor spouse having insufficient resources to meet his or her needs and the debtor spouse's ability to satisfy those needs".[79] The Scottish Law Commission in their Report on *Aliment and Financial Provision* considered first whether continuing support should be used as an objective of financial provision on divorce, on the basis that it could be seen as "a continuation of the obligation of support which existed during marriage"[80] but rejected this on the grounds that it was "inconsistent with the idea that divorce terminates a marriage."[81] They went on to consider whether, by restricting an ongoing obligation of support to relief of need, it would become a more suitable purpose for financial provision. While acknowledging that using the concept of "relief of need" would allow the courts to "escape from the notion that a divorced wife is entitled to be supported for life", they nonetheless concluded that it is "the wrong starting point".[82] A similar criticism can be made of CEFL Principle 2:3: it may be possible to accept the proposal that maintenance should only be provided where the creditor spouse is in need and

---

[76] Their original aim was to set a single purpose for financial provision but, following consultation, it was concluded that no one purpose was adequate.

[77] SLC Report, *supra* note 58, at p. 79

[78] Principle 2:2.

[79] Principle 2:3.

[80] SLC Report, *supra* note 58 at para. 3.43.

[81] *Ibid.*

[82] *Ibid* at para. 3.49.

the debtor spouse is able to provide but it would be better to look beyond this and question the desirability of ongoing obligations of maintenance.

Principle 2:4 Relevant factors

If the basic premise of an obligation of maintenance is challenged, other than within an overarching framework of property division, then analysis of the consequent detail becomes difficult. CEFL Principle 2:4 sets out a list of factors to be considered in the award of maintenance and there is clearly considerable congruence between these and the factors used in the application of the section 9 principles of the Family Law (Scotland) Act 1985. Scots law would seek to recognise the potential impact of these factors on the financial position of ex-spouses, but in the context that it is the function of financial provision to look back at the marriage rather than to the future. Section 9(1)(d) and (e) allow consideration of employment ability, age and health[83] in assessing whether provision should be made to facilitate adjustment to the loss of support or to relieve hardship. In both cases, periodical allowance may be made but only where the court is satisfied that an order for payment of a capital sum, transfer of property or pension sharing order would be inappropriate or insufficient.[84] In applying these principles, the duration of the marriage and the standard of living may also be relevant but any need for adjustment or financial hardship must be caused by the divorce itself.[85] The care of children is identified in principle 2:4 as a relevant factor in assessing maintenance and this also forms a separate principle in the Scottish statutory framework.[86] In the introduction to Part II of the Principles, one of the possible justifications put forward for a maintenance obligation is that after marriages of long duration "there is still a post-divorce solidarity between the spouses".[87] While Scots law is primarily focused on achieving a break between the spouses, their solidarity is encouraged in respect of childcare and this is reflected in section 9(1)(c) of the 1985 Act which provides for the fair sharing of the burden of childcare.[88] Principle 2:4 also recognises as a relevant factor the division of duties during the marriage. This might be considered as similar to the principle in section 9(1)(b) of the 1985 Act which allows the court to make provision for eco-

---

[83]   1985 Act s.11(4) and (5).

[84]   1985 Act s.13(2)(b).

[85]   For an interesting discussion of some of the difficulties arising from this link between the divorce and the hardship see Thomson, *Family Law in Scotland* (5th ed) 2006, Tottel, para. 7.20. It should be noted that the Scottish Law Commission rejected the preservation on divorce of the applicant's economic position during marriage as an objective of financial provision: SLC Report para. 3.47.

[86]   1985 Act s.9(1)(c).

[87]   *CEFL Principles, supra* note 21 at p. 69.

[88]   As with s.9(1)(d) and (e), an order for periodical allowance may be made in terms of this principle but again only where the other s8 orders would be inappropriate or insufficient.

nomic advantage or disadvantage which has arisen during marriage. While this is a general provision for balancing, it specifically includes the stereotypical division of roles between the breadwinner husband and the homemaker wife. That such behaviour, in the interests of the other spouse or of the family, should be taken into account on divorce is clearly accepted within Scots law but once again would be dealt with in terms of property sharing rather than as part of an ongoing obligation of maintenance.[89]

Principle 2:5 Method of maintenance provision

It is in the proposed method of financial provision rather than the underlying objectives that Scots law is at variance with the CEFL Principles. One of the principal attractions of the one-off settlement under the 1985 Act is that there can be a clean financial break between the parties which reflects the final termination of their relationship through divorce. Public opinion prior to the introduction of the legislation suggested that there was little support for ongoing obligations of maintenance: they are a burden on the party who has to pay, they prolong the dependency of the party who receives the payment and there may be practical problems of enforcement. While the 1985 Act prefers the payment of a capital sum or the transfer of property, there is, however, provision for the payment or transfer to take effect at some future specified date[90] or for payment to be made in instalments.[91]

Principle 2:6 Exceptional hardship and the relevance of conduct

Although in different terms because of the distinction between maintenance and property division, there is substantial common ground between the CEFL Principles and Scots law in respect of the impact of conduct on financial provision. As a general rule, when applying the section 9 principles, the court should not take into account the conduct of either party.[92] There is a general exception to this where "the conduct has adversely affected" the relevant financial resources[93] and in respect of orders under the readjustment principle in section 9(1)(d) or the long term hardship principle in section 9(1)(e) where "it would be manifestly inequitable to leave the conduct out of account.[94]

---

[89]   The equitable adjustment of economic advantages and disadvantages was one of the Scottish Law Commission's preferred purposes of financial provision: SLC Report para 3.46.
[90]   1985 Act s.12(2).
[91]   Ibid, s.12(3).
[92]   Ibid, s.11(7).
[93]   Ibid, s.11(7)(a).
[94]   Ibid, s.11(7)(b).

Principles 2:7–2:10 Specific issues

The specific issues dealt with in Chapter III of the CEFL Principles are of limited relevance within the Scottish system of financial provision due to the concentration on a one-off settlement. The possibility of multiple claims on one party may be taken into account in terms of the general provision in section 8(2) of the Family Law (Scotland) Act according to which any order made by the court must be reasonable "with regard to the resources of the parties". The use of ongoing periodical allowance is already strictly limited by the section 9 principles and there is provision for variation or recall of the order where there has been a material change of circumstances.[95] Principle 2:10, while dealing specifically with agreements relating to maintenance obligations, could be applied more broadly to financial provision and is in very similar terms to the provisions in Scots law. One of the aims of the 1985 Act was to encourage divorcing couples to reach their own agreement as to financial settlement. This had been hindered under previous systems by the lack of guidance and clarity as to what provision might be made by a court. While parties are encouraged to conclude their own agreement, the court retains some limited power to scrutinise and vary the provisions.[96]

4. CONCLUSIONS

In Scots law, there is a distinct split between financial support during marriage and on divorce. The obligation of support owed between spouses during marriage is one of aliment whereas on divorce either spouse may ask the court to make an order in respect of financial provision on divorce. Separate provision is made for children in terms of aliment or under the statutory scheme of child support. Although, in practice, some ex-spouses will continue to receive maintenance as part of an overall settlement, the distinct aim of the law is to move away from such ongoing obligations and therefore the Principles to a large extent are out of place within Scots law. While some of the purposes behind both the CEFL Principles of maintenance and the Scots law principles of financial provision are similar, the focus is distinct.

[It has always been the case in Scots law that the obligation of aliment between spouses ceases on divorce. Before 1964 there was no possibility of a periodical allowance after divorce. Since 1964 there has been at best the prospect of a periodical allowance at the

---

95   *Ibid*, s.13.
96   *Ibid*, s.16.

discretion of the court. No-one has ever married under Scots law in the legally justified expectation that he or she would be supported for life even after divorce.[97]

If the CEFL Principles are subsequently placed within the broader context of property division they may appear less at variance with the Scots law framework but, at present, the move towards a clean break in terms of divorce fits well with the Scottish system of financial provision which aims to secure a similarly finite economic settlement.

---

[97]　SLC Report on *Aliment and Financial Provision, supra* note 58 at para 3.12.

PART TWO
DIVERSITY IN THE NEW MEMBERS
OF THE EUROPEAN UNION:
CAN THERE BE ONE WAY FORWARD?

THE POSITION IN MALTA JUXTAPOSED TO THE PRINCIPLES OF EUROPEAN FAMILY LAW: DIVORCE AND MAINTENANCE

Ruth Farrugia

1. INTRODUCTION

In the brief assigned for this paper, the request was to provide a review of the situation in divorce and maintenance in the Maltese legal system. This was to entail the examination of the Principles of European Family Law regarding divorce and maintenance between former spouses together with an assessment of whether these Principles could be adopted with ease into the existing framework of family law in the Maltese system.

Coming from a country where obtaining a local divorce is not part of family law; my first reaction was to decline the assignment. However on further examination, it became apparent that Maltese rules relating to separation following marital breakdown are in fact closely aligned to the rules pertaining to divorce in other comparable European countries. Furthermore, recognition of foreign divorce is part of Maltese law and the legal position following this eventuality certainly bears examination within this context.

Owing to the particular circumstances pertaining in Malta, this paper examines marriage, annulment and separation before determining the relative effects on the situation post relationship. This was deemed necessary in order to incorporate alternative measures available at law in the absence of divorce. Provision for maintenance is also scrutinised within this larger scenario. Finally, the proposed principles are applied to the Maltese framework with a view to establishing to what extent, if at all, they could be incorporated into the Maltese legal system.

2. MATRIMONIAL BREAKDOWN

2.1. MARRIAGE

2.1.1. History – Canon Law – the Constitution

The Maltese concept of marriage is directly influenced by classical Roman and Canon law concepts. The Courts have repeatedly emphasised the sacramentality of marriage and the importance of monogamy and indissolubility.

Case law has reiterated the characteristics of a valid marriage within the Maltese definition declaring *"the marriage contract on this Island remains always indissoluble for whatever class of person, catholic or non catholic... the law in Malta, prior to the Council of Trent, has always retained the marriage bond as indissoluble outside the death of one of the spouses."*[1]

Under Canon law, *"a marriage which is ratified and consummated cannot be dissolved by any human power or by any cause other than death."*[2] A marriage is deemed to be ratified when the spouses are baptised and the Maltese population is said to be made up of 98% baptised persons who are subject to Canon Law simply in virtue of their being baptised. Furthermore, the Constitution of Malta specifically lists the Roman Catholic faith as the official religion of Malta:

> Article 2(1) *"The religion of Malta is the Roman Catholic Apostolic religion.*
> *(2) The authorities of the Roman Catholic Apostolic Church have the duty and the right to teach which principles are right and which are wrong."*

The Constitution of Malta makes no reference to the right to marry or the right to found a family life. Under Article 38 it makes reference to the right to privacy and there is some allusion to respect for one's private and family life in the preamble to Article 32

> *"Whereas every person in Malta is entitled to the fundamental rights and freedoms of the individual, that is to say the right, whatever his race, place of origin, political opinions, colour, creed or sex; but subject to respect for the rights and freedoms of others and for the public interest, to each and all of the following, namely—(c) respect for his private and family life."*

---

[1] *David James Low versus Marianna Micallef Low* Collected Cases, Volume XIII-243 (27/06/1892).

[2] Code of Canon Law, Canon 1141.

One should point out that the preamble is not enforceable and it has been suggested that the reference is to existing and not future family life so that there is no right to begin a family life. However, Malta ratified the European Convention on Human Rights in 1987 and is bound by interpretation of Articles 8 and 12. The European Court of Human Rights has however consistently steered away from describing divorce as a right and,

> *"furthermore, these words [right to marry] are found in a context that includes an express reference to "national laws"; even if, as the applicants would have it, the prohibition on divorce is to be seen as a restriction on capacity to marry, the Court does not consider that, in a society adhering to the principle of monogamy, such a restriction can be regarded as injuring the substance of the right granted by article 12".[3]*

Furthermore the opening statement of the Civil Code which provides for the Law of Persons does not make a direct reference to marriage or family life but declares

> Article 2(1): *"The law promotes the unity and stability of the family."*[4]

Although the National Family Commission[5] has been entrusted with the drafting of a national family policy and legislation abounds with reference to differing notions of family, to date there is no definition of "family".

The Civil Code also provides for the institution of separation whereby provision is made for a temporary or permanent response to marital breakdown. However separation does not affect the marital bond *per se* so that post separation relationships are deemed extra-marital and adulterous.[6]

2.1.2. Marriage Act 1975 Chapter 255-Laws of Malta

Until 1975, all marriages in Malta were subject to the tenets of Canon Law. The majority of couples who marry opt to marry both by civil as well as by canonical rite, although the law clearly establishes both options. It is church policy to dissuade persons from marrying by canonical rite alone.

---

3   *Johnston and others versus Ireland*, ECHR 6/1985/92/139 (18/12/1986) was closely followed by many in Malta.

4   The Civil Code, Chapter 16, Laws of Malta.

5   The author has been a member of this Commission since its inception in 2001.

6   Although adultery is no longer a criminal offence, the Civil Code apportions penalties to the spouse committing adultery by altering or eliminating maintenance allowance and allocation of community property. Such effects may take place well beyond the judgement giving rise to separation.

Article 11 (1) A marriage may be contracted either in a civil form, that is to say in the form established by this Act for civil marriage, or in a religious form, that is to say in a religious form in accordance with the provisions of this Act.

(2) A marriage, whether contracted in a civil or in a religious form, shall be valid only if all the provisions of this Act applicable thereto or to marriage generally are satisfied or observed.

(3) In the case of the non-observance of any formality or other similar requirement relating to the celebration of the marriage or preparatory thereto, a marriage may not be annulled and shall be held to have always been valid, if the demand for annulment is not made within two years after the celebration of the marriage.

Marriage may take place provided both parties are over the age of sixteen years[7] and are not related to each other in the relationships prohibited at law.[8] Any mental illness which renders a party incapable of marriage renders a marriage null and void.[9]

The advent of the Marriage Act 1975 made civil marriage possible but did not alter the position relating to monogamy and indissolubility.[10] Article 6 provides: "*A marriage contracted between persons either of whom is bound by a previous*

---

[7] Chapter 255, Article 3(1) "A marriage contracted between persons either of whom is under the age of sixteen shall be void."

[8] Chapter 255, Article 5 (1) "A marriage contracted between –
(a) an ascendant and a descendant in the direct line;
(b) a brother and a sister, whether of the full or half blood;
(c) persons related by affinity in the direct line; or
(d) the adopter and the adopted person or a descendant, or
the husband or wife, of the adopted person,
shall, whether the relationship aforesaid derives from legitimate or illegitimate descent, be void."

[9] Chapter 255, Article 4. "A marriage contracted between persons either of whom is incapable of contracting by reason of infirmity of mind, whether interdicted or not, shall be void."

[10] The National Statistics Office in a press release issued in May 2004 stated: The number of marriages registered in Malta and Gozo during the year 2003, was 2,350, which is about 6.06 per 1,000 of the mid-year population. This was exactly 110 more marriages than the previous year. Marriages celebrated in Gozo, during the past year, amounted to 181 of which 65 were civil. During the past year 803 or 34.3 per cent were civil marriages while the rest were celebrated in church. However, it has to be emphasized that the majority are non-Maltese marrying non-Maltese; and this has always been the case over the past years.
As a matter of fact, out of the 803 civil marriages, only 78 were between Maltese couples and this represented 9.7 per cent of all civil marriages. Of the 1,547 marriages celebrated in church, 1,445 or 94.1 per cent involved Maltese partners. There were 18 cases where both the bride and the groom were Irish and 12 marriages where both partners were English. Most of the remaining marriages were contracted between Maltese grooms and foreign brides, whilst in 35 cases, the bride was Maltese and the groom was a foreigner. In general, Maltese couples are still opting for a church marriage. In fact, 95 per cent of the cases in which both the bride and groom were Maltese, were celebrated in church. In cases of mixed marriages, where either the bride or the groom was a foreigner, 88 per cent opted for a civil marriage.

marriage shall be void"[11] Additionally, bigamy is a criminal offence punishable with a maximum of four years imprisonment.[12]

Divorce has been said to be deemed to be incompatible with Maltese culture and religious tradition which is founded deeply in Roman Catholicism. In Malta, a divorce may only be obtained from a foreign jurisdiction and registered in the Public Registry. The only local solution to a broken marriage is separation, following which a new relationship may lead to a state of concubinage[13] which is not regulated by law. It is also possible to request annulment of a marriage whereby a declaration is made that the marriage in question never existed.

2.2. ANNULMENT[14]

2.2.1. Definition

According to Article 19 of the Marriage Act

> *A marriage shall be void:*
> *(a) if the consent of either of the parties is extorted by violence, whether physical or moral, or fear;*
> *(b) if the consent of either of the parties is excluded by error on the identity of the other party;*
> *(c) if the consent of either of the parties is extorted by fraud about some quality of the other party which could of its nature seriously disrupt matrimonial life;*
> *(d) if the consent of either of the parties is vitiated by a serious defect of discretion of judgment on the matrimonial life, or on its essential rights and duties, or by a serious psychological anomaly which makes it impossible for that party to fulfil the essential obligations of marriage;*
> *(e) if either of the parties is impotent, whether such impotence is absolute or relative, but only if such impotence is antecedent to the marriage;*
> *(f) if the consent of either of the parties is vitiated by the positive exclusion of marriage itself, or of any one or more of the essential elements of matrimonial life, or of the right to the conjugal act;*
> *(g) if either of the parties subjects his or her consent to a condition referring to the future;*

---

[11]   The Marriage Act, Chapter 255, Laws of Malta.
[12]   Criminal Code, Chapter 9, Laws of Malta, Article 196 "A husband or wife, who during the subsistence of a lawful marriage, contracts a second marriage, shall on conviction, be liable to imprisonment for a term from thirteen months to four years." Interestingly enough the article is placed under the Title VII "Of Crimes affecting the Good Order of Families".
[13]   This is still the legal term used for relationships outside wedlock.
[14]   In 1980 there were 3 annulment cases as compared with 174 in 2003.

(h) if either of the parties, although not interdicted or infirm of mind, did not have at the time of contracting marriage, even on account of a transient cause, sufficient powers of intellect or volition to elicit matrimonial consent.

(2) Subject to the provisions of this Act, an action for the annulment of a marriage may only be commenced by one of the parties to that marriage, and this provision shall apply even where such party is, under any provision of law, incapable of suing or being sued, and in any such case the action may be commenced by such party notwithstanding such incapacity, saving any assistance or other condition the court may deem appropriate to order. Where an action has been commenced by a party to a marriage, the action may be continued by any of the heirs.

An amendment which can be seen to be directly influenced by Canon Law was introduced in 1995.

Article 19A (1) A valid marriage may be annulled at the request of one of the spouses on the grounds that the other party has refused to consummate the same.
(2) The provisions of article 19(2) shall apply to an action for the annulment of a marriage referred to in sub-article (1) as it applies to an action for the annulment of a marriage therein referred to.
(3) An action for the annulment of a marriage under this article may not be instituted before the lapse of three months from the date of the celebration of the marriage.

The reason for this final inclusion of a three month period before being able to institute an action has been put down to a deterrent to marriage of convenience. However, it seems to go directly against the very notion of the issue the article seeks to promote.

2.2.2. Effects of Annulment

The effects of the annulment are such as to bring about a reversal of status. Children born of a marriage which has been annulled are deemed to be the fruit of a putative marriage under the principle that the innocent should not suffer. This was particularly relevant in the context of legislation which penalised children born out of wedlock, known as illegitimate children, up until 2004.[15]

Article 20 also establishes penalties for the party who entered into the annulled marriage in bad faith establishing a maximum maintenance award of five years in favour of the innocent party. The article makes no mention of any obligations vis a vis children and one of the lacunae of the law lies precisely in the lack of provision for the parties and their children following the annulment. The more usual

---

[15]   Act XVIII.2004 removed relative incapacities of children and the distinction between illegitimate and legitimate children.

procedure is for the parties to enter into a public deed specifying how joint property is to be apportioned and where children are involved, elaborating maintenance rights and duties and allocation of contact and custody.

> Article 20 *(1) If a marriage is declared to be void the effects of a valid marriage shall be deemed to have existed, in favour of the spouses until the judgment of nullity has become a res judicata when both spouses had contracted the marriage in good faith.*
>
> *(2) The effects of a valid marriage shall be deemed to have always existed with reference to the children born or conceived during a marriage declared to be void as well as with reference to children born before such marriage and acknowledged before the judgment declaring the nullity.*
>
> *(3) If only one of the spouses was in good faith such effects shall apply in his or her favour and in favour of the children.*
>
> *(4) If both spouses were in bad faith the effects of a valid marriage shall apply only in favour of the children born or conceived during the marriage declared to be void.*
>
> *(5) Notwithstanding any other provision, the spouse who was responsible for the nullity of the marriage, is bound to pay maintenance to the other spouse in good faith for a period of five years, which duty shall cease if the party in good faith marries during such period.*

2.2.3. Recognition of canonical annulments

The 1995 amendments also brought about recognition of canonical annulment by the civil courts so that

> Article 25 *A decree given by the Roman Pontiff "super matrimonio rato et non consummato", when one of the spouses is domiciled in or is a citizen of Malta, shall, subject to the provisions of article 26, be recognised and upon its registration in accordance with the said article 26, shall have effect as if it were a decision given by a court and which has become res judicata annulling a marriage on the grounds of non-consummation, in accordance with article 19A.*

Furthermore, administrative steps were introduced to enable the registration of an annulment obtained before the Ecclesiastical Tribunal by its presentation in the Civil Marriage Registry following a decree of the Court of Appeal relating to its enforceability. It is restricted to persons who can prove their domicile in Malta or Maltese nationality.

> Article 26 *(1) Registration of a decree as is referred to in article 25 shall be effected by the Court of Appeal.*
>
> *(2) A request for such registration shall be made by application accompanied by an authentic copy of the pontifical decree filed in the registry of the said court, and which shall be served on the Director of the Public Registry and where it is presented by one only of the spouses, on the other spouse.*

(3) The respondents shall have a right to file a reply within twelve working days of service upon them of the application.

(4) (a) Registration shall be effected by an order of the Court of Appeal declaring the decree of the Roman Pontiff enforceable in Malta.

(b) The Court of Appeal shall register the decree if it is satisfied that it refers to a catholic marriage which was celebrated after the coming into force of this article and either of the spouses is domiciled in or is a citizen of Malta.

(5) Notwithstanding the provisions of sub-article (4) hereof, the Court of Appeal shall give a decree which refers to a catholic marriage celebrated before the coming into force of this article where the application therefore is filed by both spouses, or where it is filed by one only of the spouses, the other spouse does not oppose the registration.

The law goes as far as prohibiting the Court of Appeal from entering into the merits of the case and makes it a requisite for the judicial authority to ascertain which court was first seized of a petition for annulment. In this way a party who is anxious to have a case heard before the Ecclesiastical Tribunal can pre-empt the other party by filing proceedings before the chosen court, or vice versa. The raison d'etre of this provision seems to have been the elimination of dual proceedings with accompanying financial, psychological and logistical strain for the parties. It also aimed at relieving the burden of additional cases from already overburdened civil courts.

Article 28 In the course of an application under articles 24 and 26 the Court of Appeal shall not go into the merits of the case leading to the decision or the decree the registration of which is demanded in the application but shall limit itself to ascertain if the requirements of this Act for the registration requested exist.

In the case of a conflict between the two jurisdictions the 1995 amendments clarify that a petition whereby a case for the declaration of nullity of a catholic marriage celebrated after the coming into force of this article, is initiated before such Tribunal, the Chancellor of the Tribunal or his substitute shall deliver a certificate of such acceptance, duly authenticated, to the Registrar of Courts who shall keep the same in an appropriate register.

(2) Upon the registration as is referred to in sub-article (1), the court shall cease to be competent to deal with the matter; and where an action is pending before the court for the declaration of nullity of a marriage in relation to which a certificate has been delivered to the Registrar in accordance with sub-article (1), the court shall suspend the hearing of the case before it, and may not resume hearing the case and, in any case, shall not again be competent until the said case has, in accordance with the procedures of the Tribunal, been withdrawn from before the Tribunal or been declared abandoned.

(3) It shall be the duty of the Registrar to bring to the notice of the court any certificate which refers to that case, delivered to him in accordance with sub-article (1), as well as any decision relative thereto, registered in terms of article 24.

(4) Where an action for the declaration of nullity of a catholic marriage is brought before a court, the court shall ascertain its competence in terms of this Act.

Having said all this, the law then enters this proviso:

Article 35 *Without prejudice to articles 21 to 31, Canon Law shall, in so far as it had effect as part of the law of Malta on marriage, cease to have such effect, and all jurisdiction in relation to marriage shall vest in the courts of Malta in accordance with the relevant provisions of the Code of Organization and Civil Procedure.*

In 1995 the Republic of Malta entered into an agreement with the Holy See

The Holy See and the Republic of Malta,
– considering, on the part of the Holy See, Catholic doctrine on marriage, as also expressed in the Code of Canon Law, as well as the teaching of the Second Vatican Ecumenical Council on relations between the Church and the State, and, on the part of the Republic of Malta, the principles enforced by the Constitution of Malta;
– wanting to ensure, in line with fundamental human rights and the values of the family based on marriage, a free choice in matters of marriage; have recognized that it is opportune to reach an agreement on the recognition of civil effects to canonical marriages and to the decisions of the ecclesiastical Authorities and tribunals about the same marriages.

Article 3
The Republic of Malta recognizes for all civil effects, in terms of this Agreement, the judgements of nullity and the decrees of ratification of nullity of marriage given by the ecclesiastical tribunals and which have become executive.

Article 5
The judgements of nullity and the decrees of ratification of nullity of marriage given by the ecclesiastical tribunals are recognized as producing civil effects, provided that:
a) a request is presented, by the parties or either of them, to the Court of Appeal together with an authentic copy of the judgement or decree, as well as a declaration of its executivity according to canon law issued by the tribunal that has given the executive decision;
b) the Court of Appeal ascertains that:
(i) the ecclesiastical tribunal was competent to judge the case of nullity of the marriage insofar as the marriage was celebrated according to the canonical form of the Catholic Church or with a dispensation therefrom;
(ii) during the canonical judicial proceedings there was assured to the parties the right of action and defense, in a manner substantially not dissimilar to the principles of the Constitution of Malta;
(iii) in the case of a marriage celebrated in Malta after the 11 August 1975, there has been delivered or transmitted to the Public Registry the act of marriage laid down by the civil law;
(iv) there does not exist a contrary judgement pronounced by the civil tribunals and which has become res judicata, based on the same grounds of nullity.

The Protocol of application sets out:

> *With reference to article 1,2*
> *For the purpose of putting into effect article 1,2 the following are understood to be impediments considered mandatory or not dispensable by the civil law:*
> *a) the lack of age, which is sixteen years completed for both parties;*
> *b) the infirmity of mind of at least one of the parties which renders it incapable of contracting marriage;*
> *c) consanguinity in the direct line and up to the second degree in the collateral line;*
> *d) the subsistence of a previous marriage, valid in civil law, of at least one of the parties.*

2.2.4. Marriages of Convenience

The last amendment to the Marriage Act came about in 2004 and relates to marriages of convenience:

> *Article 38 (1) Any person who contracts a marriage with the sole purpose of obtaining -*
> *(a) Maltese citizenship; or*
> *(b) freedom of movement in Malta; or*
> *(c) a work or residence permit in Malta; or*
> *(d) the right to enter Malta; or*
> *(e) the right to obtain medical care in Malta, shall be guilty of an offence and shall on conviction be liable to imprisonment for a term not exceeding two years.*
> *(2) Any right or benefit obtained by a person convicted of an offence under subarticle (1) on the basis of the marriage referred to in that subarticle (1) may be rescinded or annulled by the public authority from which it was obtained.*
> *(3) Any person who contracts a marriage with another person knowing that the sole purpose of such other person in contacting the marriage is one or more of the purposes referred to in subarticle (1) shall be guilty of an offence and shall on conviction be liable for the same punishment laid down in subarticle (1).*

2.3. DIVORCE

2.3.1. Position in Malta

The enforcement of foreign judgements in Malta has always been possible through the provisions of Article 826 of the Code of Organisation and Civil Procedure.

> *"Saving the provisions of the British judgments (Reciprocal enforcement) Act, any judgement delivered by a competent court outside Malta and constituting a res judicata may be enforced by the competent court in Malta, in the same manner as judgements deliv-*

ered in Malta, upon a writ of summons containing a demand that the enforcement of such judgement be ordered."

In order for a person to remarry according to Maltese law, Article 18 (b) specifies that such person's *lex domicilii* at the time of the second marriage must be such as to allow capacity to contract a second marriage.

> Article 18: *"A marriage, whether celebrated in Malta or abroad, shall be invalid for all purposes of law in Malta if -*
> *(a) as regards the formalities thereof, the formalities required for its validity by the law of the country where the marriage is celebrated are observed; and*
> *(b) as regards the capacity of the parties, each of the persons to be married is, by the law of the country of his or her respective domicile, capable of contracting marriage."*

The decision as to capacity is dependent on the courts adjudication of the competence of the foreign court.

> Article 33: *"A decision of a foreign court on the status of a married person or affecting such status shall be recognised for all purposes of law in Malta if the decision is given by a competent court of the country in which either of the parties to the proceedings is domiciled or of which either of such parties is a citizen."*

2.3.2. Registration of foreign divorce judgement

Therefore while Maltese law does not provide a means for dissolution of a marriage, a foreign divorce may be registered in Malta. It has already been mentioned that Malta is the only country in Europe not to have a divorce law.[16] The debate as to its introduction has persisted over the years and a growing lobby cites the lack of such legislation as discriminatory against Maltese citizens. The issue is further complicated by the fact that it is possible to register a foreign judgment of divorce in a Maltese court which means that divorce is attainable for a small percentage of people who are married to a foreign national who has no problem obtaining a divorce in his/her country or for an even smaller number of persons who can afford the time and expense of establishing their domicile in a country that permits divorce with a view to then returning to register the judgement in Malta.

Naturally the issue is not easily resolved because of cultural and religious commitments deep-rooted in the Maltese psyche. However the mingling of foreign cultures and the free movement of persons enabled by entry into the European Union may well cause further reflection for the introduction of a civil right attain-

---

[16]   Throughout the entire world it is only Malta and the Philippines that remain without a divorce law.

able to the rest of our European neighbours. Without doubt, the introduction of such legislation will not affect a large number of Maltese people who feel strongly that marriage is a life-long commitment which is only dissolved on death.

Furthermore, the feeling among many seems to reflect the notion that the introduction of divorce will adversely affect the unity and stability of the Maltese family. This thesis seems to be strengthened by a number of studies which have been carried out in countries that have been through the divorce experience. However this attitude has done nothing to lessen the growing number of separation cases or incidence of cohabitation which also remains unregulated at law. As long as the legislator remains unsure as to the impact of divorce on the family, separation and annulment where applicable, will remain the only options. Otherwise, local people who wish to terminate their marriage must continue to seek alternative remedies beyond our shores.

2.4. PERSONAL SEPARATION

2.4.1. Chapter 16 – Laws of Malta

Separation is possible as the result of litigation or, increasingly these days, "subject to the authority of the court [...] effected by mutual consent of the spouses, by means of a public deed". In both instances the spouse or spouses must first request leave from the Family Court to proceed with the separation after attending an initial session to establish whether reconciliation is possible.

The outcome of this sitting is to recommend conciliation through counselling and therapy or to refer the spouse(s) to mediation unless there are clear indications which militate against the mediation option being applied, such as domestic violence. Prior to the onset of mediation in 2004, the court had the responsibility to try to help the spouses reach reconciliation. This responsibility was frequently perceived as an unrealistic burden placed on the shoulders of the judiciary who did not have the time or the training to address the issue, notwithstanding their noble efforts.

Following Legal Notice 397, 2003 spouses now have to attend mediation sessions in an effort to reach an amicable settlement relating to their separation. Where such agreement is not possible or is only attained partially, the court intervenes to remedy the process. Although the underlying notion is that the spouses are best suited to determine the conditions for the agreement to regulate their rights and obligations post separation, there is now the trend of remitting the proposed agreement where the judge in the Family Court feels the conditions are questionable, particularly in respect to the arrangements made on behalf of minor children.

Until 1981 all grounds for separation implied fault or attribution of guilt to at least one party. Although there remained a reluctance to eliminate guilt completely and to introduce an alternative no fault separation, the amendments to the Civil Code brought about the introduction of an additional ground whereby the spouses may plead that they "cannot reasonably be expected to live together as the marriage has irretrievably broken down". This ground is tied to the requirement of marriage for a period of not less than four years.

Prior to the introduction of this ground, separation was only possible where fault could be attributed to one or both parties. This was important because the effects such blame brought with it, particularly in relation to apportionment of community property, allocation of maintenance and at times even to the award to care and custody of minor children.

2.4.2. Grounds

Separation may be requested on one of the following grounds: adultery; excesses, cruelty, threats or grievous injury on the part of the other against the plaintiff or against any of his or her children; irretrievable breakdown, provided the marriage is of at least four years duration; and desertion for two years or more.

2.4.3. Effects according to Grounds

2.4.3.a. Adultery

Article 38: *"Either of the spouses may demand separation on the ground of adultery on the part of the other spouse."*

Adultery is viewed as the most extreme violation of the duty of fidelity within marriage. Proof of adultery is not always easy although the birth of a child by a parent other than the spouse is a classic example.

There are serious repercussions for the party found guilty of adultery and these are listed in Article 48: as depriving that spouse from rights under the law of succession; things acquired from the other spouse by donation in contemplation of marriage, during the marriage or under any other gratuitous title; any right to half the community of acquests which may have been made by the industry chiefly of the other spouse after a date to be established by the court as corresponding to the date when the spouse is considered as having given sufficient cause to the separation; and the right to compel the other spouse to supply maintenance.

2.4.3.b.   Violence

Article 40: *"Either of the spouses may demand separation on the grounds of excesses, cruelty, threats or grievous injury on the part of the other against the plaintiff or against any of his or her children..."*

Excesses is a blanket term which covers all acts of violence which endanger the life or health of the person who suffers them. They include attempted murder, assault, bodily harm and any violence of a severe nature listed under the Criminal Code. Cruelty includes all acts and ill-treatment which does not necessarily endanger life or health but violates the duty of assistance equally incumbent on both spouses and without which conjugal life is deemed to be rendered intolerable.

Threats include all words spoken or written with the intent of inflicting pain or causing fear and making life miserable. Grievous injury or gross insults encompasses all words and actions which seriously offend the honour of the person to whom they are directed or which express contempt, whether they are written or spoken, or whether they refer to real or imaginary events or issues. This last ground is frequently cited as a plea for separation.

At law, any of the acts of violence, cruelty, threats and gross insults need not be directed against the other spouse but may also be directed against any children of the plaintiff, be they children of the marriage, children of a previous marriage or children born outside marriage.

The effects of offending against this ground are left to the discretion of the court which may apply all or some of the sanctions listed in Article 48, depending on the circumstances of the case and the guilt attributable to each party.[17]

2.4.3.c.   Irretrievable breakdown

Article 40: *"Either of the spouses may demand separation [...] on the ground that the spouses cannot reasonably be expected to live together as the marriage has irretrievably broken down: ..."*

---

[17]   Article 51 and 52.

Irretrievable breakdown is a ground which was introduced into the Civil Code in 1981[18] bringing about innovation in its elimination of the notion of guilt. All the other grounds for separation are firmly entrenched in the traditional notion of *culpa* while this addition affirms the possibility of spouses requesting separation for reasons not attributable to the other party, but on the ground that conjugal life is no longer possible.

In order to invoke this ground the couple must prove that they have been married for a period of not less than four years and the court must be satisfied that the marriage has broken down. There are no sanctions applicable at law when separation is sought under this ground for the simple fact that no fault is attributable to either party.

2.4.3.d. Desertion

Article 41: *"Either of the spouses may also demand separation if, for two years or more, he or she shall have been deserted by the other, without good grounds."*

Desertion is a technical term signifying the abandonment of the matrimonial home with the intention of permanence and the failure of good grounds for so doing. The duty of cohabitation in marriage is violated by this act so that an absence of at least two years without the intention of return could lead to the petitioning for separation on this ground. Where a spouse is compelled to leave the matrimonial home for good grounds (such as violence), desertion would not apply. The effects of desertion are as serious as those of adultery and the spouse who deserts stands to make substantial losses as previously referred to under Article 48.

3. MAINTENANCE

The definition of maintenance is given in Article 19:

> *(1) "Maintenance shall include food, clothing, health and habitation.*
> *(2) In regard to children and other descendents, it shall also include the expenses necessary for health and education."*

---

18   Act XXX.1981.

3.1. SPOUSES

During marriage both spouses are bound to maintain each other. Article 3 of the Civil Code clearly sets out:

> Both spouses are bound, each in proportion to his or her means and his or her ability to work whether in the home or outside the home as the interest of the family requires, to maintain each other and to contribute towards the needs of the family.

The inclusion of work in the family has now clarified the issue before the courts once and for all so that any spouse who stays at home in the interest of the family, as in the case of caring for minor children or vulnerable persons, is deemed to be making a contribution in kind. Although this notion was implicit in previous legislation and was always taken into account on separation of community property, amendments in 1993 made the situation beyond question.

3.1.1. Competition for maintenance

When rights to maintenance are being established in competition with other person, the law states that:

> Article 5(1) In regard to maintenance the spouse shall have a prior right over the parents or other ascendants.
> (2) Where both children and spouse claim maintenance, they shall be in apposition of equality.
> (3) It shall not be lawful for either of the spouses to claim maintenance from the children or other descendents or from the ascendants if such maintenance can be obtained from the other spouse."

3.1.2. Loss of right to maintenance

The duty of one spouse to maintain the other *"shall cease if the latter, having left the matrimonial home, without reasonable cause, refuses to return thereto."*[19] The interpretation of "reasonable cause" is left to the courts and has been identified as any act which renders conjugal living impossible such as violence of any kind, both physical and mental, as well as any other act which the spouse may show has justified refusal to return.

Although the law does not specify the requirement, in practice this duty is terminated when the spouse who is bound to supply maintenance sends a judicial act

---

[19]   Civil Code, Chapter 16 Laws of Malta, Article 6.

to the creditor spouse requesting his/her return and is turned down or ignored. The correct response would be to justify the abandonment of the matrimonial home by providing a reasonable cause. This would then permit the court to make a provisional maintenance allocation to the spouse who applies for it pending resolution of the dispute, the reaching of a mediated settlement or the decision of the Family Court in contentious proceedings.

3.1.3. Quantum of maintenance

During the time the court is seized of the action for separation, either spouse may request "*a maintenance allowance in proportion to his or her needs and the means of the other spouse, and taking into account also all other circumstances of the spouses*"[20] The motive behind such allowance allocation is the preservation of the standard of living to which the creditor spouse is accustomed.[21] However factors such as the actual financial means of the debtor spouse must also be considered together with any joint financial commitments which are to the benefit of the family and where failure to honour them might prejudice the family.

Article 54 lays down the principle that *(1) The spouse against whom the separation is pronounced shall not, as a result of such separation, be relieved from the obligation of supplying maintenance to the other spouse, where [...] such maintenance is due*". Once again as in the case of maintenance *pendente lite* under Article 46A, the quantum of such maintenance is dependent on means and needs as well as the circumstances of the spouses jointly.

3.1.4. Lump sum payments

It is possible for the court to direct that maintenance be paid in lump sum format instead of in regular instalments. Although the more usual method of payment is a monthly allowance, there are increasing cases of spouses wishing to terminate the maintenance obligation by paying one sum of money once. It is also possible to stagger the payments of the lump sum compensation and pay it in instalments.

However there are some risks involved in the payment of the lump sum by instalments since a change in circumstances of the debtor spouse may lead to the remaining maintenance owing being absolved while any payment already made

---

20   Civil Code, Chapter 16 Laws of Malta, Article 46A.
21   This is in direct contrast to the plea for maintenance *pendente lite* by persons other than spouses where Article 25 specifies that interim allowance shall consist *"in such amount as is necessary for bare subsistence"*.

remains irretrievable. Lump sum payment may also take the form of the debtor's share of the matrimonial home.

The raison d'être of lump sum payment under Maltese law is to enable the creditor spouse to achieve financial independence or a position of less dependence. It expects the court to award such lump sum maintenance in cases where the creditor spouse needs the money in order to train or retrain in a profession, art, trade or other activity which would generate an income and so render him or her financially independent. In practice, lump sum payments have gained popularity as a means to simply sever ties between spouses whose marriage has irretrievably broken down.

3.2. CHILDREN

Maintenance of children is an obligation that arises out of marriage and parenthood.

> Article 3B *"Marriage imposes on both spouses the obligation to look after, maintain, instruct and educate the children of the marriage taking into account the abilities, natural inclinations and aspirations of the children."*

> Article 7 (1) *"Parents are bound to look after, maintain, instruct and educate their children in the manner laid down in Section 3B of this Code."*

3.2.1. Parental responsibility

Where the parents apply for annulment or separation their commitments towards their children are unaffected by the change in the spousal relationship. Parents have a responsibility to maintain all children up until the age of eighteen years and in some cases beyond this age.[22]

---

[22] Where a child has a disability which renders him/her dependent beyond the age of eighteen, parents remain liable for support and care, otherwise liability ceases on the child attaining the age of eighteen years. [Judgement of the Civil Court, First Hall, 05/11/1991: *George MALLIA v Teresa MUSCAT noe*] However a recent case has brought this matter into question: it concerns a father seeking to stop maintenance for two of three children on their having attained the age of eighteen. The mother argued that both children (sic) were in full time education, her maintenance allowance did not permit her to support them and this went directly contrary to the basic notion at law under Article 3B.The court decided that maintenance for children did cease at age eighteen but there was a responsibility under Article 3B for which reason the maintenance deducted from the children was awarded to the mother so that she could continue to support them in their studies. The case is under appeal.

Children are to be cared for by their parents during the separation process and the court is bound to give those directions "as it may deem appropriate, and in so doing the paramount consideration shall be the welfare of the children".[23] Where the court finds that the circumstances are such that the children should be removed from the parental authority of one or both parents, it may direct that the child(ren) be placed in alternative forms of care. However even in this case, the parents remain duty bound to *"watch over the maintenance and education"* of the children and *"shall still be bound to contribute thereto, according to law"*. In this way the law states that the obligation of parents to supply maintenance is not tied to physical care and custody of the child and indeed though the parent may have no contact whatsoever with the child for a variety of reasons, s/he is still bound to supply maintenance.[24]

3.2.2. Court intervention

The court is empowered to intervene in any separation agreement in order to ensure that the provisions do in fact respect the best interests of the child. Even where parents reach an amicable settlement which makes specifications for the care of the child, the court may opt to exercise its option to intervene and order a revision of the draft in order to ensure the children's best interests are upheld.[25]

4. LINK TO BRUSSELS II – REGULATION 2201/2003

The Code of Organisation and Civil Procedure provides in Article 742(6)

> "Where provision is made under any other law, or, in any regulation of the European Union making provision different from that contained in this article, the provisions of this article shall not apply with regards to the matters covered by such other provision and shall only apply to matters to which such other provision does not apply".

Malta is a party to Brussels II Bis relating to the recognition and enforcement of judgements,[26] so that when the court is faced with a case regarding divorce, annulment or parental responsibility it has to determine whether or not it has jurisdiction to hear the case. This is done by looking at the regulation rather than at the rules establishing jurisdiction as found in the Code of Organisation and Civil Procedure so that the court is bound to tackle the issue of domicile and

---

23   Civil Code, Chapter 16 Laws of Malta, Article 47.
24   *Ibid*, Articles 56 and 57.
25   *Ibid*, Articles 56, 57 and 61.
26   EC Regulation 2201/2003.

habitual residence which has been the subject of much discussion for many years.

4.1. JURISDICTION

The rules of jurisdiction in Article 3 of Regulation 2201/2003 state that:

> *I.   In matters relating to divorce, legal separation or marriage annulment jurisdiction shall lie with the courts of the Member State*
> *(a)   in whose territory:*
> *i.   the spouses are habitually resident, or*
> *ii.   the spouses were last habitually resident, insofar as one of them resides there, or*
> *iii.   the respondent is habitually resident, or*
> *iv.   in the event of a joint application, either of the spouses is habitually resident, or*
> *v.   the applicant is habitually resident if he or she resided there for at least a year immediately before the application was made, or*
> *vi.   the applicant is habitually resident if he or she resided there for at least six months immediately before the application was made and is either a national of the Member state in question or, in the case of the United Kingdom and Ireland, has his or her "domicile" there;*
> *vii.   the nationality of both spouses or, in the case of the United Kingdom and Ireland, of the "domicile" of both spouses.*

The interpretation of this article will have an effect on access of Maltese nationals to divorce in Member States, often subject to less rigorous rules than were previously applicable. The opposite eventuality of non-Maltese spouses seeking redress in Malta remains to be seen in keeping with this development. For instance, it will be interesting to see what happens when spouses who obtained a divorce by talaq or gett[27] and are declared free to marry in another European state attempt to marry in Malta. Another anomaly might present in relation to the provision in Dutch law enabling spouses to convert their marriage into a cohabitation contract[28] since Malta has no legislation relating to cohabitation let alone to registered partnerships.

The Code of Organisation and Civil Procedure in Article 825A states:

> *Where regulations of the European Union provide, with regard to the matters regulaed under this title, in any manner different than in this title, the said regulations shall pre-*

---

[27]   Both these forms of divorce are not acceptable at Maltese law because they are not the decision of a competent court as cited under Article 33 of the Marriage Act.

[28]   Dutch Civil Code, Article 77A.

vail, and the provisions of this title shall only apply where they are not inconsistent with the provisions of such regulations or in matters not falling within the ambit of such regulations.

4.2. RECOGNITION AND ENFORCEMENT

Therefore in the case of recognition and enforcement of judgements relating to divorce, annulment or parental responsibility, the procedure is governed by the rules found in the Regulation 2201/2003 rather than according to the Code of Organisation and Civil Procedure. However Article 33 of the Marriage Act continues to apply so that automatic recognition as envisaged by the Regulation 2201/2003 may possibly be stalled if compliance is lacking on some issue.

Furthermore Article 25 of the Regulation provides that judgements cannot be refused recognition when *"the law of the Member State in which such recognition is sought would not allow divorce, legal separation or marriage annulment on the same facts"*. Only time will tell how this application fares locally.

5. JUXTAPOSITION AND COMPARISON WITH PRINCIPLES

5.1. PERMISSION OF DIVORCE: PRINCIPLE 1:1

The very first principle causes a problem for Maltese legislation as the law does not permit divorce. As has been illustrated, the law permits the recognition of a divorce obtained through a foreign judgement but there is no mechanism for the granting of divorce within domestic legislation. Therefore, all following principles will be applied in relation to separation on the pretext that if they are applicable in this context they should also be applicable if or when divorce legislation is introduced in Malta.

Under separation law, there are requirements relating to minimum duration of marriage. These apply where the grounds of separation, which the spouse(s) cite as grounds, are desertion (two years) or irretrievable breakdown (four years). No such time limits apply in the cases of violence or adultery.

In view of the fact that these time limits are imposed in order to give the parties ample opportunity to effect reconciliation, it would seem unlikely that a total elimination of time constraints would be met with favourably.

5.2. DIVORCE PROCEDURE: PRINCIPLE 1.2

Rules pertaining to recognition of foreign divorces in Malta already make it amply clear that divorce procedure must be determined by law. The interpretation of Article 33 of the Marriage Act has required a judgement by a competent foreign court indicating the requirement of a judicial process. It remains to be seen whether a decision of an administrative body declared so competent, would be acceptable.

5.3. TYPES OF DIVORCE: PRINCIPLE 1:3

By analogy to the law on separation, a principle which permits divorce by mutual consent and divorce without the consent of one of the spouses should be applicable.

5.4. MUTUAL CONSENT: PRINCIPLE 1:4

Within the context of Maltese separation law, the grounds on which the application is made determine the extent of applicability of this principle. For instance at present it is inconceivable to prospect separation on the grounds of irretrievable breakdown on the basis of mutual consent within a period under the four years requisite at law. It is irrelevant whether the parties are living together or are separated for this time. For this reason mutual consent alone may not be considered the determining factor in permitting separation.

However it is acceptable at law and common practice in non contested cases, for spouses to file a joint application for separation. This does not imply the automatic granting of the separation requested as the law requires an agreement to be concluded relating to post separation rights and obligations. Prior to Legal Notice 397.2003 mentioned above, it was possible to file a joint consensual separation draft agreement before the court and following its acceptance on court scrutiny, be granted separation within a matter of weeks. The introduction of mandatory mediation has made this process longer but consensual separation can be a very brief process, particularly when there are no children to the marriage. This latter consideration included as a provision relating to children in the agreement is subject to court examination and may be turned down if it fails to prove that it is in the best interests of the child(ren).

In the case of annulment, the issues are even more relevant as within the civil law context where the case is contentious, the consent of both parties may often lead to the notion that there is collusion between the spouses in order to dissolve what may have been a valid marriage. The Ecclesiastic Court renders the process one against the validity of the marriage bond itself so that the *difensor vinculi* is appointed to defend the union. In this context, mutual consent of both spouses in favour of the inexistence of the marriage is totally irrelevant.

5.5. REFLECTION PERIOD: PRINCIPLE 1:5

Such period of reflection is outside the practice of current separation law in Malta.

5.6. CONTENT AND FORM OF THE AGREEMENT: PRINCIPLE 1:6

All the notions contained in Principle 1:6 are in keeping with Maltese separation law. It is not possible to effect a legal separation in the absence of an agreement or judicial decree detailing all the elements listed in the said Principle. Any separation agreement must make provision for division of community property, where this is applicable [29] and for allocation of matrimonial home, preferably following agreement of the parties, but where this is lacking, at the order of the court.

Where there are children to the marriage [30] the spouse(s) must make provision for the care and custody (residence and contact) and maintenance of such children. Failure to do so will entail the court ordering whatever provisions are deemed suitable in the best interests of the child. Even where the spouse(s) decide on these issues, the court has the authority and responsibility to review them and may order the resubmission of the draft agreement or may make its own proposals

---

[29]   The community of acquests is the matrimonial regime automatically applied to all marriages celebrated in Malta or to those spouses taking up domicile in Malta. Alternatives are the regime of community of residue under separate administration which was introduced in 1993 and which is still largely unknown and separation of estates which is not very popular. Both latter regimes must be entered by public deed prior to the marriage or if subsequent to the marriage, following authorisation of the court.

[30]   Children are defined as any persons who have not attained the age of eighteen years although this applies equally to adult children who are unable to support themselves owing to disability or some other incapacity at law.

until such time as it is satisfied that the agreement truly serves the best interests of the child(ren).[31]

5.7. DETERMINATION OF THE CONSEQUENCES: PRINCIPLE 1:7

This is the current practice in Maltese law applicable to separation. Apart from the scrutiny concerning articles of the proposed agreement relating to minor children, the court also ascertains whether the contents of the agreement relating to allocation of matrimonial home, division of community property and assignment of maintenance appear to be fair *prima facie*. The court has an obligation to ensure that the parties fully understand the consequences of the agreement they are about to sign where an amicable settlement is reached and enters its own provisions in the case of a judicial decree.

5.8. FACTUAL SEPARATION: PRINCIPLE 1:8

In the framework of separation, consent is not required in the case of violence, adultery or desertion. Neither is a time imposed for separation in the cases of adultery or violence so that a spouse may sue for separation on these grounds immediately following marriage. A time limit applies in relation to desertion where the spouses must have been separated for a period of not less than two years. It is worth noting here that as there is no divorce law in Malta, separation is viewed as a suspension of marriage rather than its termination and to this end it is unnecessary to establish the commencement of separation *de facto* in order to apply for separation itself.

5.9. EXCEPTIONAL HARDSHIP TO THE PETITIONER: PRINCIPLE 1:9

This provision is not applicable in view of its being superseded by alternative provisions cited above.

---

[31] A recent example was a proposal agreed to by the spouses to divide the children to the marriage. The court felt such separation would be detrimental to the children, ordered a psychological report and a child advocate to hear the children's views whereupon the parents reconsidered the proposal and kept the children together [Judgement of the Court of Appeal (Civil Superior), 23/11/2004: *Pauline MUSCAT gia MALLIA v David MALLIA*].

5.10. DETERMINATION OF THE CONSEQUENCES: PRINCIPLE 1:10

These issues are observed under Maltese separation law.

5.11. RELATIONSHIP BETWEEN MAINTENANCE AND DIVORCE: PRINCIPLE 2:1

The allocation of maintenance in the context of separation in Malta is dependent on apportionment of fault, unless the parties reach an amicable settlement. Where separation is based on fault in cases of adultery, violence or desertion, a maintenance award may be and usually is made to the aggrieved party. The quantum of maintenance depends on the economic position of the guilty party although the court determines the amount according to the needs of the applicant and the means of the spouse against whom the separation is pronounced.

The law makes reference to both the award of maintenance *pendente lite* and following the conclusion of the separation. In the former scenario either spouse may apply for maintenance and it is up to the court to reach a prima facie decision relating to which spouse, if either, is the deserving recipient of maintenance. In the latter case, proof would have been brought to show which party is liable to continue payment of maintenance once the separation is declared.

> Article 46A *During the pendency of the action for separation, either spouse, whether plaintiff or defendant, may demand from the other spouse a maintenance allowance in proportion to his or her needs and the means of the other spouse, and taking into account also all other circumstances of the spouses...*

> Article 54 (2) *The amount of such maintenance shall be determined having regard to the means of the spouse bound to supply maintenance and the needs of the other spouse, taking into account also all other circumstances of the spouses.*

Maintenance of children is not notionally connected to this issue at all since the allocation of maintenance for children is linked directly to parental responsibility and has no bearing on spousal support.[32]

---

[32]   In practice it is true that spousal and child support are often merged into one allowance allocation.

5.12. SELF SUFFICIENCY: PRINCIPLE 2:2

There is no standard means for calculation of maintenance although the court is expected to view the assets and liabilities of both spouses in relation to their community property and paraphernal property when determining the quantum of maintenance. Insurance and pension awards also form part of income and are weighted accordingly. However the notion of maintenance as a means of penalising the guilty spouse is still applicable under Maltese law on separation and is enforced in cases of violence and adultery.

5.13. CONDITIONS FOR MAINTENANCE: PRINCIPLE 2:3

The courts are very strict in expecting the debtor spouse to honour commitments relating to maintenance and would only agree to decrease or remove the responsibility in special circumstances when the debtor spouse can prove that s/he is manifestly unable to honour the obligation. Loss of employment for instance must be shown to be unconnected to any action of the debtor spouse. The courts have decreed that where a debtor spouse deliberately quits a job to spite the creditor spouse and not be in sufficient funds to make maintenance payments, the debt would still be due and enforceable. Failure to pay maintenance is a criminal offence and is punishable with imprisonment.

5.14. DETERMINING CLAIMS FOR MAINTENANCE: PRINCIPLE 2:4

The law on separation does not list any specific criteria for determination of maintenance but the underlying notion is that the innocent spouse should not suffer any loss in standard of living where possible. Where fault is not an issue, both spouses are equally deemed to be in a position to support themselves, unless the contrary can be proved to the satisfaction of the court. Caring for the children or for vulnerable members of the family is acceptable as a reason for failing to be economically independent. However any person who is fit and of an age to work is expected to join the labour market and support him/herself unless the contrary can be proved.

Where the separation is based on the guilt of one of the spouses the creditor spouse need not prove any such inability to work although recent trends have tended away from the award of long term maintenance as a penalty and rely on the apportionment of community assets in a way as to favour the creditor spouse according to law. Furthermore, the spouse who stays at home to care for children is assumed to be unable to be economically independent unless the debtor spouse can prove the contrary and for this reason allocation of care and custody is linked to the award of maintenance. The duration of the marriage has no bearing on the award of maintenance.

The event of a new marriage or long-term relationship would have no bearing on the award of maintenance by the debtor spouse unless the circumstances of the creditor spouse had changed to assure maintenance by a third party or new partner. In the case of annulment for instance, although maintenance may be awarded to the innocent party for a period not exceeding four years, this obligation is automatically terminated on new marriage. In post separation proceedings the obligation to financially support the innocent spouse may be altered where the innocent spouse acts contrary to the obligations of marriage, such as committing adultery.[33]

5.15. METHOD OF MAINTENANCE PROVISION: PRINCIPLE 2:5

The general rule is periodical payment in advance, usually on a monthly basis in keeping with salary collection, although the court may direct otherwise according to the means and needs of the spouses.

A lump sum payment may be deemed appropriate in lieu of the whole or part of the maintenance although the law specifies that such a measure would more usually be taken in the attempt to render the spouse to whom the maintenance is due financially independent or less financially dependent.

> Article 54(3) specifies that *"…the court shall, among the circumstances, consider the possibility of the person to whom the maintenance is due, of receiving training or retraining in a profession, art, trade or other activity or to commence or continue an activity which generates an income and order the lump sum for that purpose"*

---

[33] Trends in case law are also changing here. A recent case dealt with the application of a husband whose marriage had been suspended on the grounds of his adultery where he had agreed to pay maintenance to his innocent wife. A few years subsequent to the judicial separation, the wife had an adulterous relationship and the husband sued for cessation of maintenance and a refund of the maintenance paid since the commencement of the relationship. The court of first instance acceded to his request but the Court of Appeal established that the relationship in question had been a 'one night stand' and reversed the decision. The question now centres round what constitutes an adulterous relationship [Judgement of the Court of Appeal (Civil Superior), 03/06/2005: *BORG v BORG gia BUGELLI* and *vide* also more recent judgement of the Court of Appeal (Civil Superior), 03/11/2006: *Dennis FARRUGIA proprio et nomine v Carmen FARRUGIA ROMANO* (ref. 1136/2002/1)].

Payment of the lump sum may be made in equal or unequal payments and may consist of the assignment of property in ownership, usufruct, use or habitation. Problems may arise when the circumstances of the person who is bound to pay such lump sum change.

> Article 54(7) *"Where there is a supervening change in the means of the spouse liable to supply maintenance or the needs of the other spouse, the court may, on the demand of either spouse, order that such maintenance be varied or stopped as the case may be. Where however, a lump sum or an assignment of property has been paid or made in total satisfaction of the obligation of a spouse to supply maintenance to the other spouse, all liability of the former to supply maintenance to the latter shall cease. Where instead the lump sum assignment of property has been paid or made only in partial satisfaction of the said obligation, the court shall, when ordering such lump sum payment or assignment of property, determine at the same time the portion of the maintenance satisfied thereby and any supervening change shall in that case be only in respect of the part not so satisfied and in the same proportion thereto."*

5.16. EXCEPTIONAL HARDSHIP TO THE DEBTOR SPOUSE: PRINCIPLE 2:6

In Maltese legislation, in cases where fault is attributed to one of the spouses, the penalty is the withholding of maintenance. For this reason circumstances of exceptional hardship described as domestic violence and mistreatment are automatically listed under fault and are penalised accordingly.

5.17. MULTIPLICITY OF MAINTENANCE CLAIMS: PRINCIPLE 2:7

The position of the child within Maltese separation law receives paramount consideration. It is not expressly stated that the maintenance claim of the child supersedes that of the creditor spouse, however, in effect all issues relating to children are given priority in relation to other claims. Article 57(1) *"Whosoever may be the person to whom the children are entrusted, the father and mother shall maintain their right to watch over their maintenance and education, and shall be bound to contribute thereto, according to law."*

In relation to the rights of spouses when they have an obligation towards a new spouse, the law in Malta does not mention such an eventuality although it is possible through remarriage post annulment or divorce obtained following the judgement of a foreign court.

Maintenance obligations no longer apply to the relatives of spouses since the amendments of Act XXI.1993. Even within marriage itself there is now no obligation to provide any form of maintenance to in-laws, although support to the spouse's family during marriage through use of community property is accepted in practice.

5.18. LIMITATION IN TIME: PRINCIPLE 2:8

The underlying principle of maintenance in marriage is ongoing support which is not extinguished through separation. For this reason there is no time bar attached to the award of maintenance subsequent to separation. An exception exists in relation to lump sum payments by instalments but the nature of such payment innately requires a time frame established at law. It is a matter for discussion whether this time limit would be deemed just in relation to a divorce where marriage is terminated and where fault is still attributed to one of the spouses.

5.19. TERMINATION OF THE MAINTENANCE OBLIGATION: PRINCIPLE 2:9

The issue of maintenance obligations ceasing on remarriage has already been treated and applies only where annulment provisions so require. With reference to long-term relationships, it should be pointed out that in Malta cohabitation is not recognised at law, regardless of whether short or long term in duration.

As the first option does not apply the second cannot take effect either.

Death does bring about the cessation of maintenance obligations under Maltese separation law so that this provision under Principle 2:9 (3) should be readily acceptable at law.

5.20. MAINTENANCE AGREEMENT: PRINCIPLE 2:10

It would be *contra* public policy to permit arrangements to be made regulating separation prior to the breakdown of the marriage. Before the amendments of 1993 when the institution of *dotarium* was removed, it was possible to ensure that a sum of money would be payable to the wife at the end of the marriage, but in the interests of equality this provision was eliminated (together with the institute of *dota* which was also only in favour of women).

DIVORCE AND MAINTENANCE BETWEEN FORMER SPOUSES IN ESTONIA AND THE CEFL PRINCIPLES

Triin Göttig, Liis Hallik and Triin Uusen-Nacke

1. INTRODUCTION

1.1. HISTORY OF DIVORCE LAW

The first important source of Estonian private law is the Baltic Civil Code, which entered into force in 1865.[1] In the sphere of divorce law it primarily regulated the property consequences of divorce, leaving divorce itself and the prerequisites thereof mainly within the competence of the ecclesiastical law. After the emancipation of the Republic of Estonia in 1918, a decision was taken to substantially decrease the competence of the church concerning marriage law and to recognise civil marriage. As a result, in 1922 the Law on Marriage[2] and in 1925 the Law on Marital Status[3] were passed.

In the context of the European divorce law of that time the 1922 Law on Marriage was comparatively innovative, enabling divorce within a comparatively short period and extending the grounds for divorce.[4] Both spouses had the right to demand that the marriage be dissolved and divorce on the basis of an agreement between the spouses was recognised. The consequences of divorce were still regulated by the Baltic Civil Code[5], pursuant to which the spouse at fault for the divorce was obliged to support the other spouse according to the latter's needs.

---

[1]   Provinzialrecht der Ostseegouvernements. Dritter Theil. Liv-, est- und curlaendisches Privatrecht: zusammengestellt auf Befehl des Herrn und Kaisers Alexander II. St. Petersburg, 1864.

[2]   Abieluseadus (*Law on Marriage*). Riigi Teataja (in the Following: RT) (*The State Gazette*) 1922, No. 138, Art. 88.

[3]   Perekonnaseisuseadus (*Law on Marital Status*). RT 1925, 191/192, 110.

[4]   J. Lõo. Perekonnaseisu ja abielu seaduse eelnõud (*The drafts of the Law on Marital Status and Law on Marriage*). – Õigus 1922, No. 2, pp. 40 and 46; Seletuskiri Tsiviilseadustiku 1935. a eelnõu nelja esimese raamatu juurde (*Explanatory letter to the first four books of the 1935 Draft Civil Code*), compiled by J. Uluots, Tartu 1936, p. 44.

[5]   See §31 of the Law on Marriage.

The maintenance obligation terminated upon the remarriage of the other spouse.[6]

After the establishment of the Republic of Estonia the drafting of our own Civil Code was commenced; the draft was prepared and was presented to the Riigikogu (Estonian parliament) for adoption in the wording of 1940.[7] In regard to divorce law the principles of the Law on Marriage of 1922 as well as the prerequisites of divorce thereof were adopted.[8] Also, the right of a divorced spouse to receive maintenance was established in a wording similar to that of the Baltic Civil Code.[9] The referred draft was not passed as a law due to the Soviet occupation.

During World War II, under the occupation regime, the Law on Marriage, Family and Custody Code of the Russian Soviet Socialist Republic (SSR),[10] the Baltic Civil Code, and the Law on Marriage and the Law on Marital Status were in force in the territory of Estonia. In 1944 the laws of the USSR and Estonian SSR were enacted and subsequently family relationships were regulated by the Law on Marriage, Family and Custody Code of the Russian SSR. Pursuant to the latter the marriage could be dissolved on the basis of an agreement between spouses or in the court in the event of the lack of agreement; pursuant to the amendment of the Code in 1945, only in the court. After divorce only a needy spouse incapacitated for work had the right to maintenance on the condition that the other spouse was capable of providing maintenance.[11]

In 1970 the Marriage and Family Code of the Estonian SSR[12] came into force, according to which the marriage could be dissolved upon an agreement of the spouses in a 'vital statistics office' if the spouses had no minor children and there

---

6   Provinzialrecht der Ostseegouvernements. Dritter Theil. Liv-, est- und curlaendisches Privatrecht, §124.
7   Tsiviilseadustiku eelnõu (*The Draft Civil Code*). EV Riigivolikogu erikomisjoni 12. märtsi 1940. a redaktsioon (*The wording of the select committee of the Parliament of 12 March 1940*). Tartu 1992.
8   See *Explanatory letter to the first four books of the 1935 Draft Civil Code*, note 4, p. 47.
9   §299 of the Draft Civil Code.
10   Кодекс законов о браке, семье и опеке (СУ1926, 82, 612) с изменеиями до 1 июнья 1937 г. Москва, 1937.
11   Eesti NSV territooriumil kehtiv Vene NFSV abielu, perekonna ja eestkoste seaduste koodeks. Ametlik tekst muudatustega kuni 5.12.1952 (*Law on Marriage, Family and Custody Code of the Russian SSR valid on the territory of Estonian SSR. Official text consolidated up to 5.12.1952*). Tallinn, 1952.
12   Eesti NSV abielu- ja perekonnakoodeks (Marriage and Family Code of Estonian SSR). Passed on 31.07.1969. ENSV Teataja (State Gazette of ESSR) 1969, 31, appendix. Last amendment RT I 1992, No. 11, Art.168.

was no dispute concerning the consequences of divorce. Vital statistics offices are the administrative authorities competent in divorce matters.[13]

In all other cases the marriage was dissolved in the court upon the request of a spouse if further cohabitation of the spouses and the preservation of the family proved impossible.[14] The right of a divorced spouse to receive maintenance was guaranteed only in cases enumerated in law and, as a rule, in the case of incapacity for work but without a time limit. The amount of support depended on the need of the dependant person and on the financial situation of the spouses. Support was to be provided by periodic monetary payments. Upon remarriage of the spouse his or her right to maintenance terminated.[15]

After the restoration of independence in 1992 it was decided that the civil law of the Republic of Estonia should be drafted on the basis of the principles of the 1940 draft of the Civil Code[16], but an exception was made concerning family law and the law then in force was taken as a basis. That is why the conceptual bases of the Family Law Act, which entered into force on 1995[17], to a great extent originate in the Marriage and Family Code of the Estonian SSR.[18] It was then held that any change in family law affects emotionally the whole of the society and that radical reforms of the sphere should be more than ordinarily prudent.[19]

---

[13]   Vital statistics offices are structural units of local governments, in the sphere of government of the Ministry of Internal Affairs. See Vabariigi Valitsuse seadus (*Government of the Republic Act*). Adopted on 13.12.1995. RT I 1995, No. 94, Art. 1628. Last amendment RT I 2006, No. 14, Art. 111. The draft Acts Related to Civic Status Act brings no principal changes to the competence of vital statistics offices. The general competence of vital statistics offices upon divorce arises from §64 of the Draft Family Law Act—a vital statistics office shall grant a divorce solely upon mutual consent of the spouses, if both spouses reside in Estonia. Pursuant to §3(4) of the draft Acts Related to Civic Status Act it will be the county governments as administrative authorities who shall grant divorces in the future.

[14]   Marriage and Family Code of Estonian SSR, §§35–46.

[15]   Marriage and Family Code of Estonian SSR, §§30–33.

[16]   Eesti Vabariigi Ülemnõukogu 6. juuli 1992. a otsus Eesti Vabariigi pankrotiseaduse rakendamise kohta (*Resolution of the Supreme Council of the Republic of Estonia of 6 July 1992 on the implementation of the Bankruptcy Act of the Republic of Estonia*), §7.7. RT 1992, No. 31, Art. 404. See also: VARUL, P, Eesti õigussüsteemi taastamine (*Restoration of Estonia's legal system*). – Juridica I/1999, pp. 2–4; VARUL, P, Legal Policy Decisions and Choices in the Creation of New Private Law in Estonia.—Juridica International V/2000, pp. 104–118.

[17]   Perekonnaseadus (*Fmily Law Act*). Passed on 12.10.1994. RT I 1994, No. 75, Art. 1326. Last amendment RT I 2005, No. 39, Art. 308. The English language versions of the Acts of the Republic of Estonia are accessible at: http://www.legaltext.ee.

[18]   SALUMAA, E, Abielu- ja perekonnakoodeksi uus redaktsioon tulekul (*A new version of the Marriage and Family Code on its way*). Juridica I/1993, p. 14.

[19]   VARUL, P, Juridica 1995, No. 1, foreword.

1.2. CONTEMPORARY DIVORCE LAW

Currently, the institutions of marriage and family are constitutionally protected in the Republic of Estonia. First of all the Constitution of the Republic of Estonia[20] establishes the principle that the state shall not interfere with family life.[21] At the same time the Constitution provides for a positive obligation of the state to guarantee the protection of the family, including the institution of marriage[22], the equal rights of the spouses[23] and the duty of the family to care for its members.[24]

The present regulation of divorce and the legal consequences thereof has been enacted on the basis of the principles referred to. Divorce is regulated in Chapter 5 of the Family Law Act, entitled "Termination of Marriage" (§§26–30 of the Family Law Act), and maintenance of the divorced spouses primarily in Chapter 4, entitled "Maintenance of Spouse" (§§21–25 of the Family Law Act).

Actually, the Ministry of Justice of the Republic of Estonia has completed a Draft Family Law Act[25] and a draft of Acts Related to Civic Status Act[26], which do provide for somewhat different details concerning divorce and maintenance of the divorced spouse, but will not bring about essential changes concerning divorce and maintenance of divorced spouses.[27]

---

[20] Eesti Vabariigi Põhiseadus (*Constitution of the Republic of Estonia*). Adopted by a referendum held on 28 June 1992. RT 1992, No. 26, Art. 349. Last amendment RT I 2003, No. 64, Art. 429.

[21] Eesti Vabariigi Põhiseadus §26. See also: Eesti Vabariigi põhiseadus: kommenteeritud väljaanne (*Constitution of the Republic of Estonia with commentaries*). Tallinn, 2002, p. 227; Eesti Vabariigi Põhiseaduse Ekspertiisikomisjoni lõpuaruanne (*Final report of the committee for expert analysis of the Constitution of the Republic of Estonia*). Accessible at: http://www.just.ee/10725 (1 May 2006).

[22] Constitution of the Republic of Estonia, §27 (1).

[23] Constitution of the Republic of Estonia, §27 (2).

[24] Constitution of the Republic of Estonia, §27 (5).

[25] Perekonnaseaduse eelnõu ja seletuskiri 15.05.2006. a redaktsioonis (*Draft Family Law Act and Explanatory Letter in the wording of 15 May 2006*). Accessible at: http://eoigus.just.ee (25.05.2006)

[26] Perekonnaseisutoimingute seaduse eelnõu ja seletuskiri 15.05.2006. a redaktsioonis (*Draft of Acts Related to Civic Status Act and Explanatory Letter in the wording of 15 May 2006*). Accessible at: http://eoigus.just.ee (25 May 2006).

[27] Both drafts were submitted to the Government of the Republic on 18 May 2006 and should enter into force on 1 January 2008.

2. DIVORCE

2.1. GENERAL

2.1.1. General principles of divorce

According to Estonian family law, divorce may be granted by a 'vital statistics office' upon agreement of the spouses and by a court if the spouses disagree.[28] Divorce shall be granted by a court if the spouses disagree about the divorce or if together with the divorce a spouse desires to resolve a dispute concerning a child or concerning the division of joint property or desires support to be ordered. A divorce also falls within the competence of courts if one of the spouses does not reside in Estonia.[29]

In granting a divorce a court ascertains that continuation of the marriage is impossible.[30] A vital statistics office does not ascertain the fact of the breaking down of conjugal relations.

In this context a difference of starting points can be observed concerning the Commission on European Family Law (CEFL) Principles and Estonian law—and a difference not only with the Estonian law but with several other legal orders which the CEFL Principles have rejected to establish the breakdown principle and proceed solely from two grounds: divorce upon agreement of spouses and divorce when a spouse disagrees about divorce. Estonian law proceeds also from other grounds.

Nevertheless, Estonian divorce law is in conformity with the general principle, manifested in CEFL Principle 1:1 (1), that the law should permit divorce. Neither is it required, under Estonian divorce law, that the marriage should have lasted for a certain period (cf. CEFL Principle 1:1 (2)).[31] These general principles of Estonian divorce law shall not be amended by the Draft Family Law Act.

---

[28] The competence of the vital statistics office has been considerably extended when compared to the Marriage and Family Code of ESSR: earlier the spouses with minor children were not allowed to divorce their marriage in a vital statistics office. Pursuant to §§64 and 65 of the Draft Family Law Act the grounds for divorce will in principle remain the same.

[29] See §27 (2) of Family Law Act.

[30] The wording of §29 (2) of the present Family Law Act. Compare this to §67(1) of the Draft Family Law Act, which provides as one of the grounds for a court to grant a divorce the irretrievable termination of conjugal relations. The concept of irretrievable termination of conjugal relations will be dealt with in more detail below under 2.3. In principle, both cases are manifestations of the breakdown principle.

[31] Short duration of marriage as an obstacle to divorce is neither provided by law nor recognised in judicial practice. E.g. Tallinn City Court, by its judgment of 12.08.2002 No. 2/4/228–7644/01

2.1.2. About divorce statistics in Estonia

The number of marriages dissolved in a court (i.e. if there is a dispute) is almost three times smaller than the number of marriages dissolved by vital statistics offices (i.e. upon an agreement between spouses).[32]

Among other things the statistical data shows that the divorce rate in Estonia has not changed considerably year-on-year. The ratio of divorces as compared to marriages has increased due to the decrease of the number of marriages.[33]

The statistics reveal that at the end of 1980s the percentage of marriages broken down after a very short period of cohabitation was significantly higher than in the late 1990s, which can be explained by the fact that in the eighties the age at marriage was very low and the prevalent practice was that when a woman got pregnant, marriage was considered not only desirable but was rather an obligation; today the percentage of short marriages among divorces has decreased due to the decrease of such forced marriages, as free marriage has become a generally accepted form of cohabitation.[34]

---

divorced a marriage which had lasted but 5.5 months.

[32] Number of marriages dissolved by vital statistics offices has been: in 2001–3073, in 2002–2992, in 2003–2929, in 2004–3102 and in 2005–3080, only a very few of these (in 2001–6, in 2002 and in 2003–3 divorces) where divorces on the basis of a petition of one spouse and a court judgment, because the other spouse had been declared missing or lacking active legal capacity (this ground of divorce existed until 1 January 2006). Number of marriages dissolved by courts has been: in 2001–1239, in 2002–1082, in 2003–1044, in 2004–1058 and in 2005–991. The data is accessible at the homepage of Estonian Statistical Office http://www.stat.ee (18 April 2006), whereas the figures for 2004 and 2005 are estimates, that is the interim summary of events entered into registries.

[33] The statistics of marriages and divorces on the basis of different criteria is available at the homepage of Estonian Statistical office http://www.stat.ee.

[34] HANSSON, L, Lahutusjärgsete perede kohanemis- ja toimetulekuraskused. – Lahutus: probleemid ja lahendused (*Adaptability and coping problems of post-divorce families. – Divorce. Problems and solutions*). Rahvusvaheliste ja sotsiaaluuringute instituut (*Institute of International and Social Studies*): Tallinn 2003, pp. 33–34. On the basis of various sample studies the percentage of non-married cohabiting persons is estimated to be up to 15%. The statistics have been pointed out by: TIIT, E-M, KAARIK, E (2000) Sündimuse dünaamika Eestis. Mõjutused, trend ja prognoos Euroopa rahvastikuprotsesside taustal (*The dynamics of births in Estonia. Influences, trends and prognosis against the background of population processes*); available at www.riik.ee/rahvastik/ (20 April 2006), Bureau of Minister of Population Affairs.

2.1.3. Competent authorities in the divorce proceedings and the date of termination of marriage upon divorce

Estonian divorce law provides for judicial as well as administrative proceedings for divorce.[35]

Competent courts in divorce matters are the courts of general jurisdiction, that is, there are no separate family courts in Estonia. In civil matters the first instance courts are the County Courts, against the judgments of which appeals can be filed with the Circuit Courts and—in the third and the last instance—with the Supreme Court. In the County Courts, as the courts of first instance, divorce matters are adjudicated by judges sitting alone, in Circuit Courts the disputes are adjudicated collegially by panels of three, and in the Supreme Court also collegially by panels composed of at least three justices.[36]

Thus, both possibilities provided for in CEFL Principle 1:2 are being implemented in Estonia—both courts and administrative bodies are authorities competent to grant divorce. Also, in conformity with CEFL Principles, Estonian law[37] does not allow the so called "private/informal divorces".[38]

The law also prescribes the procedure for divorce, as required by CEFL Principle 1:2 (1).

In order to dissolve a marriage in a vital statistics office, as a rule (exceptions will be discussed in more detail below under 2.2.2), the spouses have to submit a joint written application, if they agree on the divorce.[39] For divorcing in a court, an action has to be filed indicating the names of common minor children, their dates of birth, who maintains and raises the children, with whom the children live and a proposal as to the further arrangement concerning parental rights and raising of the children.[40]

---

[35] The courts and administrative authorities will remain competent bodies in the future, too, in the Draft Family Law Act, §§64 and 65.

[36] See §§9, 11 and §§16–18 of the Code of Civil Procedure. Tsiviilkohtumenetluse seadustik *(Code of Civil Procedure)*. Adopted on 20.04.2005. RT I 2005, No. 26, Art. 197. Last amendment RT I 2006, No. 7, Art. 42.

[37] It will remain so pursuant to the Draft Family Law Act.

[38] See BOELE-WOELKI, K (ed.). *Principles of European Family Law Regarding Divorce and Maintenance Between Former Spouses*, (2004) Comment 3 under Principle 1:2.

[39] The forms of applications submitted to vital statistics offices and of certificates issued thereby were approved by Regulation No. 2 of the Minister of Regional Affairs of 18 April 2006. Riigi Teataja Lisa *(Appendix)*, 2006, No. 34, Art. 609. The form of divorce application is in appendix 2 of the Regulation.

[40] See §§102 and 363 of the Code of Civil Procedure.

Whereas in a vital statistics office the spouses have to submit their application in person, in a court the spouse/spouses has/have the right to participate in the proceedings either in person or through a representative.

Upon a divorce granted by a vital statistics office, the marriage terminates as of divorce registration, upon divorce granted by a court, as of the entry into force of the court order.[41] There is no need to re-register the divorce granted by a court in a vital statistics office. Pursuant to §29(5) of the Family Law Act it is necessary to send a copy of the court order to the vital statistics office where the marriage was contracted within ten days after the entry into force of a court order granting a divorce.

2.2. AGREEMENT AS A GROUND FOR DIVORCE

2.2.1. Divorce by mutual consent as an independent ground for divorce

In Estonia, divorce upon mutual consent of the spouses is an independent ground for divorce, similar to CEFL Principles.[42] Thus, it can be argued that Estonian law is in conformity with CEFL Principle 1:3, which gives primacy to divorce by mutual consent among the grounds for divorce,[43] and with CEFL Principles 1:1 (2) and 1:4, giving preference to divorce by mutual consent.[44] It is desirable in every respect that parties reach an agreement in such a situation. Thus, Estonian divorce law adheres to the idea on which CEFL Principles are also based: "The mutual consent of the spouses is to be considered to be of overriding importance. [...] there is no justification for binding spouses against their corresponding clear and free will for any time at all."[45]

Neither does Estonian divorce law prescribe for a period of factual separation as a condition for divorce by mutual consent, which would be in conflict with CEFL Principles 1:1 (2) and 1:4 (1). Even Estonian judicial practice does not obstruct a divorce when the marriage lasted for a very short period and the spouses have not been factually separated for a certain period.[46] It is probable, though, that such judicial practice (in cases of divorce when there is a dispute, not in the cases of

---

41   See §30(2) and (3) of the Family Law Act. The regulation of the date of termination of marriage will remain the same under the Draft Family Law Act (see §66 of the Draft Family Law Act).

42   See BOELE-WOELKI, K (ed.), *supra* note 38, Comment 1 under Principle 1:4.

43   *Ibid*, Comment 2 under Principle 1:3: "Due to its growing importance, a divorce by mutual consent is expressly recognised as the first type of divorce."

44   *Ibid*, Comment 2 under Principle 1:1.

45   *Ibid*, Comment 3 under Principle 1:4.

46   See *supra* note 30.

divorce by consent) is not in full conformity with the standpoint of CEFL Principles, because pursuant to the latter, a body granting divorce should require a reflection period even when the spouses submit a joint application for divorce (that is upon divorce by mutual agreement), as problems could arise after the commencement of divorce proceeding.[47]

2.2.2. Divorce proceedings upon divorce by mutual consent

As a rule, for a divorce by mutual consent, the spouses must submit a joint petition to a vital statistics office in person.[48] Only when a spouse cannot appear at a vital statistics office in person for submission of a joint petition, may he or she submit a separate notarised petition.[49]

It proceeds from the spirit of the Act that at least one of the spouses must appear at a vital statistics office in person for submission of a joint petition. As a rule, upon registration of divorce also, both spouses must appear at a vital statistics office in person.[50] A divorce may be registered without the presence of one spouse if that spouse cannot, with good reason, appear at a vital statistics office and the notarised consent of the spouse to the divorce is submitted without his/her presence.[51]

A spouse living in a foreign country may submit a written petition on which the signature of the petitioner is confirmed by a consular officer of the Republic of Estonia.[52] And if a spouse living in a foreign country cannot, with good reason, appear at a vital statistics office for the registration of divorce, he or she may also submit a written consent on which the signature of the petitioner is confirmed by a consular officer of the Republic of Estonia.[53]

As upon mutual consent, divorce is granted not earlier than one month after submission of a petition; the spouses have to appear at a vital statistics office twice—

---

[47]   See BOELE-WOELKI, K (ed.), *supra* note 38, Comment 2 under Principle 1:1.
[48]   See §28(1) of Family Law Act.
[49]   See the first sentence of §28 (2) of Family Law Act, by which the legislator intended to avoid unfounded recourse to the courts for getting a divorce. The solution where a marriage can be dissolved in a vital statistics office if spouses do not disagree about the divorce has also been regarded reasonable by the judges, because up to 1995 divorces in which spouses had no dispute made up a considerable percentage of all civil cases. See the opinion of Tallinn Circuit Court judge SEPPIK, M, 5. peatükk. Abielu lõppemine (*Chapter 5. termination of marriage*). Juridica 1995, No. 1, p. 4: "Nüüd on kohtutel võimalus pühendada rohkem aega vaidluste lahendamisele (*Now the courts can devote more time to solving disputes*)."
[50]   §120(1) of Family Law Act.
[51]   First sentence of §120(2) of Family Law Act.
[52]   Second sentence of §28(2) of Family Law Act.
[53]   Second sentence of §120(2) of Family Law Act.

first for the submission of petition and for the second time for the registration of divorce.[54]

2.2.3. Reflection period

It is only upon divorce at a vital statistics office, i.e. upon divorce by an agreement of the spouses, that the divorce may be granted not earlier than one month and not later than three months after submission of a petition. The term of one month should contribute to the prevention of rash divorces.

According to CEFL Principle 1:5 (2) a reflection period is not necessary if the spouses have no children under the age of 16 and they have agreed upon all legal consequences of the divorce. Perhaps it would be reasonable, even in such cases, in order to avoid rash divorces, to provide for a mandatory reflection time, when the divorce is granted pursuant to administrative procedure.[55] Upon a divorce by a court the time of proceeding in itself constitutes sufficient reflection time.

When establishing the regulation of Estonian divorce law it would be wise to consider the implementation of CEFL Principle 1:5 and provide for a period longer than three months, if the spouses have not reached an agreement concerning the circumstances of divorce and they have children under the age of 16. At present, the duration of the reflection period depends on the discretion of a vital statistics official and is not dependent on the circumstances relating to divorce, although it should be to a certain extent.

2.2.4. Agreement of spouses on the consequences of divorce

The spouses may divorce at a vital statistics office even if there is a dispute as to the consequences of divorce and without having to submit their agreement or a proposal as to the solution of the dispute to a vital statistics office. The achievement of such an agreement is an objective during a possible subsequent dispute in a court. Thus, in Estonia an administrative agency does not determine the legal

---

54   The procedure for divorce upon mutual consent shall not in essence be changed by the Acts Related to Civic Status Act. Only a special regulation shall be provided due to the fact that as of 1 January 2008 the Ministry of Internal Affairs is planning to implement a system of computerised registering of vital records. It will be possible to submit petitions in person and in writing or electronically, certified by person's digital signature. A person will not have to appear at a vital statistics office for the submission of a petition if he or she submits a petition certified by his or her digital signature. Also, the entries in the register shall be signed digitally. A prerequisite of a registration to enter into force is the signing thereof by an official of a vital statistics office competent to make such entries.

55   Otherwise the simplification of divorce to such an extent would be in substantial conflict with the general principles of marriage (marriage for a lifetime, etc.).

consequences of divorce and does not exercise control over the agreement reached between the spouses. If the spouses have dissolved their marriage at a vital statistics office and have not agreed upon the consequences of the divorce, the issues disputed over shall be adjudicated on by a court.[56] If there is no dispute, there is no scrutiny of the consequences.

CEFL Principles have been developed with the aim of not relating the divorce and the consequences thereof.[57] Thus, a total lack of interdependence between these two, as it is currently the situation in Estonian law, is not in conformity with CELF Principles, especially when considering the interests of the child, because pursuant to CEFL Principles at least in cases when the interests of children come into play upon divorce, there must be control over the consequences of the divorce when granting one.

Therefore the principle that an agreement regarding the circumstances of divorce should be in writing, as expressed in CEFL Principle 1:6, deserves recognition. At the same time a question arises of whether this will make it too difficult for the spouses to exercise their right to divorce upon mutual consent (the principle, which is provided for in CEFL Principle 1:2 (2)), as the spouses will definitely need the help of a legal counsellor for preparing the written agreement referred to in CEFL Principle1: 6, whereas there would be no need for such legal counselling service when simply submitting a joint petition for divorce with an administrative body without the need to submit such an agreement. It is clear, though, that in the present form Estonian law provides for a so called simplified divorce, but this can hardly be the reason why the divorce rate in Estonia is one of the highest in the world.

What is also disputable is that when according to CEFL Principle 1:7, a competent authority must, to a certain extent, have control over the agreements on the consequences of divorce, then is it at all conceivable that besides a court, an administrative body could be such a competent body and when, if ever, a divorce in another competent authority, which is not a court, would be possible?

There is no doubt that the position adopted in CEFL Principle 1:6 (1) (a), that when divorcing, the spouses must agree upon issues pertaining to their parental responsibility, as well as the rule in CEFL Principle 1:7 (1), that the body granting a divorce shall bear in mind the best interests of the children, are very positive.

---

[56]   See below 2.3.4.
[57]   BOELE-WOELKI, K and MARTINY, D, *Prinzipien zum Europäischen Familienrecht betreffend Ehescheidung und nachehelicher Unterhalt. – Zeitschrift für Europäisches Privatrecht.* 1/2006, p. 15.

Although both the present Estonian Family Law Act and the Draft Family Law Act put an obligation on the parents to take responsibility for children even after divorce, the idea enshrined in the law is not implemented in real life—joint raising of children after divorce or joint custody is not common in Estonia, and disputes about who shall raise the children are very rare, because pursuant to our predominantly traditional role model, as a rule the children will be left to be raised by the mother.[58] Perhaps the introduction of a principle similar to the one introduced by CEFL Principle 1:6 (1) (a) would contribute to raising the awareness of parents that both of them have a duty to participate in the raising and taking care of the child also after divorce.

Thus, Estonian law and the Principles differ in regard to the consequences of divorce by agreement of the spouses. Estonian law permits divorce by mutual consent even if the spouses have a dispute concerning the legal consequences of the divorce. For the resolution of such disputes a separate action has to be filed with a court, otherwise divorce could be granted by an administrative body. CEFL Principles aim at preventing divorce without agreement concerning the consequences thereof. For this reason a reflection time is provided for. If no agreement is reached, the consequences shall be determined by a competent authority. Although under Estonian law agreement of the spouses concerning the consequences of the divorce is not required for getting a divorce, this is not, in substance, in conflict with the Principles.[59]

---

[58] HANSSON, *supra* note 34, pp. 42–43; PALL, K., Lahutusjärgsed pered ja ametlikud tugisüsteemid. – Lahutus: probleemid ja lahendused (*Families after divorce and official support systems. – Divorce. Problems and solutions*). Rahvusvaheliste ja sotsiaaluuringute instituut (*Institute of International and Social Studies*): Tallinn 2003, pp. 55–61: "Perede lahutusjärgsed käitumismallid on erinevad ning paraku on ühiskonnas olemas ka hoiak, et lahutus "päästab" mehe pere kütkeist ja edasisest vastutusest (*The post-divorce behavioural patterns of families are different and, unfortunately, there is an attitude within the society that a divorce „liberates" a man from the shackle of family and from further responsibility*)".

[59] See BOELE-WOELKI, K. (ed), *supra* note 38, Comment 6 under Principle 1:4: "There is no precondition that an application for the dissolution of the marriage must be accompanied by an agreement with respect to the consequences of the divorce. The Principles aim to favour consensual divorce."

2.3. DISSOLUTION OF MARRIAGE AS A GROUND FOR DIVORCE

2.3.1. Ascertainment of dissolution of marriage

The second ground for divorce in Estonian divorce law is the impossibility of continuation of the marriage, which the court has to ascertain upon granting the divorce.[60]

As compared to the present law, the Draft Family Law Act provides for somewhat more precise criteria on the basis of which a court can decide on the dissolution of the marriage: a separation period of certain duration (two years) is being provided for, in which case it can be presumed that the spouses will not restore their conjugal relations.[61] The Draft Family Law Act also provides for the irretrievable termination of conjugal relations, which means that the spouses no longer have conjugal relations and there is ground to believe that these will not be restored.[62]

Following judicial practice, when ascertaining the dissolution of marriage, it is currently not the objective circumstances that have to be taken into account, instead what is decisive is whether the concrete cohabitation of spouses has irretrievably terminated from the subjective point of view of the partners.[63]

According to the previous law the divorce was granted when the court ascertained that further cohabitation of the spouses and the preservation of the family were no longer possible. Thus, at that time, too, the law did not provide for more specific grounds for divorce. Pursuant to the judicial practice a divorce was granted, e.g. when the spouses continually lived separately and conjugal relations had terminated in fact, when a new family had been set up and new children had been born of a new cohabitation, also when one of the spouses abused alcohol, was infertile, in the case of infidelity, in the case of systematic display of disre-

---

[60] See §29 (2) of Family Law Act.
[61] See §67 (2) of Draft Family Law Act.
[62] See the second sentence of §67 (2) of Draft Family Law Act.
[63] See e.g. judgment of Tallinn Circuit Court No. II-2/32/98, quashing the judgment of Tallinn City Court, because the latter had, when deciding on the possibility of continuation of the marriage, proceeded primarily from an objective point of view: „The parties have been married for more than 50 years. The Court found that the relations between the parties do not fully meet the wishes and ideas concerning a harmonious marriage, but the relations are understandable bearing in mind the age of the spouses and the situation which has developed in the joint dwelling of the parties." The chamber of Tallinn Circuit Court found that "... the continuation of the marriage in not possible, because the parties themselves do not consider such a marriage a proper one and the time given by the court to the spouses for conciliation did not yield results as the conjugal relations were not restored."

spect towards the other spouse, or when the spouse did not take care of the children. It was not considered possible in principle to establish an exhaustive list of grounds for divorce in law, because such a list could have excluded an otherwise justified divorce if the grounds thereof did not fall under any of those enumerated in the law.[64]

As the conceptual foundations of the present Family Law Act are primarily to be found in the law that was valid earlier, the causes of divorce today are similar to the earlier ones also.[65] Similar to previous times when the legislator sensed a danger in providing for too many casuistic grounds for the breakdown of marriage, the present law establishes only two basic divorce grounds: agreement and impossibility of continuation of marriage. This is in conformity with the idea expressed in CEFL Principle 1:3 that a divorce is permissible on two grounds.[66] Also, Estonian divorce law recognises the idea that the fact of having children is not of decisive importance regarding the grounds for divorce; the same view underlies CEFL Principle 1:3.[67]

Although, pursuant to the CEFL Principles, the scrutiny of the breakdown of conjugal relations has been abandoned,[68] the present Estonian law, and the planned family law reform[69] state that the ascertainment of breakdown of conjugal relations is a prerequisite for a court to granting a divorce. Though these two are conceptually different approaches, they yield results that perhaps do not differ that much after all. Under CEFL Principle 1:9, too, in exceptional hardship, the divorce may be granted before a separation for one year, that being the primary ground for divorce when the spouses have a dispute.

---

64   Eesti NSV Abielu- ja perekonnakoodeks: kommenteeritud väljaanne (Marriage and Family Code of Estonian SSR: commented issue). Tallinn, 1974, pp. 58–59.

65   Although infidelity is being pointed out as one of the justifications of divorce, the fault or infidelity of a spouse is not a ground for divorce in Estonian divorce law. It is the fact of termination of conjugal relations that constitutes a ground for divorce. Thus, in Estonian divorce law the breakdown principle is valid, not the principle of fault.

66   See BOELE-WOELKI, K.(ed.), *supra* note 38, Comment 1 under Principle 1:3: "Other circumstances (separation, agreement as to the consequences etc) are either a question of the conditions for divorce or its consequences and do not justify a multitude of divorce forms".

67   *Ibid*, Comment 1 under Principle 1:3: "The existence of children should therefore only have an impact on the consequences of the divorce, not on the divorce itself" and also Comment 1 under Principle 1:4.

68   The scrutiny of the breakdown, without the provision of a time criterion is losing its significance in different national legal systems, and thus the verification of the breakdown of conjugal relations as a principle has become outdated. See BOELE-WOELKI, K. and MARTINY, D., *supra* note 57, p. 15.

69   German law has served as the primary model in this context.

But when no required separation period has been established as a prerequisite of divorce, as is the situation in Estonian law, it is certainly difficult to check whether conjugal relations have irretrievably terminated, and that is why the factual separation for one year as an objective criterion provided for in CEFL Principle 1:8 must be considered as positive. Furthermore, one year should be sufficient. The provision for a two-years' separation as a prerequisite of termination of conjugal relations in the Draft Family Law Act can be attributed to a different conceptual approach.[70]

2.3.2. Factual separation

Factual separation of fixed duration is neither required by the present law nor by the Draft Family Law Act. Yet, under the Draft Family Law Act, the termination of conjugal relations is assumed if the spouses have been separated for at least two years.[71] The present Family Law Act does not embody such an assumption, but when ascertaining the possibility of continuation of marriage the courts do take into account the separation criterion.[72]

As the factual separation is regarded as a prerequisite of the termination of conjugal relations under the Draft Family Law Act, which sets out no other conditions concerning separation and in regard of which there is no judicial practice, it is impossible to state with certainty whether the separation has to be an intended one or whether a separate residence will be required.

According to judicial practice evolved under the present law the continuation of marriage has been considered unacceptable when the spouses live in separate rooms.[73]

---

70 This is probably a compromise in regard to the German version (as a rule three years and one year only when the spouses submit a joint petition), on the basis of which one can argue that against the background of the trend of Estonian divorce law the solution of simplification of divorce law has been chosen.

71 Whereas there will be no need the prove the termination of conjugal relations by other means. See Explanatory Letter to the Draft Family Law Act.

72 See e.g. judgment of Jõgeva County Court of 3.10.2005 No. 2–353/05, in which the court pointed out that no information has been presented to the court on the basis of which one could hope that the marriage will be preserved or restored, and that it has been ascertained that the parties have been living separately for years. See also judgment No. 2–512/05 of Rapla County Court of 2.12.2005; judgment No. 2–1063/05 of Lääne-Viru County Court of 13.12.2005; judgment No. 2–530/05 of Jõgeva County Court of 14.11.2005; judgment No. 2–370/05 of Põlva County Court of 15.12.2005; judgment No. 2–394/05 of Järva County Court of 11.11.2005; judgment No. 2–3233/05 of Ida-Viru County Court of 12.12.2005.

73 Tallinn Circuit Court, as a court of second instance, has expressed a view in its judgment No. 2–2/1581/04 of 29.12.2004 that "living in one and the same flat does not in itself mean the continuation of conjugal relations." See also judgment No. 2–344–05 of Põlva County Court of 1.12.2005; judgment No. 2–423/05 of Rapla County Court of 15.12.2005.

Factual separation should certainly be interpreted not to mean separate dwellings, because in many cases this would simply be unfeasible for economic reasons. It would also be important to take into account the fact that the spouses may intend to live separately. CEFL Principle 1:8 is worded very generally, although the referred issues have been taken into account when rendering meaning to the principle.[74]

2.3.3. Reflection period

Tough according to the present Family Law Act, a court does not have to grant the spouses a reflection period, courts have done so, when necessary.[75] According to

---

[74]   In fact, according to the drafters of CEFL Principles the latter should be read taking into account the commentaries. See BOELE-WOELKI, K (ed.), *supra* note 38, Comment 7 under Principle 1:8, also referring to these circumstances when giving meaning to the concept of "factual separation".

[75]   As a rule the reflection time ordered by the courts has been 2 to 3 months. See e.g. judgments of Harju County Court of 27.06.2003 No. 2/1–186/02/03; of Tallinn City Court of 7.02.2002 No. 2/3/23–4824 This is probably a compromise in regard to the German version (as a rule three years and one year only when the spouses submit a joint petition), on the basis of which one can argue that against the background of the trend of Estonian divorce law the solution of simplification of divorce law has been chosen.
   Whereas there will be no need to prove the termination of conjugal relations by other means. See Explanatory Letter to the Draft Family Law Act.
   See e.g. judgment of Jõgeva County Court of 3.10.2005 No. 2–353/05, in which the court pointed out that no information has been presented to the court on the basis of which one could hope that the marriage will be preserved or restored, and that it has been ascertained that the parties have been living separately for years. See also judgment No. 2–512/05 of Rapla County Court of 2.12.2005; judgment No. 2–1063/05 of Lääne-Viru County Court of 13.12.2005; judgment No. 2–530/05 of Jõgeva County Court of 14.11.2005; judgment No. 2–370/05 of Põlva County Court of 15.12.2005; judgment No. 2–394/05 of Järva County Court of 11.11.2005; judgment No. 2–3233/05 of Ida-Viru County Court of 12.12.2005.
   Tallinn Circuit Court, as a court of second instance, has expressed a view in its judgment No. 2–2/1581/04 of 29.12.2004 that "living in one and the same flat does not in itself mean the continuation of conjugal relations." See also judgment No. 2–344–05 of Põlva County Court of 1.12.2005; judgment No. 2–423/05 of Rapla County Court of 15.12.2005.
   In fact, according to the drafters of CEFL Principles the latter should be read taking into account the commentaries. See BOELE-WOELKI, K.(ed.), *supra* note 38, Comment 7 under Principle 1:8, also referring to these circumstances when giving meaning to the concept of "factual separation".
   As a rule the reflection time ordered by the courts has been 2 to 3 months. See e.g. judgments of Harju County Court of 27.06.2003 No. 2/1–186/02/03; of Tallinn City Court of 7.02.2002 No. 2/3/23-/01; of Põlva County Court of 9.12.2002 No. 2–080/2002; of Põlva County Court of 23.12.2002 No. 2–173/2002; of Tartu County Court of 4.04.2003 No. 2–1853/2002; of Harju County Court of 27.06.2003 No. 2/1–186/02/03; of Ida-Viru County Court of 14.11.2003 No. 2–2486/03; of Lääne-Viru County Court of 9.02.2005 No. 2–810/04; of Rapla County Court of 15.12.2005 No. 2–423/05. It could be said that the reflection time is provided for under previous law and practice, because then the courts were obliged, when adjudicating divorce matters, to take measures for reconciliation of the spouses and they had the right to grant the spouses a conciliation time.

judicial practice, the granting of reflection time to spouses has so far been a right, not an obligation of the courts.[76] Thus, the courts grant divorce even when one of the spouses does not consent to divorce and wishes that a conciliation time be granted.[77] Even in the second instance courts it has been pointed out:

> Conciliation and continuation of marriage requires the will of both parties. The fact that a spouse is unwilling to divorce cannot, in itself, be a ground for dismissing the request for divorce, if the court has ascertained that the conjugal relations of the parties have terminated and one of the spouses no longer wishes to be conciliated with the other and to restore conjugal relations.[78]

The new Code of Civil Procedure requires that a court stay the divorce proceedings (it is possible only once and for the duration of up to six months) if there is a ground to believe that it would be possible to save the marriage. When doing this the court shall point out to the parties the possibility of conciliation and the possibility of seeking help from a counsellor in family matters. The court shall not stay the proceedings if the spouses have been separated for a longer period and neither consents to the stay of proceedings.[79]

The Draft Family Law Act also provides for the duty of the courts to take measures to conciliate the parties and to grant them a conciliation period of up to six months, except when this proves impossible due to concrete circumstances of the case.

---

[76]   See judgment No. 2–2-231/05 of Tartu Circuit Court of 17.06.2005; judgment No. 2-2-189/05 of Tartu Circuit Court of 20.06.2005; judgment No. 2–2/767/05 of Tallinn Circuit Court of 4.07.2005.

[77]   See e.g. judgment No. 2–296/05 of Jõgeva County Court of 20.10.2005, where the defendant did not agree to the divorce and asked the court to grant a conciliation time believing that the problems could be solved with the help of a marriage counsellor, but the court nevertheless granted a divorce justifying its decision stating that "as a marriage, in essence, is a contract between two persons, it will not be possible to continue the marriage if one of the parties is convinced in the impossibility of the continuance thereof". See also judgment No. 2–509/05 of Rapla County Court of 7.12.2005, where the marriage had lasted for 26.5 years and the defendant did not consent to the divorce and asked the court that it grant a conciliation time, but the court did not grant one and granted the divorce arguing that "a marriage is a voluntary union of two persons. If one of the parties excludes further cohabitation the continuation of the marriage is impossible and a divorce has to be granted"; see also judgment No. 2–2/161/04 of Tallinn Circuit Court of 4.03.2004,where the court justified the divorce arguing that "if one of the spouses is unwilling to continue the marriage and the wish is corroborated by the termination of conjugal relations and unwillingness to restore the conjugal relations, the continuation of the marriage is impossible. A court cannot, by a judgment, oblige anyone to continue a marriage."

[78]   See judgment No. 2–2-231/05 of Tartu Circuit Court of 17 June 2005.

[79]   See §357 of Code of Civil Procedure.

2.3.4. Agreement of spouses on the consequences of divorce

As a divorce can only be granted by a court if the spouses have a dispute concerning the circumstances related to the divorce, this means that the spouses do not have to submit to the court an agreement concerning these issues. The very reason for recourse to the courts is that the spouses have a dispute concerning the circumstances of the divorce and they wish the court to resolve it. At the same time it is also possible that the court grants just the divorce, without determining the consequences thereof.

Thus, pursuant to the present law, the consequences of divorce have to be treated separately from the granting of the divorce, and the consequences are determined by a court only if a spouse has submitted a pertinent claim. As the claim is a separate one, the court does not have to adjudicate these two matters jointly and one does not affect the other.

Upon divorce by a court, the party who seeks the resolution of a dispute may submit his or her proposal concerning the solution of the dispute about the consequences of the divorce, and this is usually the case. Yet, the solution of such a dispute does not have to, but may, take place within the divorce proceeding. The claims submitted by the spouses are adjudicated independently, and thus, if a matter is extremely complicated, a claim may be separated and dealt with in an independent proceeding.

The court is not bound by the proposal of the spouses. The court has to resolve the dispute between the spouses and the court itself determines the consequences of the divorce.[80] Naturally, the court may follow the proposal of a spouse, but in that case the court must give reasons why it settled the dispute the way it did. Upon settling disputes concerning a child the court must, pursuant to §58 of the Family Law Act, proceed from the interests of the child. The court must consider the wishes of a child who is at least ten years of age. The wishes of a child younger than ten years of age shall also be considered if the level of the child's development so permits.

§§68 and 69 of the Draft Family Law Act provide for more precise possibilities for the courts for determining the further usage of the hitherto joint housing and the household facilities thereof. §68 (1) of the Draft stipulates that the court shall consider, first of all, the welfare of the child and other important circumstances if

---

[80] See first sentence of §29 (3) of Family Law Act: " Upon granting a divorce, a court shall, at the request of the spouses, settle disputes concerning a child and disputes concerning support or division of joint property."

the spouses do not agree upon divorce, on the further usage of the dwelling and the standard furnishings thereof. On the request of one spouse, the court has to divide the items of the standard furnishing in the joint ownership of the spouses in a fair and expedient manner.[81] Similar to the present law, the Draft establishes that the court must, when adjudicating matters pertaining to children, render a judgment proceeding first and foremost from the interests of the child.[82] In this regard Estonian divorce law is in full conformity with the CEFL Principles.[83]

3. MAINTENANCE BETWEEN FORMER SPOUSES

3.1. GENERAL REMARKS ON MAINTENANCE BETWEEN FORMER SPOUSES

3.1.1. The principle of self-sufficiency and state assistance

In a state based on social justice everyone has in principle three sources of income for meeting his/her needs: income earned from work, maintenance received from members of the family and social benefits.[84] Hypothetically, every member of society ensures the means necessary for satisfaction of his or her needs by work. A person should be entitled to the assistance of family members or the state only if under certain circumstances he or she is not able to support himself or herself.

Due to the recognition of the referred principle the right to maintenance by a former spouse in Estonian law is not very extensive, originating, as such, in the Soviet times.[85] A prerequisite of the principle of equality of spouses, recognised at that time, was a working-woman, capable of supporting the family and being self-sufficient. Consequently, the spouses were obliged, as a rule, to support themselves after the divorce, too. It was only in rare cases stipulated by law that a former spouse was entitled to receive maintenance from the other.

Today Estonia recognises the principle that a marriage is based on the partnership of two independent individuals and consequently both spouses are responsible for guaranteeing the means necessary for their lives and for satisfying their

---

81   See §69 (1) of Draft Family Law Act.
82   See §123 of Draft Family Law Act.
83   See *CEFL Principles, supra* note 38, Principle 1:7 (1).
84   TAVITS, G, Sotsiaalhooldusõigus (*Social care law*) (2006) p. 17.
85   During the Soviet era equality of men and women was recognised on the territory of Estonia. It was argued that both men and women worked outside their home and thus both were capable of supporting themselves and the family. See Marriage and Family Code of Estonian SSR: commented issue, *supra* note 64, pp. 6–12.

respective personal needs.[86] Arising from the aforesaid, the principle of self-sufficiency is such a widespread concept that it has not even been written down in the law in black and white.[87] Nevertheless, this can be deducted from the Constitution, which establishes the principle that the spouses have equal rights.[88] The equality of the spouses means firstly, among other things, that they have equal opportunities for acquiring education, for the choice of occupation and earning of income, which in turn guarantees everyone the possibility to provide for his or her own support, and secondly, that even after a divorce the spouses are bound to earn their own living and to support themselves.

At the same time the state has to ensure that the individuals are capable of subsistence. The Constitution lays down positive obligation of the state to guarantee also the subsistence of divorced spouses, through regulating the maintenance obligation[89] and through offering state assistance.[90]

One of the aims of social benefits is to provide, in certain cases, a source of income to a person and to increase the income of a person who has the obligation to maintain his or her family.[91] As state benefits either substitute or supplement the income of beneficiaries, they also affect the subsistence of spouses after the divorce, guaranteeing a former spouse, in certain cases, a source of income or supplementing the existing one. The Estonian social welfare system supports a divorced spouse first and foremost in cases where he or she has no income due to caring for a child or incapacity to work, as well as in the event of the death of maintenance provider.[92]

The loss of income of parents arising from the raising of a child is compensated for by maternity benefits[93], parental benefits[94] and child care allowances[95],

---

[86] KULLERKUPP, K, *Family Law in Estonia. – The International Survey of Family Law*. 2001, p. 103.
[87] *Ibid*, p. 102.
[88] §27 (2) of the Constitution. See also section A. I. *supra*.
[89] §27 (1) of the Constitution. See in more detail: *Constitution of the Republic of Estonia with commentaries), supra* note 20, pp. 246–250.
[90] §28 (2) of the Constitution.
[91] TAVITS, *supra* note 84, p. 17.
[92] The current family policy of Estonia proceeds from the traditional family model, emphasising the role of the family in helping out its members in difficulties, and attributing the formal support systems but a secondary role. See HANSSON, *supra* note 34, p. 43.
[93] Ravikindlustuse seadus (*Health Insurance Act*). Passed 19 June 2002. RT I 2002, No. 62, Art. 377. Last amendment RT I 2005, No. 71, Art. 546.
[94] Vanemahüvitise seadus (*Parental Benefit Act*). Passed on 10 December 2003. RT I 2003, No. 83, Art. 549. Last amendment RT I 2005, No. 39, Art. 308.
[95] Riiklike peretoetuste seadus (*State Family Benefits Act*). Passed on 14 November 2001. RT I 2001, No. 95, Art. 587. Last amendment RT I 2005, No. 65, Art. 497.

which reduce the necessity of a divorced spouse to receive maintenance from the former spouse.[96]

To compensate for the reduction or loss of income in the case of incapacity to work the pension for incapacity to work, old-age pension and national pension are provided.[97] The referred pensions may be below the minimum means of subsistence and thus, these pensions do not always guarantee the actual subsistence of a person incapacitated to work.[98]

Furthermore, a person is entitled to receive survivor's pension upon the death of a provider, including a former spouse, or if a court has established the fact that the provider is missing,[99] and this pension practically substitutes for the maintenance received from the deceased spouse.

In principle, the family or its needy members are entitled to apply for state assistance only when the family itself is not capable of caring for its needy members.[100] Nevertheless, in practice state assistance does not depend on the impossibility of family members to assist each other. State assistance could rather be considered as a supplementary source of income, guaranteed by the state to a person if pertinent preconditions are fulfilled. Yet, state allowances are not meant to guarantee full subsistence to a person and the ultimate responsibility for the subsistence of a person lies with his or her family members.

3.1.2. Right to receive maintenance from a family member, including a former spouse

As stated in the Constitution, the primary duty to care for needy family members lies with the family itself.[101] Because the Constitution does not specify the circle of the subjects of the maintenance obligation or the grounds for and extent of the obligation, it is up to the legislator to decide which members of a family are obliged to provide maintenance to one another. In addition, under the Family Law Act a former spouse has the maintenance obligation. At the same time the Constitution confines the obligation to care for family members to the clause that the family member be in need for assistance—if a family member is not in need for assist-

---

[96] Until the child reaches 14 months of age the average income is guaranteed to the parent caring for the child, thereafter only supplementary allowance is guaranteed.
[97] Riikliku pensionikindlustuse seadus (*State Pension Insurance Act*). Passed on 5.12.2001. RT I 2001, No. 100, Art. 648. Last amendment RT I 2005, No. 39, Art. 308.
[98] Statistics accessible at http://www.stat.ee/ (28 April 2006).
[99] §20 (2) 5) of State Pension Insurance Act.
[100] TAVITS, *supra* note 84, p. 45.
[101] §27 (5) of the Constitution.

ance, the other members of the family have no obligation to provide his or her maintenance.

The main aim of the right to receive maintenance from a former spouse is to guarantee to the spouse who had been dependent on the other the economic support and possibility of sustenance after divorce. As the employment rate of women is comparatively high and approximately at the same level as the employment figures for men,[102] both men and women are basically on the same footing for earning the income necessary for satisfying their needs. That is why, as a rule, the unconditional and full maintenance of a former spouse by the other spouse is not necessary, and this is confirmed in practice.[103]

Women, due to caring for children,[104] are inevitably in a situation where earning an income through wages is more difficult and receiving of income from a former spouse proves necessary. This may also be attributed to lower wages of women.[105] It is also necessary to point out in this context that the day care of children is organised by the state, but does not always guarantee the possibility for day care. Neither do the old-age pension, national pension or pension for incapacity to work always guarantee sufficient subsistence for a divorced spouse. In these cases the divorced spouse may need a supplementary income for subsistence, and in certain cases this could be provided by a former spouse.

Thus, the maintenance of a former spouse is justified only in cases when a divorced spouse is not capable of sustaining himself or herself. As a rule, a former spouse does not need maintenance, and thus, under the present law, the divorced spouses have but a marginal maintenance obligation.

---

[102] When the employment figures are for men under 40, they are somewhat higher than the corresponding figures for women under 40, but from that age on the employment figures for women are higher than the corresponding figures for men. The differences are not big, though. Data accessible at http://www.stat.ee/ (28 April 2006).

[103] Generally, in practice, maintenance is not requested even in the case of need, which in turn is conditioned by the general attitude that a divorced spouse should sustain himself or herself and not admit the need for assistance. See: HANSSON, *supra* note 34, p. 37.

[104] Traditionally, in Estonia the children are left with the mother to be raised. See above B. II. 4.

[105] E.g. the average wages of women in 1998 were but 63% of the average wages of men, in 2002 the figure was 69%. In 1998 as much as 76% of single mothers with minor children worked, yet their income did not always guarantee the subsistence of the family. See e.g. DERMAN, N, Üksikemade majanduslikud ja emotsionaalsed probleemid. – Lahutus: probleemid ja lahendused (*Economic and emotional problems of single mothers – Divorce. Problems and solutions*). Rahvusvaheliste ja sotsiaaluuringute instituut (*Institute of International and Social Studies*): (2003) pp. 64–65.

Maintenance of a former spouse only in exceptional cases is in conformity with CEFL Principle 2:2, according to which each spouse should generally provide for his or her own support after divorce.

3.1.3. Relationship between a former spouse's right to maintenance and joint property regime and the grounds for divorce

In Estonian law, the marital property regime and the spouse's (including former spouse) right to maintenance are regulated separately. Marital property law regulates the division, upon divorce, of joint property acquired during the marriage, irrespective of the need for assistance of the spouses and, as a rule, on the principle of equal shares of spouses. The maintenance of a divorced spouse, on the other hand, is based on the need for assistance of the spouse requesting maintenance and on the ability of the other spouse to provide maintenance, and is related to the right to receive maintenance as established in the Family Law Act. The right to receive maintenance is not directly dependent on the division of joint property and the material benefits acquired thereupon.

The judicial practice has so far supported the view that the division or non-division of joint property is irrelevant to ordering support.[106]

On the other hand, the financial situation of a divorced spouse may improve as a result of the division of joint property upon divorce. Consequently, due to the property received as a result of division of joint property there may be no ground for maintaining a former spouse, as the latter is capable of sustaining himself or herself thanks to his or her proprietary situation. This is confirmed by judicial practice, especially when upon the division of joint property a financial compensation has been ordered to a spouse.[107] Again, in keeping with judicial practice, the property acquired upon division of joint property can be taken into account when assessing the proprietary situation of a spouse, because the financial compensation ordered in favour of the obligated spouse upon division of joint property enables him or her to provide maintenance to the divorced spouse.[108] Thus, the judicial practice does recognise a certain connection between the right of a former spouse to receive support and the way joint property is divided, although under the regulation of family law the maintenance of a former spouse does not depend on the joint property regime.

---

[106] See e.g. judgment of Tartu Circuit Court of 26.06.2003 in civil matter No. 2–2-255/2003; judgment of Viru Circuit Court of 16.12.2003 in civil matter No. 2–2-220/03.

[107] E.g. judgment of Tallinn Circuit Court of 30.04.2003 in civil matter No. 2–2/74/03; judgment of Viru Circuit Court of 22.01.2002 in civil matter No. II-2–53/02.

[108] E.g. judgment of Tallinn City Court of 22.03.2002 in civil matter No. 2/5/230–1461/01.

Under Estonian law the right of a divorced spouse to receive maintenance or the extent thereof does not generally depend on the reasons behind the divorce or whether the divorce was granted on the basis of an agreement or by a court. Neither does the termination of conjugal relations have any relevance. Until the formal divorce of a marriage the obligation to provide maintenance, as a legal consequence of marriage, is valid and the fact of separation has no relevance for the right of a divorced spouse to receive maintenance. The aforesaid is in conformity with CEFL Principle 2:1, pursuant to which maintenance between former spouses should be subject to the same rules regardless of the type of divorce.

3.2. SPECIFIC ISSUES CONCERNING MAINTENANCE BETWEEN FORMER SPOUSES

3.2.1. Creation of the right to receive maintenance.

The obligation to provide maintenance to a divorced spouse is created upon divorce, which under the present law means divorce registration or the entry into force of the court order granting divorce.[109] The general conditions for the creation of the maintenance obligation are a spouse's need for assistance and the financial ability of the other spouse to provide maintenance.

The divorced spouse's need for assistance may not arise from the divorce. Neither is it necessary that the need for assistance arose during the marriage or during the divorce procedure. The need for assistance may also arise after the divorce.

Need for assistance means the lack or insufficiency of resources for meeting immediate personal needs and the lack of possibilities to receive such resources in the form of wages, pension or other income.[110] In the judicial practice the need for assistance of a divorced spouse is ascertained by comparing the income of the spouse requesting maintenance and the expenses necessary for subsistence. The property owned by him/her out of which it would be possible to support him/herself, is also taken into account.

In addition to the need for assistance of one spouse, the financial situation of the other allowing for satisfying the needs of the needy spouse is also a prerequisite for the creation of the maintenance obligation. The fact that a divorced spouse owns property is a sufficient ground for granting maintenance to the other

---

[109] §39 2) and 3) of Family Law Act.
[110] Marriage and Family Code of Estonian SSR: commented issue, *supra* note 64, p. 51.

spouse.[111] The courts evaluate the financial situation of a divorced spouse on the basis of comparing his or her income to necessary expenditure. The aggregate financial situation of the person is taken into consideration, that is, in addition to income, the property the person owns, as well as his or her obligations, including maintenance obligations in regard to other persons (spouse, co-habiting partner, child).[112]

Since, in establishing the maintenance obligation, the law proceeds from the need for assistance of a creditor spouse and from the ability of the debtor spouse to provide maintenance, depending on his or her financial situation, it can be argued that regarding the issue under discussion the Estonian law in essence conforms to CEFL Principle 2.3, pursuant to which the maintenance of a divorced spouse should be dependent upon the creditor spouse having insufficient resources to meet his or her needs and the debtor spouse's ability to satisfy those needs. Although Estonian law does not proceed from the obligated spouse's subjective ability to provide maintenance and instead proceeds from the objective financial situation, it does not mean that the law contradicts the spirit of the principles. CEFL Principles, too, stipulate that in determining the need for assistance of the entitled spouse and the ability to provide maintenance of the obligated spouse, account should be taken of the income and property of both spouses.[113]

Nevertheless, under Estonian law the maintenance obligation of a divorced spouse is not created merely if the general conditions—need for assistance and financial means for providing maintenance to a divorced spouse—are met. Pursuant to the Family Law Act the obligation to provide maintenance to a divorced spouse is born on very limited grounds enumerated in the Act, and resembling the circumstances that serve as the basis for receiving social benefits.[114]

A divorced spouse has the right to receive maintenance from his or her former spouse on three grounds only:[115] the spouse became incapacitated to work during the marriage; the spouse became disabled within three years after the divorce, if the marriage had lasted at least twenty-five years; and pregnancy and child-care

---

111   The valid law has abandoned the concept of ability of a divorced spouse to provide maintenance and this has been substituted by the assessment of the spouses financial situation. Fulfilment of objective criteria is sufficient for the creation of maintenance obligation. SEPPIK, *supra* note 49, p. 3.

112   E.g. judgment of Tartu Circuit Court of 26.06.2003 in civil matter No. 2-2-255/2003; judgment of Tallinn Circuit Court of 20.05.2002 in civil matter No. 2-2/930/02.

113   See BOELE-WOELKI, K.(ed.), *supra* note 38, Comment 2 under Principle 2:3.

114   See *supra* 3.1.2.

115   §22 of Family Law Act.

until the child attains three years of age if the child was conceived during the marriage.

The divorced spouse's incapacity to work is determined as a percentage of his or her capacity to work. Previously a person was considered to be incapacitated to work when he or she reached pensionable age or became disabled. Currently the courts substantiate the concept of incapacity to work on the basis of actual ability of a person to work. Thus, a person does not become incapacitated to work automatically, upon attaining a certain age. The attainment of pensionable age in itself does not guarantee the creation of the right to receive maintenance.[116] On the other hand, the incapacity to work of a person who has not attained pensionable age is not regarded as a factual condition and this person is only considered to be incapacitated to work if he/she has been declared as such by a decision of a medical assessment committee.[117] There is no uniform approach in the judicial practice about how big the loss of capacity to work has to be for becoming entitled to receive maintenance.[118]

The spouse's pregnancy and child-care until the child attains three years of age are considered to be equivalent to incapacity to work. It is presumed that the divorced spouse will temporarily be unable to work and therefore will need maintenance.

Thus, the Family Law Act makes the creation of the right to receive maintenance dependent upon the divorced spouse's loss of capacity to work, including the loss due to age or disease, as well as upon the duration of a marriage and the need to care for a child if the child was conceived during the marriage. Furthermore, the spouse claiming maintenance must be in need of assistance and the financial situation of the spouse bearing the maintenance obligation must allow for provision of maintenance. If none of the conditions exist the right of a divorced spouse to receive maintenance is not created.

The CEFL Principles, also, stipulate the circumstances to be taken into account upon determining the right to receive maintenance. Pursuant to CEFL Principle 2:4 particular consideration should be given to the spouses' employment ability, age and health; the care of children; the division of duties during the marriage; the standard of living during the marriage and the existence of any new marriage or long-term relationship. The list is not exhaustive and the circumstances

---

[116] E.g. judgment of Harju County Court of 14.02.2005 in civil matter No. 2–1775/01/05.
[117] E.g. judgment of Viru Circuit Court of 22.02.2006 in civil matter No. 2–04–209.
[118] The courts have considered persons to be incapacitated for work if the loss of capacity for work was 40% or more. See e.g. judgment of Viru Circuit Court of 22.02.2006 in civil matter No. 2–04–209.

included therein do not necessarily constitute conditions for the creation of maintenance obligation, but in addition to other possible relevant circumstances these have to be taken into account when determining the maintenance obligation. Consequently, it is possible that the maintenance obligation arises even when the sole conditions are a spouse's need for assistance and the ability of the other spouse to provide maintenance. However, Estonian law recognises the right to receive maintenance only if additional circumstances exist, primarily the incapacity to work of a divorced spouse and the care of a child. On the other hand, although the other circumstances enumerated in CEFL Principle 2:4 are not considered conditions for the creation of the right to maintenance obligation, these can and should be taken into account when ordering maintenance to a divorced spouse.

3.2.2. Termination of the maintenance obligation

The right of a divorced spouse to receive maintenance depends on the existence of the conditions stipulated in law, and when these conditions cease to exist the right to receive maintenance terminates.[119] Thus, the provision of maintenance to a divorced spouse terminates when the person receiving maintenance is no longer in need for assistance, his or her capacity to work is restored or the financial situation of the spouse providing maintenance changes and no longer allows for provision of maintenance.[120] As the CEFL Principles do not establish when the right to receive maintenance shall terminate, it has to be concluded on the basis of the spirit of the Principles that the duration of the right to receive maintenance depends on the cessation of the existence of the conditions for providing maintenance.[121]

The duty to provide maintenance terminates also if the creditor spouse receiving maintenance remarries.[122] Upon contracting a new marriage his/her new spouse will have a legal duty to provide maintenance to his or her spouse and the debtor spouse's duty to provide maintenance terminates.[123] The aforesaid is in conformity with CEFL Principle 2:9, pursuant to which the maintenance obligation of a debtor spouse terminates if the creditor spouse remarries. Furthermore, CEFL Principle 2:9 provides for the termination of maintenance obligation also when

---

[119]   §25 of Family Law Act.
[120]   In this case the divorced spouse providing maintenance may request that he or she be relieved of the duty to provide maintenance. Cf. Marriage and Family Code of ESSR: commented issue, *supra* note 64, pp. 54–55.
[121]   Although, as a rule, upon ordering the provision of maintenance the payment thereof must be limited in time. See below under 3.2.3.
[122]   §25 of Family Law Act.
[123]   Cf. Marriage and Family Code of ESSR: commented issue, *supra* note 64, p. 55.

the creditor spouse establishes a long-term relationship, which in turn excludes the possibility of the creditor spouse retaining the right to receive maintenance through intentionally avoiding contracting a new marriage.[124]

Although it is not explicitly stipulated in the Family Law Act, the maintenance obligation may terminate under Estonian law if the spouse receiving maintenance commences a new permanent cohabitation without remarrying. Although the non-married cohabiting partner has no obligation to provide maintenance to his or her partner and consequently the duty to provide maintenance is not transferred to him or her, the need for assistance of the spouse receiving maintenance may cease to exist when his or her partner actually supports him or her. Nevertheless, unlike a new marriage, a long-term relationship does not always constitute a ground for termination of the duty to provide maintenance.

The creditor spouse's right to receive or and the debtor spouse's duty to provide maintenance terminate upon the death of the other spouse. Although this does not directly proceed from the Family Law Act, the divorced spouse's right to receive or duty to provide maintenance are inseparably bound to the person and, as a rule, cannot be transferred to other persons.[125] Nevertheless, if a debtor spouse dies, a third person may have the duty to provide maintenance to the creditor spouse instead of the deceased spouse,[126] but even in this case the debtor spouse's maintenance obligation terminates and is replaced by other sources of income established by law. On the basis of analogy, the duty to provide maintenance terminates upon the death of the spouse entitled to receive maintenance.

The termination of the right to receive maintenance upon the death of either spouse proceeds also from CEFL Principle 2:9. The Principle has been established because the claims for maintenance are personal claims which cease upon the death of the person.

---

[124] See BOELE-WOELKI, K.(ed.), *supra* note 38, Comment 1 under Principle 2:9.

[125] See Pärimisseadus (*Law of Succession Act*). Passed on 15.05.1996. RT I 1996, No. 38, Art. 752. Last amendment RT I 2005, No. 39, Art. §6 (1) of Tsiviilseadustiku üldosa seadus (*General Part of the Civil Code Act*) Tsiviilseadustiku üldosa seadus (*General Part of the Civil Code Act*). Passed on 27.03.2002. RT I 2002, No. 35, Art. 216. Last amendment RT I 2005, No. 39, Art. 308. See also §2 of Pärimisseadus (*Law of Succession Act*). 308.

[126] Võlaõigusseadus (*Law of Obligations Act*) §129 (3). See Võlaõigusseadus (*Law of Obligations Act*). Passed on 26.09.2001. RT I 2001, No. 81, Art. 487. Last amendment RT I 2005, No. 61, Art. 473.

3.2.3. Payment of maintenance

If a former spouse fails to perform the duty to provide maintenance voluntarily, although the above conditions exist, the creditor spouse may claim maintenance by judicial process, and the court shall order the payment of maintenance to the creditor spouse it the debtor spouse violates the duty to provide maintenance,[127] does not pay support or does so in insufficient amounts or irregularly.[128]

The divorced spouse's right to receive maintenance is, by nature, not limited in time. A divorced spouse may file a claim for support at any time if the conditions for the right to receive maintenance exist. As a rule, the support is ordered as of the filing of the claim. In exceptional cases support may be ordered retroactively for up to one year before filing of the claim for support.[129]

Similarly, the debtor spouse's duty to provide maintenance is generally not limited in time and lasts until the conditions for maintenance cease to exist. Therefore, support is ordered for an unspecified term or until the cessation of the conditions. In the case of permanent loss of capacity to work the debtor spouse's maintenance obligation is practically lifelong. Maintenance duty on the condition of taking care of a child is limited until the child attains three years of age. Nevertheless, when ordering support the court may take into account the fact that the divorced spouse's capacity to work may be restored or the spouse taking care of a child may go back to work before the child attains three years of age, and the court may order support to continue until the restoration of capacity to work or until the other spouse returns to work.[130]

On the basis of the aforesaid, as a rule support is ordered for an unspecified term but in exceptional cases, including upon a good reason to be established by the court, until a specified date.[131]

CEFL Principles state that the maintenance obligation of a divorced spouse should generally be limited in time. Therefore, the creditor spouse's unlimited right to receive maintenance is not in conformity with CEFL Principle 2:8, according to which maintenance should be granted to a divorced spouse for a limited period and it is only in exceptional cases that the maintenance may be ordered without

---

[127] §23 of Family Law Act.
[128] See judgment of the Supreme Court of 23.04.2004 in civil matter No. 3-2-1-57-04. RT III 2004, No. 12, Art. 155; judgment of the Supreme Court of 8.02.2006 in civil matter No. 3-2-1-121-05, RT III 2006, 7, 62. Accessible at: www.riigikohus.ee (1 April 2006).
[129] §70 of Family Law Act.
[130] See e.g. judgment of Tallinn Circuit Court of 4.04.2002 in civil matter No. 2-2/231/02.
[131] §24 of Family Law Act. In more detail see below under 3.2.5.

specifying the time limit. The time-limit of a creditor spouse's maintenance obligation is endorsed by the principle that a debtor spouse has a duty to guarantee the income necessary for his or her support.[132]

Since under Estonian law the divorced spouse has the right to receive maintenance only in very exceptional cases, the fact that the support is generally not limited in time is probably in conformity with the CEFL Principle that maintenance may exceptionally be granted without a time limit. The time limits to ordering support are not stipulated in the planned amendments to Estonian family law, either.[133]

In addition to the time limits of providing maintenance it is also important that the payments be regular. Support shall be paid to a creditor spouse in the form of monthly payments in Estonian law.[134] Payment of a lump sum is not possible and the courts do not order such payments. Yet, in certain cases the ordering of payment of a lump sum may prove necessary and justified. Together with maintenance being limited in time, this would make possible to end the after-effects of divorce as soon as possible and would motivate the divorced spouse in need for assistance to obtain his or her own income. Still, maintenance payable as a lump sum would be seen to constitute compensation for the damage caused by divorce and would not proceed from meeting the needs of the divorced spouse in need for assistance, whereas the latter is the fundamental principle of Estonian regulation.

According to the planned amendments to family law it will be possible to order the payment of a lump sum, if the entitled person so requires, but there must be good reason and the obligated persons must not be unfairly burdened; but as a general rule maintenance shall be provided at regular intervals. It is not important that both spouses agree to such an arrangement. The court, when ordering the payment of a lump sum, has to consider the interests of both divorced spouses and the financial ability of the obligated spouse.[135]

Under CEFL Principle 2:5, also, maintenance to a divorced spouse should be provided at regular intervals, however, taking into consideration the circumstances of the case, a lump sum payment may be ordered upon the request of both spouses. Although Estonian law does not recognise the payment of a lump sum, the referred principle will be observed when amending the present law.

---

[132] BOELE-WOELKI, K and MARTINY, D, *supra* note 57, p. 18.
[133] See §§72–73 of Draft Family Law Act.
[134] §23 (1) of Family Law Act.
[135] See §75 (2) of Draft Family Law Act.

3.2.4. The amount of support

The amount of support payable to a divorced spouse depends primarily on the financial situation of each spouse and the need for assistance.[136] The Family Law Act does not specify the grounds for determining the amount of support and, in the case of a dispute, the amount will be determined by a court, taking into consideration the concrete circumstances of the case.

No procedure for calculating the amount of support has been established. As the amount of support does not depend only on the income of the spouse obligated to provide maintenance, the amount of support has not been determined as a proportion or percentage of the spouse's income. Neither do the courts order support as a proportion or percentage of the obligated person's income. Pursuant to the judicial practice the support is ordered in the form of monthly payments of fixed amounts.

The support payable to a divorced spouse must, at least, cover his/her ordinary needs. The law provides neither for the maximum nor for the minimum amounts of support.[137]

Consequently, the court should assess the financial situation and need for assistance of the spouses in each concrete case. Ordinarily, the court first ascertains the amount of expenses necessary for the maintenance of a divorced spouse and if the spouse is not able to cover the expenses due to his or her insufficient income, the court shall assess the financial situation of the other spouse, whereupon it shall decide whether and to what extent the financial situation of the latter allows for the provision of maintenance to the former.

When ascertaining the need for assistance the court shall decide on the justified amount of maintenance expenses taking into account the circumstances of each specific dispute. The courts have held that a divorced spouse claiming support does not always have to prove the amount of his or her maintenance expenses. Bearing in mind that these are needs, not actual expenses, it is impossible to produce documentary evidence of such expenses,[138] therefore, the minimum monthly wage established by the Government of the Republic can be regarded as the amount of expenses necessary for the maintenance of a former spouse.[139]

---

[136]   §23 of Family Law Act.
[137]   Although §61 (4) of Family Law Act establishes the minimum amount of monthly support payment for one minor child, which is half of the minimum monthly wage established by the Government of the Republic, there is no relevant provision concerning the support of adults.
[138]   E.g. judgment of Viru Circuit Court of 22.06.2005 in civil matter No. 2–2-98/05.
[139]   See judgment of Viru Circuit Court of 22.01.2002 in civil matter No. II-2–53/02.

Just as upon ascertaining the existence of the need for assistance and the financial resources necessary for granting maintenance, the financial situation of the divorced spouses must be assessed taking into account the income and necessary expenditures of both. When doing this the aggregate financial situation of a spouse has to be considered, i.e. in addition to income, the property owned by the person, as well as his or her obligations, including housing expenses, expenditure on food, medicines, etc;, and maintenance obligations in regard to other persons (spouse, co-habiting partner, child).[140] Among other things the amount of support depends on whether the obligated spouse had been paying a certain amount of support before the order of support, or if he or she had assisted the divorced spouse in some other manner, e.g. by providing free housing.[141] What is also taken into account is whether the divorced spouses are pensioners[142] or whether the primary income of the obligated spouse is social allowances.[143] What is decisive is the financial situation and need for assistance at the time of claiming maintenance.

As support is ordered according to the need for assistance of a divorced spouse and the financial situation of each spouse, once ordered the support is generally not increased by indexation as the cost of living rises.[144] As a rule, the amount of support is changed upon the change of the circumstances on the basis of which the support was ordered. If the need for assistance of a creditor spouse or the financial situation of either spouse has changed the increase or decrease of the amount of support may be requested.[145]

CEFL Principles do not provide bases for calculating the amount of support, because there is no international consensus as to the circumstances to be taken into account or the calculation methods.[146] Thus, the calculation of the amount of support, the circumstances forming the bases for such calculation, as well as the calculation methods are for each legal system to decide and these issues have been regulated quite differently by different states. Estonian law has left the amount of support in each specific case to be decided by the courts.

---

[140] See e.g. judgment of Tartu Circuit Court of 26.06.2003 in civil matter No. 2–2-255/2003; judgment of Tallinn Circuit Court of 20.05.2002 in civil matter No. 2–2/930/02.
[141] See judgment of Tartu Circuit Court of 11.12.2002 in civil matter No. 2–2-275/2002.
[142] See judgment of Tallinn Circuit Court of 30.04.2003 in civil matter No. 2–2/74/03.
[143] See judgment of Tartu Circuit Court of 22.02.2006 in civil matter No. 2–05–382.
[144] Nevertheless, pursuant to judicial practice it is possible to link the amount of support to the change of the minimum monthly wage established by the Government of the Republic, as a result of which the support automatically increases upon establishment of a higher minimum monthly wage. See judgment of Tartu Circuit Court of 11.12.2002 in civil matter No. 2–2-275/2002.
[145] §23 (2) of Family Law Act.
[146] See BOELE-WOELKI, K.(ed.), *supra* note 38, p. 81.

3.2.5. Exemption from and restriction of maintenance obligation

A court may, with good reason, release a spouse from the duty to provide maintenance to the other spouse or limit the duty with a time period, primarily if the behaviour of the spouse requesting support was indecent during the marriage or if the marriage lasted a short time.[147] As the Family Law Act does not establish an exhaustive list of circumstances upon the existence of which the maintenance obligation could be restricted or a person could be exempted from the obligation, it is the courts who shall, in each case, ascertain the existence of sufficient cause for the restriction or exemption.

Judicial practice shows that the debtor spouses have predominantly requested that they be exempted from the obligation to provide maintenance to the creditor spouses, invoking the indecent behaviour of the other spouse as well as other circumstances, including the short duration of marriage and the fact that the person from whom support is claimed is himself or herself dependant.[148]

The open list concerning the restriction of and exemption from maintenance obligation is in conformity with CEFL Principle 2:6, which states that the competent authority may deny, limit or terminate maintenance because of the entitled spouse's conduct. Estonian law establishes a somewhat wider ground—a good reason does not have to be related to the conduct of the spouse. As there is no obligation, under the CEFL Principles, to establish an exhaustive list of grounds for the restriction of maintenance obligation,[149] the law in Estonia is in conformity with the provisions of this Principle.

3.2.6. Multiplicity of maintenance claims

Estonian law does not establish the order of persons entitled or obligated to provide maintenance upon the multiplicity of maintenance claims, and it is up to the courts to decide on case-to-case basis whether to take into consideration the support of a child or a new spouse when ordering support for a divorced spouse.

According to judicial practice, when ordering support to a former spouse, it is not necessary to take account of the fact that the other spouse maintains a new cohabiting partner or his or her descendant relatives. The primary duty of a divorced spouse is to maintain his or her former spouse,[150] although, in another view the

---

[147] §24 of Family Law Act.
[148] See e.g. judgment of Supreme Court of 16.11.2004 in civil matter No. 3-2-1-125-04. RT III 2004, No. 33, Art. 347. Accessible at: www.riigikohus.ee (1.04.2006).
[149] See BOELE-WOELKI, K.(ed.), *supra* note 38, Comment 2 under Principle 2:6.
[150] See judgment of Tartu Circuit Court of 11.12.2002 in civil matter No. 2-2-275/2002.

income remaining to a debtor spouse after fulfilling the duty to provide mainte-nance to his or her former spouse should guarantee him or her the possibility to also maintain his or her new family (partner and common child).[151] According to the predominant approach a divorced spouse must first and foremost maintain his or her minor child. A person is obliged to maintain his or her former spouse only if his or her financial situation allows for it after satisfying the needs of a child.

As the law does not establish the order of the persons entitled to receive or obliged to provide maintenance upon submission of a maintenance claim or fulfilling the maintenance obligation, and the courts have no clear guide lines for deciding such issues, the family law amendments intend to provide for an order of persons entitled to receive maintenance. Accordingly, a minor child is given priority over other children, children are given priority over other relatives in descending line, a relative in descending line is given priority over relatives in ascending line, and among the latter, priority shall be given to close relatives. A spouse is considered equivalent to a minor child and maintenance shall be ordered to him or her before it is accorded to an adult child or a married minor child and other relatives. The obligated persons will also be put into order and the primary duty to maintain a divorced spouse shall lie with the former spouse.[152]

CEFL Principle 2:7, states that in determining the debtor spouse's ability to satisfy the needs of the creditor spouse, the competent authority should give priority to any maintenance claim of a minor child of the debtor spouse and take into account any obligation of the debtor spouse to maintain a new spouse.

This issue is currently not regulated by Estonian law. The order of persons entitled to receive or obliged to provide maintenance has not been unambiguously deter-mined in the judicial practice either. However, the courts take into account, upon ordering support and assessing the financial situation of the obligated person, whether the latter has minor dependent children or a spouse. The planned law amendments shall guarantee the priority of the child over a divorced spouse in receiving support, but the amendments do not explicitly take into account the duty to maintain a new spouse. If the law was to be amended following the CEFL Principles, it would be wise to consider the establishment of the priority of the new spouse over the former one. Yet, this issue could be solved by the courts, who could take into account the obligation of a spouse to his or her new spouse when assessing the financial situation of the obligated spouse.

---

[151] See e.g. judgment of Tartu Circuit Court of 26.06.2003 in civil matter No. 2-2-255/2003.
[152] See §§98 and 107 of Draft Family Law Act.

3.2.7. Maintenance agreement

In addition to the maintenance obligation provided for by law the spouses are allowed to agree upon a maintenance obligation different from that stipulated by law.

Estonian Family Law Act does not provide for a separate maintenance agreement as such. Nevertheless, the spouses may determine reciprocal proprietary rights and obligations by a marital property contract differently from that provided in the Act,[153] including the reciprocal maintenance obligations upon termination of the marriage. A marital property contract may not deny a spouse or divorced spouse the right to receive maintenance on the bases provided for in the Family Law Act,[154] i.e. in a marital property contract the spouses may agree on a maintenance right more extensive than that stipulated by law.

A marital property contract may be entered into before or during marriage.[155] A marital property contract may not be entered into after a divorce, yet the spouses may, on the basis on the principle of freedom of contract, agree on a maintenance obligation, although there is no specific regulation concerning such agreements. Thus, in principle it is possible to agree on the maintenance of a divorced spouse both during marriage and after divorce. The agreement entered into during marriage must be notarised and it shall be void if the mandatory form is not observed; the contract may prove void or invalid on the basis of general provisions concerning invalidity of transactions or upon annulment of the marriage.[156] The law does not provide for a mandatory from of a contract entered into after a divorce, consequently, this may also be entered into either orally or deduced from relevant behaviour. Neither are the restrictions concerning marital property contracts applicable to such contracts, rendering it theoretically possible to agree on a more restricted maintenance obligation than stipulated by law.

The planned amendments to the Family Law Act shall regulate the entering into a maintenance contract after divorce, however, it will no longer be possible to agree on the maintenance of a divorced spouse within a marital property contract. The formal requirement of notarisation will remain in force. Reasonable restriction of the duration and extent of maintenance obligation will be allowed,

---

[153] In practice such contracts are comparatively rare, and even more rare are the clauses concerning the maintenance of a spouse or a divorced spouse. As of 1 January 2006 only 2548 registry cards have been opened in the marital property register. Statistics available at: http://www.just.ee (1 May 2006).

[154] §§8 (1), 9 (1) 5 and 9 (2) 2) of Family Law Act.

[155] §10 (1) of Family Law Act.

[156] §§10 (4) and 12 of Family Law Act.

and it will be possible to agree on the manner of paying the support and termination of payments. It will not be possible to waive the right to receive maintenance.[157]

Pursuant to CEFL Principle 2:10 the spouses should be allowed to make an agreement about maintenance after divorce. The agreement may concern the extent, performance, duration and termination of the maintenance obligation, as well as renouncement of the claim to maintenance. Such an agreement should be in writing.

As the current law does not consider the contract of maintenance, the Estonian regulation does not conform to the provisions of the referred Principle and does not guarantee the divorced spouses the possibility to enter into maintenance agreements after divorce. Although there is no regulation conforming to the CEFL Principles, nevertheless, in practice, it is possible to regulate maintenance relations by a contract. The amendments scheduled for the near future should eliminate this drawback. The principle that the right to receive maintenance cannot be waived will be retained, though. Bearing in mind the principle that everyone must have the income necessary for his or her support, the introduction of the referred amendment into Estonian law is worth consideration.

4. CONCLUSIONS

By and large Estonian law concerning divorce and maintenance of divorced spouses is in conformity with the CEFL Principles. Although certain differences or discrepancies can be observed in relation to some individual issues, the majority of these will be eliminated by the planned law amendment. Also, other solutions offered by the CEFL Principles are worth to being taken into account by the Estonian legislator.

Both the CEFL Principles and Estonian divorce law proceed from the general trend of European divorce law, withdrawing from divorce on the principle of fault and moving towards divorce upon consent. Differently from the CEFL Principles, the Estonian Family Law Act provides for a second ground for divorce—the breakdown of marriage—which is a widespread ground also elsewhere in Europe. There is no doubt that the national legislator should introduce into the law certain separation period, be it one or two years, which would serve as an objective criterion for ascertaining the termination of conjugal relations.

---

[157]   §§42 and 78 of Draft Family Law Act.

As the Principles leave individual matters to be solved by national legislators, it can be argued that in fact the Estonian divorce system wherein both the courts and administrative bodies are competent to grant divorce is in conformity with the Principles, although the system is exceptional as compared to other European states.

It is already in the preamble that the CEFL Principles recognise the interests of the child as the primary one in regard to the consequences of divorce, therefore the Estonian legislator should take much more account of this. Presently there is no scrutiny whether, upon divorce by consent, the spouses have agreed on the consequences, but this would be necessary if the divorcing spouses had minor children.

As regards the maintenance of a divorced spouse, Estonian law is very much in conformity with the CEFL Principles and as compared to many other European states the principle of self-support is deeply rooted in Estonia. Following the CEFL Principles it would be expedient to consider giving priority to a new spouse over the divorced one when amending the law. At the same time, bearing in mind the high number of non-married partnerships in Estonia, the right of a divorced spouse to receive maintenance could be terminated not only upon re-marrying, but also when he or she establishes a lasting relationship, that is upon starting a non-married cohabitation. Certainly, the former spouses should be permitted to enter into a maintenance agreement and the possibility of entitling the spouses to renounce the claim to maintenance should be considered.

LEGAL REGULATION OF DIVORCE IN THE CIVIL CODE OF THE REPUBLIC OF LITHUANIA AS COMPARED TO THE CEFL PRINCIPLES

Inga Kudinaviciute-Michailoviene

1. INTRODUCTION

Prior to the Civil Code of 2001, there were two procedures for dissolution of marriage in Lithuania[1]: marriage could be dissolved either in a court or in a civil registry office. If both spouses agreed to dissolve the marriage, had no minor children and no disagreement regarding common property or maintenance, marriage was dissolved in a civil registry office within three months of the application for divorce. Registry offices also dissolved marriages for persons where one spouse was declared missing by the court; was declared legally incapacitated owing to insanity or imbecility; or was condemned to imprisonment for more than three years. In all other cases marriages were dissolved in court. The Code defined only one exception which applied to both procedures: a husband had no right to divorce a wife who was pregnant or during one year after the birth of a child.

The court had to establish the background of the divorce and check that the ground was acceptable for granting dissolution of the marriage. The claim would be rejected if the court determined that grounds for the dissolution of marriage were insufficient. The Code did not name the grounds for dissolution. Considering the particular circumstances the Court could attempt to reconcile the spouses. The Court would accept the claim for a divorce only after being assured the spouses could not live together and that the family could not be preserved, having broken down irretrievably. The Court had discretion in evaluating the grounds for divorce.

Comparing the norms regarding divorce in the former Marriage and Family Code of the Republic of Lithuania with the 2001 Lithuanian Civil Code,[2] one

---

[1] Lithuanian Republic Marriage and Family Code – Vilnius: Ministry of Justice Press, 1990 m.
[2] This Code came into force on 1 July 2001.

could conclude that after 2001 for all cases the Civil Code prescribes only one procedure of marriage dissolution: in court. Comparing its norms with the "Principles of European Family law concerning divorce and maintenance between former spouses" we see that the 2001 Civil Code's choice of only one procedure of marriage dissolution does not coincide with some of the Principles of the European Family Law which express more progressive norms of family law and defend the interests of former spouses more coherently.

After having compared the CEFL Principles with the norms regarding divorce and maintenance between former spouses of the Lithuanian Civil Code (CC) of 2001, an attempt will be made to establish which CC norms or their parts do not correspond with the CEFL Principles and to present the conclusions and suggestions as to how to harmonise them.

Since the middle of the 1960's the number of divorces has started to increase in Lithuania. Between 1970 and 1993 there were 2.2–3.7 divorces per 1000 persons.[3] In the last decade of the 20th century the number hardly changed and there were 3.9–4.1 divorces per thousand persons. Nowadays about 11 thousand spouses divorce per year.[4]

Part III of Article 38 of the Constitution of Lithuania claims that: "Marriage shall be entered into upon the free consent of man and woman". This means that a man and a woman can enter marriage only by their free agreement. Considering that the principle of voluntary marriage stated in Article 3.3 of the Civil Code presupposed freedom of divorce, it follows that divorce should not be limited by a marriage period, by a period of factual separation, or by compulsory agreement regarding the consequences of dissolution of marriage. Although many theorists and practicing family lawyers evaluate norms regarding divorce only from one side—how it helps to preserve the family, and seeks methods of how to suspend or forbid divorce—, when broken marital life prejudices spouses and their children and damages society, restraints on divorce in order "to save marriage at any cost" is only a virtual protection of family life.

2. DIVORCE

Articles 3.49–3.72 of the Third Book "Family Law" of the Civil Code regulate dissolution of marriage and its legal consequences. They define three ways of divorce: 1) marriage can be dissolved by mutual agreement of spouses; 2) by the applica-

---

3   STANKUNIENE, V, *Management of demographic processes.* (1995). Vilnius: Technika.
4   MASLAUSKAITE, A, *Lithuanian family: between market and policy* (2005), pp. 37–38.

tion of one of the spouses or 3) because of the fault of one or both of the spouses. Each of these has conditions for implementation and also conditions regarding conciliation of the spouses. Part 1 of the second section of Article 3.51 "Divorce by the mutual consent of the spouses" under "Dissolution of Marriage", the fourth chapter of the Civil Code states certain conditions, all of which must be met if marriage is to be dissolved by mutual consent: 1) a year must have elapsed since the commencement of the marriage; 2) the spouses must have made a contract in respect of the consequences of their divorce (property adjustment, maintenance payments for the children, etc.) and 3) both spouses must have full legal capacity.

The first condition of part 1 of Article 3.51 of the Civil Code does not fit CEFL Principle 1:1 (2) which states that "No duration of marriage should be required". The comment on this part of Article 3.51 of the Civil Code points out that the legislator prescribing the length of marriage was striving to protect marriage stability, to prevent spouses from careless, reckless, impulsive solutions and fictitious marriages. It was a sufficient period during which spouses could find out if their further common life was possible.[5] However, very often marriage is already broken down when spouses apply for divorce: spouses do not live in marital life, nor conduct common economy; they have other partners with whom they live as if married. Therefore, suspension of a divorce for a longer time gratuitously limits freedom of divorce and prevents the contract of a new marriage. CEFL Principle 1:1 (2) is considered to be more appropriate to the interests of divorcing persons, and the norm related to the duration of marriage of the Civil Code should be abolished.

The second condition of part 1 of Article 3.51 of the Civil Code states that marriage can be dissolved by mutual consent if the spouses have made a contract in respect of the consequences of their divorce. This does not fit part 3 of CEFL Principle 1:7 which states that if the spouses have not made an agreement or have reached only a partial agreement regarding property division and spousal maintenance, the competent authority should resolve these matters.

According to Article 3.51 of the Civil Code dissolution of marriage by mutual consent is possible only if spouses agree not only regarding dissolution of marriage but regarding all its legal consequences. Spouses who agree that their marriage is broken down and wish to dissolve it with a simplified procedure[6] should

---

5   MIKELENAS, V, KESERAUSKAS, S and OTHERS, *Comment on Civil Code. Third book. Family Law* (2002), p. 112.

6   Cases regarding divorce by mutual consent of the spouses or by application of one of spouses are considered by special rules of procedure// Civil Procedure Code of the Republic of Lithua-

make an agreement concerning its legal outcomes. If spouses agree that their marriage is broken down, but do not agree (or partially agree) on its legal consequences, they cannot dissolve their marriage in this manner. The court will not supplement the agreement and solve this problem.[7] In our opinion, the norm in part 3 of Principle 1:7 coincides more with the interests of persons wishing to divorce. Therefore, in order to improve Article 3.51 of the Civil Code, divorce, which is an exceptional personal right of spouses, should not be associated with property outcomes. It could be discussed as a separate claim in court and only in debates concerning the division of property and mutual consent of the spouses.

The first part of Article 3.51 of the Civil Code states that application for divorce by mutual consent should be made to the local court in the place of residence of one of the spouses. This arrangement should be reconsidered in the light of part 2 of CEFL Principle 1:2, which states that "Divorce should be granted by the competent authority which can either be a judicial or an administrative body". Divorce by mutual consent is the simplest way of marriage dissolution when there is no dispute regarding marriage dissolution or its legal consequences and it can be accomplished in registry offices. Nevertheless, according to the present legal regulation of family relations, marriage dissolution is exclusively in the competence of the court and this does not depend on the type of the divorce. The comment explains that the norm of part 1 of Article 3.51 of the Civil Code was chosen by the legislator as divorce causes serious legal consequences for spouses and for third parties (children of spouses, creditors etc.). Consequently, it should be supervised by the court, since according to part I of Article 6 of the ECHR every person has civil rights and duties to be resolved in an independent and objective court.[8] It is thought that to apply to the court is a personal constitutional right and not a duty, so the Civil Code should support the opportunity for spouses to have their marriage dissolved by administrative bodies as well as by courts.

Part 1 of Article 3.52 states that spouses should make a mutual application to the court for divorce and that the application should contain reasons why, in the opinion of the spouses, their marriage has broken down (CC part 3 Article 3.52). This approach is narrower than part 3 of CFEL Principle 1:4, which says that agreement may be expressed either by a joint application of the spouses or by an application by one spouse with the acceptance of the other. The Civil Code could be complemented with such a norm.

---

nia // State news. 2002 No. 36.

7   Article 138 of Civil Procedure Code.

8   MIKELENAS, V., *supra* note 5 at p. 110.

When granting a divorce decree, the court approves the contract of the spouses as to the consequences of divorce and the content of the contract is incorporated in the divorce decree (CC part 3 Article 3.53). The Civil Code does not state the form of such agreement as it is stated in part 2 of CFEL Principle1:6 that agreement of spouses should be in written form. Part 3 of Article 3.53 of the Civil Code does not present a finite list of all outcomes that should be discussed by the spouses, but states that the maintenance payments for minor children and each other, the residence of the minor children, their participation in the education of the children and other property rights and duties should be discussed. In our view, this approach of the Civil Code regarding the context of the agreement is not precise, because the spouses themselves should make an agreement concerning communication with children, division and usage of property, common creditors, and surnames of spouses if to be changed. If the above-mentioned agreement contradicts public order or violates the rights and legal interests of minor children or one of spouses, the court will not confirm it and the divorce case will be suspended pending a new agreement (CC part 4 Article 3.53). It should be noted that if creditors of the spouses (or one of spouses) make demands concerning the divorce, the case is suspended until creditors' demands are settled.[9] This approach contradicts the principle of free divorce, because as the divorce case is suspended, the right of the spouses to divorce is postponed for an indeterminate time and depends on third persons.

Article 3.54 of the Civil Code defines conciliation of spouses which in comparison with CEFL Principle 1:5 could be improved. This article determines the principle that the duty of the court is to enable the parties to solve their dispute peacefully. So part 1 of Article 3.54 states that the court must take measures to encourage the reconciliation of the spouses. However, settled court practice and systematic explanation of the legal norms show that reconciliation is implemented when the court has reason to think that partners can reconcile. Therefore, this should be treated as the right of the court, but not its duty. The term for conciliation cannot be longer than six months and unlike CEFL Principle 1:5, Article 3.54 of the Civil Code does not differentiate the length of the term in relation to the existence of children or their age, or other circumstances. Article 3.54 of the Civil Code states that the term for conciliation can be settled by the application of one of the spouses or on the court's initiative. There are also cases when such term is not imposed: 1) if neither of the spouses petitions for divorce within a year of the beginning of the reconciliation period or 2) where the spouses have lived apart for over a year or the reconciliation period is essentially contrary to the interests of one of the spouses or those of their children, or 3) where both the spouses require a substantive consideration of their case. In our opinion, the construction of

---

[9] Civil Procedure Code// State news. 2002 No. 36, article 540.

CEFL Principle 1:5 is more progressive and its norms could be introduced into Article 3.54 of the Civil Code. The period of conciliation should be related to the presence of children and to the agreement regarding the outcome of divorce.

In any case, if after the period for conciliation a spouse implements his/her right openly and declares his/her will to divorce and sustains it, this right should be independent of the subjective position of the other spouse or third persons, should not be denied or gratuitously constricted because the fifth norm of Article 38 of the Constitution of Lithuania which states that "rights of spouses are equal". This means that after marriage spouses have equal rights and equal civil responsibility regarding period of marriage and its dissolution.

Article 3.55 of the Civil Code regulates the dissolution of marriage by application of one of the spouses. In this case marriage can be dissolved if: 1) the spouses have been separated for over a year; 2) after the formation of the marriage one of the spouses was declared legally incapacitated by the court; 3) one of the spouses was declared missing by the court; 4) one of the spouses has been serving a term of imprisonment for over a year for the commission of a non-premeditated crime. Each condition is independent, which means that one of the conditions is sufficient ground for divorce by unilateral application of one of the spouses. The first point of part 1 of Article 3.55 of the Code "the spouses have been separated for over a year", means that separation should be confirmed by the court according to the procedure stated in Articles 3.73–3.80 of the Code.[10] This differs from CEFL Principle 1:8, which does not include factual separation unconfirmed by the court. Moreover, separation always means legal separation, but not always the physical separate lives of the spouses. So after confirmation of separation spouses could live in the same flat or house, though not as one family: they must not conduct common economy nor share marital life. In other words, if spouses want to divorce they should first present a court decision confirming separation. The Law does not state any exception to the separation term; thus, marriage can be dissolved by application of only one of the spouses after separation of one year. In other circumstances stated in points 2–4 of Article 3.55, if after the formation of the marriage one of the spouses has been declared legally incapable by the court; one of the spouses has been declared missing by the court; or one of the spouses has been serving a term of imprisonment for over a year for the commission of a non-premeditated crime, the demanding of a separate life or its duration are not defined as is stated in CEFL Principle 1:9. The term is not settled if marriage is

---

[10]   Separation is the first step to divorce. One spouse or both spouses can apply to the court for confirmation of separate life, if their common life because of circumstances, became impossible or can essentially damage the interests of their minor children or spouses are not interested to continue their common life. Article 3.73 of Civil Code).

terminated in case of the application of one spouse, since in the latter case the term would not correspond with its purpose.

After the evaluation of part 3 of Article 3.57 of the Civil Code which claims "the court having regard to the age of one of the spouses, the duration of marriage, the interests of minor children of the family, may refuse to grant a divorce decree if the divorce may cause significant harm to the property and non-property interests of one of the spouses or their children", it must be said that this conflicts with part 3 of Article 38 of the Constitution of Lithuania. It violates the rights of spouses to be in marriage by free agreement, and part five, which states: "rights of spouses are equal". Therefore, after marriage spouses have equal rights and equal civil responsibility in their relations regarding period of marriage and divorce, and this norm does not conform to CEFL Principle 1:1 which indicates that law should allow divorce and cannot demand a certain period of marriage.

Article 3.59 of the Code stipulates the outcome of divorce upon one spouse's application. It includes all the same questions as for divorce by mutual consent and it matches CEFL Principle 1:10 (1 a) and (1 b): the court should determine parental responsibility, including residence and contact arrangements for children and child maintenance; and questions of one spouse's maintenance and common property division, except in cases where common property was divided by common agreement confirmed by a notary. However, the norms of the Code do not include the opportunity to solve questions of property after divorce, as does the second part of CEFL Principle 1:10. It appears that acceptance of such a principle would improve norms of the Code regarding divorce.

Also, unlike the norms of the Principle, the fourth section of chapter 4 of the Civil Code regulates divorce on the basis of the fault of one or both of the spouses. The legislator defined this mode of divorce as a sanction and indicated several intentions: 1) to protect the innocent spouse from the other spouse, who violates marital duties, and to establish responsibility for the break down of the marriage in this way thus providing some satisfaction for the aggrieved spouse; 2) to establish the principle that fault in family law has a preventative and educational role.[11]

A spouse can obtain divorce if the marriage has broken down through the fault of the other spouse (CC part 1 Article 3.60). The interpretation of this approach allows one to think that a guilty spouse cannot apply to the court, but the Supreme Court opined that a claim for divorce can be based not only on the circumstance of marriage break down through the fault of the other spouse (the defendant spouse), but also on the fact that the marriage has broken down because of the

---

[11]   MIKELENAS, V *supra* note 5 at p. 130.

claimant's fault or if both spouses are guilty.[12] Part 3 of Article 3.60 states: a marriage shall be presumed to have broken down through the fault of the other spouse where he or she has been convicted of a pre-meditated crime or has committed adultery or is violent toward the other spouse or the other members of the family or has deserted the family and has not been caring for them for over a year. Demand for divorce because of the fault of one spouse should also be related to the duration of marriage. The respondent in a divorce suit may argue against his or her fault and put forward facts to prove that the other spouse is at fault in the breakdown of the marriage. The court having regard to the circumstances of the case may declare that both parties are at fault for the breakdown of the marriage (CC Article 3.61 part 2).

In my opinion, presumptions of fault in part 3 of Article 3.60 should be assessed critically. Part 2 of Article 3.60 of the Code states that the fault of a spouse for the breakdown of the marriage shall be established if he or she has seriously breached the duties determined in the Code; the reason why matrimonial life has become impossible is to be established. This could be one of the conditions of divorce stated in point 5 of part 1 of Article 3.55 of the Code and this would fit Principle 1:3, which describes possible ways of divorce without the criteria of fault.

After analysing court practice in Lithuania, we see that many cases for divorce start with the claim based on the fault of one of the spouses (CC Article 3.60), but during the deliberations in the court, spouses make another application: for divorce by mutual consent. The marriage is then dissolved on this second ground (CC Article 3.51), whereupon the judicial debates regarding fault ceases and stamp-duty is returned to the claimant. Thus, spouses can implement their right to choose the way of divorce.

3. MAINTENANCE BETWEEN FORMER SPOUSES

Spouses must be loyal and respectful to each other. They must support each other morally and financially and contribute toward the common needs of the family or the needs of each other in proportion to their respective capabilities. Where due to objective reasons one of the spouses is unable to make a sufficient contribution toward the common needs of the family, the other spouse must do so in accordance with his or her abilities. Circumstances, where one spouse does not take care of the other spouse, hides his/her income or does not use it for family purposes, could be grounds for reducing his/her share in the division of the common prop-

---

[12]   Supreme Court of Lithuania. Consultation of Civil Cases Department 8 April, 2004, No. A3–103. http://www.lat.litlex.lt.

erty (CC part 3–4 of Article 3.123). The proper achievement of spousal duties is considered together with the question of maintenance and the court can reject a spouse's claim for maintenance from the other spouse if he/she had not taken care of his/her spouse.

In cases when a marriage is dissolved by mutual consent, the question of maintenance of the former spouse should be solved either by application of a spouse or through the fault of a spouse.[13] There is an implicit connection between divorce and the fulfilment of duty of maintenance. Article 3.72 of the Civil Code regulates maintenance of the spouses. This is a kind of property relationship between spouses. The right to demand maintenance and the duty to provide maintenance exist not only in marriage, but after divorce, and after the declaration of the marriage as invalid or confirmed separation.

The fourth part of Article 3.72 of the Code states that the spouse responsible for the breakdown of the marriage should have no right to maintenance and makes no exceptions. Most foreign states have not admitted the fault of spouses in the breaking down of marital life for quite some time, as divorce for fault is based on simple sociology and therefore is subjective. CEFL Principles do not allow the fault of a spouse or spouses to be a ground for divorce. Therefore, in order to improve the Lithuanian Civil Code, divorce should not be based on fault (CC Articles 3.60–3.65); thus, the imbalance between such norms and CEFL Principle 2:1, which states that maintenance between former spouses should be subject to the same rules regardless of the type of the divorce, would be avoided. In this way, the statement that divorce by the fault of a spouse (spouses) is one of the types of divorce and Principle 2:1 can be used together and this would not contradict CEFL Principle 1:3 defining only two ways of divorce: by mutual consent and without consent of one of spouses.

Maintenance between spouses is to be regulated by: 1) marital contract (CC part 4 Article 3.104); 2) agreement of the spouses concerning the consequences of divorce (CC part 3 Article 3.53); 3) or, if the questions related to maintenance have not been regulated by spousal agreement, the spouse who demands maintenance has the right in case of divorce to ask the court to rule on maintenance. If a spouse does not claim maintenance during marriage or during the debates of the case in court, he/she cannot do so at a later date: for example, if the marriage was dissolved by mutual consent and the agreement stated that "neither spouse requires maintenance from the other", even if circumstances change, spouses cannot request maintenance.

---

13   Civil Procedure Code of Lithuanian Republic, Articles 385 and 386.

Such an approach does not coincide with Principle 2:10, which creates the opportunity for spouses to agree on maintenance after divorce as well as during divorce proceedings. A clause regarding maintenance is to be inserted into the agreement in some form and for some amount. When circumstances change, such a clause in the agreement could also be amended. This right is fixed in part 3 of Article 3.53, which states that when there is an essential change in the circumstances (illness of one of the former spouses, incapacity for work, etc.), both the former spouses or one of them may petition the court to reconsider the terms and conditions of their contract as to the consequences of divorce. Only specifications regarding the maintenance payments for children and each other, and the residence of their children could be changed, but specifications regarding division of property cannot, because it could violate third party interests (for example, creditors).

Concerning Principle 2:2 stating that each spouse should provide for his or her own support after divorce, Principle 2:3 stating that maintenance after divorce should be dependent upon the creditor spouse having insufficient resources to meet his or her needs and the debtor spouse's ability to satisfy those needs, Principle 2:4 stating that in determining a claim for maintenance, account should be taken in particular of the following factors: the spouses' employment ability, age and health; the care of children; the division of duties during the marriage; the duration of the marriage; the standard of living during the marriage and any new marriage or long-term relationship, it can be said that the Lithuanian Civil Code states particular criteria, based on which questions regarding the necessity of maintenance and realisation of the duty to provide it could be solved. Article 3.72 of the Civil Code relates a spouse's right of maintenance to his/her property status, so a spouse has no right of maintenance if his/her assets or income are sufficient to fully satisfy his/her needs. "Assets and income sufficient for complete satisfaction of ones needs" means a level of life when property and income under rational use are enough to satisfy minimal needs of accommodation, food and clothing. It is expected that the solution of such a problem should follow the criteria of Minimum Monthly Wages (MMW) and part 2 of Article 6.461 of the Civil Code, which states that the value of the total amount of monthly maintenance cannot be less than one minimum monthly wage and should be implemented by analogy. In such case the application of the analogy is based on part 2 of Article 6.439, which claims that the duty to pay rent might be established by law or by court judgement. Such criteria are implemented taking into account whether the spouse who must pay maintenance has financial means to do so. Therefore, maintenance could be decided upon only if the debtor spouse had at least an income equal to the minimum monthly wage left after the deduction of the maintenance payment. However, the implementation of such criteria (MMW) depends on certain circumstances.

Whereas, the duty of maintenance between spouses is based on principles "according to the needs and opportunities", the right of maintenance could be admitted to a spouse whose monthly income is more than MMW if the property status of the other spouse is sufficient to provide maintenance. Maintenance of a spouse is presumed to be necessary if: he/she is bringing up a minor child of the marriage or is incapacitated for employment because of his/her age or state of health (CC part 2 Article 3.72). Such presumptions can be challenged, so the defendant has a right to prove that even if the latter circumstances are present, the other spouse has no right of maintenance, because he/she has enough assets or income to maintain himself/herself. For example, if he/she is an old age pensioner, but the superannuation is enough to satisfy his/her necessary needs; the spouse who asked for maintenance is incapacitated for employment because of his/her state of health, and the other spouse is incapacitated for employment because of his/her age, then the court considers property status, state of health and other ways of providing their needs. In the case of almost equal income of both parties, it must be established whose expenses are greater. For example, a spouse incapacitated for employment because of his/her state of health may need medicine which may not be necessary for the other spouse also incapacitated for employment, for instance, because of his/her age; or both sides may have immovable property, but the spouse who is incapacitated for employment because of his/her age has a better opportunity to maintain and provide for himself/herself using this property—for example, age doesn't impede him from work in agriculture or fishing. However, on the whole, such possibilities for a spouse incapacitated for employment because of his/her state of health are limited.[14]

The third part of Article 3.72 of the Civil Code states that a spouse not able to obtain any qualification for work (complete his or her studies) because of the marriage, common interests of the family or the need to care for the children, shall have a right to demand from the former spouse support to cover the costs related to the completion of his or her studies or retraining. This would not apply if the studies were not completed or qualification not acquired were unrelated to the marriage, for instance, where a spouse was excluded from study because of low achievement or his/her refusal to continue studies. Expenses for study or further education and training include reimbursements, payment for studies, expenses for equipment, textbooks and so on.

---

14   Decision of Lithuanian Republic Supreme Court in civil case on 2003 04 09 No. 3K-3-500/
      2003.

Inga Kudinaviciute-Michailoviene

The maintenance order is the basis for the pledge of the respondent's assets. If the former spouse defaults on his or her obligation to pay maintenance, his or her assets may be used to provide payments according to the procedure laid down by the law (CC part 10 Article 3.72). In my view Article 3.72 of the Civil Code would be improved if the norms of CEFL Principle 2:4 regarding distribution of duties, standard of living and long term relationship in marriage were to be incorporated into the Civil Code.

The fifth part of Article 3.72 of the Civil Code sets the criteria on which a court decision regarding the question of maintenance and its amount should be based: a) the duration of the marriage, b) the need for maintenance, c) the assets owned by the former spouses, d) their state of health, e) age, f) capacity for employment, g) the possibility of the unemployed spouse finding employment and h) other important circumstances, which could apply to a person who should pay maintenance and who has other dependants such as minor children from a new marriage or maintenance of parents. In such cases, whether the spouse who needs maintenance (the creditor spouse) has the opportunity to receive maintenance from others such as adult children could be considered. Considering that Principle 2:7 foresees the opportunity of the debtor spouse satisfying the needs of the creditor spouse, sections (a) and (b) of Principle 2:7 could be added to part 5 of Article 3.72 of the Civil Code.

In the Lithuanian Civil Code, the amount of maintenance is reduced, made temporary or refused in one of the following circumstances: 1) the marriage has lasted for a period of less than a year; 2) the spouse entitled to maintenance has committed a crime against the other spouse or his or her next of kin; 3) the spouse entitled to maintenance has created his or her own difficult financial circumstances through his or her own irresponsible acts; 4) the spouse requesting maintenance did not contribute to the growth of their community assets or has wilfully prejudiced the interests of the other spouse or the family during the marriage (CC part 6 Article 3.72).

The eighth part of Article 3.72 of the Civil Code states that the court may order maintenance as: a) a lump sum; b) periodical (monthly or quarterly) payments or, c) property adjustment, both movables, such as a car, agricultural equipment etc., and immovables such as a house or flat, the use of which could be used for income. After comparing this approach to Principle 2:5, it can be concluded that the Civil Code solves the problem of maintenance in better ways, by stating that maintenance can be ordered on property. Principle 2:5 confined itself to only providing maintenance "at regular intervals and in advance", and of payment of a lump sum only on the request of either or both spouses taking into account the circumstances of the case.

Where the maintenance order is for periodical payments and the circumstances change significantly this may warrant the application by either of the former spouses for an increase, reduction or termination of maintenance payments (CC part 11 Article 3.72). Article 3.72 of the Civil Code does not state particular terms of payments. According to the circumstances stated in parts 5 and 6 of Article 3.72 of the Civil Code the court can order maintenance for a limited period. For example, if the marriage has lasted for less then one year and the spouses have no common children, maintenance cannot be ordered or ordered only for a limited period, such as only for two years, or until the creditor spouse finishes his/her studies. Maintenance could be paid throughout the life of the creditor spouse if maintenance is ordered by periodical payments (CC part 11 Article 3.72). Therefore, the period of the maintenance may also depend on the manner in which it has to be paid. For example, if maintenance is ordered in kind, the creditor spouse has no right to demand another way of maintenance, as the duty of maintenance is fulfilled and it is not for a lifelong period as would be a possibility if payments were periodic. We can conclude that this rule in Article 3.72 coincides with Principle 2:8, that maintenance should be granted for a limited or an unlimited period.

Part 12 of Article 3.72 states that after the death of the debtor spouse, the obligation to pay maintenance is devolved to his or her successors to the extent of his or her estate irrespective of the way the estate is accepted by the successors. This does not fit the third part of Principle 2:9, which states that "The maintenance obligation should cease upon the death of either the creditor or the debtor spouse." Considering that maintenance of a spouse is closely linked to the person and former marital-family relations of the debtor spouse, the Lithuanian civil law norms regarding inheritance cannot be implemented for personal rights, and therefore part 12 of Article 3.72 of Civil Code should be removed.

Part 13 of Article 3.72 of the Civil Code states that if the dependant dies or remarries the maintenance payments are terminated. On the payee's death, the right to demand arrears of maintenance payments devolve to the payee's successors. The dissolution of the new marriage creates a right to apply for the renewal of maintenance payments if the payee is bringing up a child by his or her former spouse or is caring for a disabled child by his or her former spouse. In all other cases the duty of the subsequent spouse to maintain the payee shall take precedence over that of the first former spouse. Comparing this approach with parts 1 and 2 of Principle 2:9 which states that "The maintenance obligation should cease if the creditor spouse remarries or establishes a long term relationship" and, after its termination this duty does not re-appear if a new marriage or long term relationship comes to an end, we can conclude that norms of part 13 of Article 3.72 of the Civil Code regarding the renewal of maintenance, if the former spouse is bringing up a child by his or her former spouse or is caring for a disabled child by his or her former spouse, could be changed. It could be determined that in such cases the duty of maintenance should not cease even if the spouse remarries, and in other cases it should fit parts 1 and 2 of Principle 2:9 and supplement the norm in Article 3.72 of the Civil Code regarding long term relationships.

4. CONCLUSION

In conclusion, after an analysis of the norms of the Lithuanian Civil Code regarding divorce and maintenance between former spouses and the CEFL Principles, in my opinion, some articles of the Civil Code could be improved in view of the progressive nature of the Principles and the opportunity they provide for ensuring more effective protection of the interests of the spouses in the realisation of the rights of divorce and the implementation of duty to maintain a former spouse.

PART THREE
AN ASPIRANT CANDIDATE:
DO VALUES CLASH?

TURKISH FAMILY LAW FACING THE PRINCIPLES OF EUROPEAN FAMILY LAW

Esin Örücü

1. INTRODUCTION

The Turkish Republic aspires to membership of the European Union. For this reason alone it would be interesting to investigate the accord or otherwise of the norms, principles and values of Turkish Family Law with the "Principles of European Family Law regarding Divorce and Maintenance between Former Spouses". Before making this juxtaposition and comparison however, it would be worthwhile to give a general picture of Family Law in Turkey as far as is relevant to our inquiry.[1]

The Ottoman Empire collapsed and the Turkish Republic came into existence in 1923. In 1926 Turkish Family Law was reshaped and secularised with the adoption of a Civil Code adapted from the Swiss. The desire of the *"élite dirigeant"* of the Turkish Republic to westernise and modernise Turkish society, and to embrace secularism (laicism) transformed Family Law totally.[2] However, certain charac-

---

[1] This overview is provided because Turkish Family law was not one of those considered when the Principles were being drawn up and there is no Turkish report to accompany the research that went into producing the Principles. For this see the publication of national reports: BEOLE-WOELKI, K, BRAAT, B and SUMNER, I (eds) *European Family Law in Action: Volume I. Grounds for Divorce and Volume II. Maintenance Between Former Spouses* (2003).

[2] Until 1917 Family law in the Ottoman Empire was based on the Şeriat (*shari'a*) and reflected Sunni beliefs and the Hanafi School's interpretation. See ESPOSITO, JL, *Women in Muslim Family Law* (1982) pp. 26–39 for Family law in Islam and specifically divorce = *talaq* (divorce proper, delegated divorce, mutual divorce, divorce by judicial process and divorce by apostasy), its consequences and maintenance. In 1916 two imperial edicts (*İrade*) were promulgated granting wives the right to sue for divorce in cases of desertion and a husband's contagious disease making conjugal life dangerous. These were followed in 1917 by the first ever officially adopted codification of Muslim Family law: the Ottoman Family Law (*Aile Hukuku Kararnamesi*), again seeking to establish grounds that would enable wives to sue for judicial divorce: contagious diseases of a husband, mental illness, not providing support for the family and incompatibility (Section 122); and also to limit a husband's exercising repudiation, by putting marriage and divorce under state control. The effects of this codification spread only to urban areas and remained controversial, since conservatives and minority religious groups

---

teristics of the law still reflected the special Turkish blend. In addition, though the concept of equality between the spouses was a fundamental principle of the Civil Code, "some were more equal than others" as seen in some of the Code provisions, such as those stating that the husband was the head of the family and chose the abode, and that the wife carried his surname and had no say in decisions concerning the home and the children. In case of divorce, she was only entitled to property legally registered under her name. Nevertheless, the 1926 Code was considered revolutionary both in Turkey and abroad when it was adopted in a country of Muslims. Yet it failed to keep up with the times. Moreover, until the 1961 Constitution there was no higher law demanding total equality between the sexes.

Both the 1961 Constitution and the present 1982 Constitution contain articles that make sex equality a constitutional principle, but in Family Law most provisions of the Civil Code remained unchanged. A few were amended by the legislator. For instance, legitimate and illegitimate children gained equal status (1990); the wife could retain her own surname (1997); and in 1990, by annulling the relevant article of the Code, the Constitutional Court (*Anayasa Mahkemesi*)[3] enabled the wife to work outside the home without her husband's permission.

In October 2001, a package of Constitutional amendments was introduced in an effort to further harmonise Turkish laws with the European Union *acquis,* the European Convention on Human Rights and the laws of the European Union member states. In addition to the already existing provision in Article 10 on "equality before the law", which states that: "All individuals are equal before the law without any discrimination, irrespective of language, race, colour, sex, political opinion, philosophical belief, religion, sect, or any such consideration", an additional clause was introduced into the framework Article 41 on "the protection of the family" which originally read: "The state shall take the necessary measures and establish the necessary organisation to ensure the peace and wel-

---

resisted it and nationalists and westernisers found it inadequate. In 1919 this codification was abrogated in the Ottoman state, although it remained in effect in Syria, Lebanon, Jordan, Israel and Iraq for much longer. In Turkey this was a transitional law (*kanunu muvakkat*), paving the way to efforts based on it in 1923 and 1924 to regulate family law and finally to the 1926 Civil Code.   See for an evaluation KURNAZ, Ş, *II.Meşrutiyet Döneminde Türk Kadını* (1996) pp. 107–114, and KURNAZ, Ş, *Cumhuriyet Öncesinde Türk Kadını,* (1997), pp. 89–91. For further information on Family Law in the Republic see, ÖRÜCÜ, E, "Turkey: Reconciling Traditional Society and Secular Demands" (1987–88) 26 *Journal of Family Law,* 221- 236; and on the then divorce law in particular see 27–34 of ÖRÜCÜ, E, "Turkish Divorce law", 2(96) *Migrantenrecht.*

3   It must be noted here that the decisions of the Constitutional Court (*Anayasa Mahkemesi*) are binding for all, but apart from the "unification of judgments" of the Court of Cassation (*Yargıtay*), judicial decisions do not form binding precedents in the Turkish legal system.

fare of the family, the protection of the mother and the children in particular, and for family planning education and practical application." Article 41 now has a first paragraph which reads: "The family is the foundation of Turkish society and is based on equality between the spouses."

Efforts to update the Civil Code had been made over a number of decades unsuccessfully, but with this added impetus for change, the Civil Code was extensively revised on 22 November 2001 and the new Civil Code came into force on 1 January 2002.

This is not a brand new Civil Code, but an amended one and many of the old provisions are the same apart from their numbering and modernising of the language. In the field of Family Law however, there are extensive amendments, the most important being related to equality.[4]

2. SETTING THE TURKISH SCENE

2.1. THE IMPORTANCE OF CIVIL MARRIAGE FOR THE OFFICIAL LEGAL SYSTEM

Laicism (secularism) is in the essence of Family Law in Turkey. Therefore, only a civil marriage is legally recognised. Section 237/4 of the then Penal Code, criminalised religious unions (*imam nikahı*) entered into without prior civil marriage, and imposed a prison sentence of from two to six months on the man and the woman, as well as criminalising and imposing a prison sentence on persons performing such religious ceremonies without seeing the official certificate of marriage. This Section was challenged as violating several Articles of the Constitution: Article 2 (the principle of laicism), Article 10 (equality), Article 12 (the character and the scope of fundamental rights and freedoms) and Article 24 (freedom to conduct religious services and ceremonies). The Constitutional Court (the *Anayasa Mahkemesi*), referring to Article 13 of the Constitution on the limitation of rights and freedoms, stated that Section 237 had been inserted into the Penal Code in 1936 to give support to civil marriage, that without this Article, polygamous unions would become possible and that, though such unions have no legal consequence, they pose a threat to the concept of family, being detrimental to the social order. The Court stated that if couples enter such illegal unions, women cannot use their rights arising from marriage, children are illegitimate

---

4   Family Law is now regulated in the Second Book of the Civil Code between Sections 118 and 494 (previously Sections 82–438), and Succession in the Third Book between Sections 495 and 682 (previously Sections 439–617).

and lose their inheritance rights; civil marriage must be strengthened in order to protect the family and the rights of women and children. The Court then went on to say that there is no violation of the principle of equality here between those who live together with no marriage of any kind and those with only a religious "marriage", as was claimed, since the first group do not wish their unions to be regarded as marriage. Equality before the law does not mean that everyone must be treated alike, differentiation based on Article 13 is not unconstitutional. The Court saw the Civil Code as a fundamental building block in the structure of the bridge to a contemporary and laic legal system for the Turkish Republic, said that civil marriage, being in the essence of that block, is also specifically protected by Article 174 of the Constitution and that to keep law and religion separate is the most important function of laicism. As a religious ceremony after the civil marriage is not banned, the Court saw no violation of laicism or any fundamental right and decided unanimously that Section 237/4 did not violate the Constitution.

The above decision sets the scene for Turkish secular Family Law. This scene did not change after the introduction of the New Penal Code in 2005.

In fact, as pointed out earlier, neither the legal framework nor the Court of Cassation (*Yargıtay*) accept in essence the fact that couples living out of wedlock can be regarded as in a relationship to be protected by law. For instance while the *Yargıtay* was determining what is an "engagement" in order to decide on whether gifts beyond the ordinary should be returned upon the breaking of the relationship, it was careful to differentiate between the breaking up of an "engagement", that is a promise to marry, in which case gifts beyond the ordinary would be returned, and of "living together without a valid marriage act", in which case they need not be returned.[5] In the second instance, since both parties act outside legality, the law protects the possessor.

Nevertheless, the *Yargıtay,* in its effort to tune the law to the needs of society, has sometimes taken a milder position. For example, while considering compensation for the death of the partner in work-related accidents, the *Yargıtay* extended the right to compensation to the unmarried cohabiting women (*nikahsız eş*), but on a different basis from that for married women, on a percentage lower to that which would be the due of a married wife, "her chance of getting re-married being much higher than that of a married woman".[6] In another case[7] when the insured

---

[5]   98/10173; 98/12105; 24/11/1998; 25 *Yargıtay Kararlar Dergisi* 1999, 170.

[6]   96/1606; 96/1661; 21/3/1996, 22 *Yargıtay Kararlar Deregisi* 1996, 1291.

[7]   97/3331; 97/4819; 8/7/1997 23 *Yargıtay Kararlar Dergisi* 1997, 1785. The Court was of the opinion that, her age, social status, position and family ties mean that she is not in the same posi-

died again in a work-related accident, the partner, who was this time referred to by the *Yargıtay* as the "cohabiting partner", was eighteen and had a child. According to the Court she had more than a 35% chance of getting re-married which is the accepted percentage for an official widow

2.2. A WOMAN'S SURNAME

It is also worthwhile mentioning another pivotal case. In Turkish Family Law, a woman still acquires the surname of her husband upon marriage; but, she can add her surname before that of her husband's upon written request to the marriage registrar at the time of marriage, or subsequently to the administration for personal status (Section 187). As stated above, this was already possible as a result of a legislative amendment in 1997.[8] However, the feminist camp regards this as an archaic clause not reflecting the current trends in an otherwise modern Civil Code. Nevertheless, a decision of the *Anayasa Mahkemesi* illustrates the general attitude to equality between the spouses in Turkey. In fact this decision is as relevant today as it was then. In this decision,[9] only published four years after it was delivered, the Court did not find the then Section 153 (now Section 187) of the Civil Code to be unconstitutional. The case arose when a married woman who wanted to use her maiden name only, objected to Section 153. The challenge was that this provision violated Articles 10, 12, and 17 of the Constitution related to equality, fundamental rights and freedoms, personality rights and rights to development of personality. Following a very conservative interpretation of the family and the place of the woman in it, and referring to "long established traditions", the *Anayasa Mahkemesi* saw no violation of any of the Articles mentioned. However, in the dissenting opinion, three judges saw a violation of Article 10, 13 and 17 and the Convention on the Elimination of All Forms of Discrimination Against Women, which Turkey ratified in 1985. They stated that the Constitution should be read in the light of International Conventions and contemporary developments. Making reference to the German Family Law amendments of 1976 and a decision of the German Constitutional Court in 1991, indicating that spouses should be able to choose either surname, these judges observed that it might be extremely important for the development of a spouse's personality and identity, to carry the surname acquired at birth. Obviously, the fact that it took four years before the decision was published indicates how even the *Anayasa Mahkemesi*

---

tion as a married woman who expects to live in the family home for an indefinite period and can expect support throughout her life. The compensation arising out of section 43 of the Code of Obligations therefore should be reduced in keeping with fairness and equity.

8   See for an analysis, ÖRÜCÜ, E, "Improving the Lot of Women and Children", in BAINHAM, A (ed), *The International Survey of Family Law 1997*, (1999) 465, at pp. 470–471.

9   1997/61; 1998/59; 29/9/1998; 15 November 2002, *Resmi Gazete*: 24937.

finds it extremely difficult to pass judgement in cases related to equality of the sexes in Turkey.

3. SPECIFIC ISSUES RELEVANT TO OUR RESEARCH AREAS

3.1. MATRIMONIAL PROPERTY

Matrimonial property regime was previously one of the most serious problem areas of family law. Separation of property was the codal regime in the old Code and worked to the detriment of the wife. The new codal regime is "participation in acquisitions" (Section 202) and again follows the Swiss pattern.[10] The other three regimes, separation of property (the previous codal regime), community property (in two forms: limited community and community of acquisitions) and shared separation, can be opted for by contract.[11] If there is no contract, "participation in acquisitions" applies automatically to marriages taking place after 1 January 2002.

This regime covers all goods acquired during the marriage and the personal property of each spouse (Section 219). Section 219 also defines "acquisitions" as goods acquired by either spouse as payments during marriage, including wages and salaries, social security and social benefit payments such as disability payments and unemployment benefits, income from personal property and goods replacing payment. In order to protect the economic integrity of the family or to provide for financial obligations arising from the marriage union, a judge, upon the request of one of the spouses, can decide that certain properties be designated for these purposes and that transactions on these can only be undertaken with the consent of the other spouse. The judge can ban one of the spouses from such transactions on this property and this will be entered into the property register (Section 199).[12] If a house bought by one of the spouses with the money made through work during marriage is sold, then the payment received, or a replacement property, counts as acquisition. Personal property is defined as goods for the sole personal use of one of the spouses such as jewellery and the like, goods belonging to one of the spouses before the marriage or acquired as a result of inheritance or without pay-

---

10 Participation in acquisitions—"*edinilmiş mallara katılma*"—(*Errungenschaftsbeteiligung*) was also accepted in Switzerland (the source legal system for Turkish Civil Law) on I January 1988 as the codal regime.

11 The contract to opt out can be drawn up by the notary before or after the marriage. The spouses can draw up the contract themselves and then have it authenticated by a notary, or they can decide and give a written request to the marriage registrar (Section 203).

12 2.H.D. 2005/5879;2005/8335, 30.5.2005, (2005) 31 *Yargıtay Kararlar Dergisi*, 1531.

ment, compensation for moral damages and replacement goods for personal property (Section 220). The spouses may decide by contract, that income from personal property shall not be part of the "participation in acquisitions" regime. Each spouse has the right to manage, use, and benefit from acquisitions (Section 223). Though new, this is a controversial provision.

In addition, by accepting a wife's work at home as a contribution, a feeling of equality within the marriage union has been created. In the event of the marriage coming to an end, the current market value of all acquisitions is added together. It includes the value attributed to the wife's work in the home. Obligations to others are subtracted and the rest is divided equally.[13]

In exceptional circumstances, the judge can decide on a return to "separation of property" upon the request of one of the spouses (Section 206). This may have unfortunate consequences. Also, there is a return to "separation of property" upon bankruptcy (Section 209), which is salutary.

Section 221 regulates the status of professional property. Section 227, dealing with contribution to the increase in value of property, is also new. The non-owner spouse is entitled to half of any increased value, unless the union has ended in divorce for adultery or threat to life, whereupon the judge gains discretion (Section 236), This is yet another new provision.

Upon the death of one of the spouses, the surviving spouse can ask for recognition of rights of occupation and *fructus* on the "family home" and furniture in return for the contribution percentage and, if not sufficient, for payment, in order to maintain his/her living standard (Section 240). The judge can recognise property rights instead, with the consent of the other heirs. This is a most significant innovation.

The Civil Code of 2002 introduced a new concept, the "matrimonial home" or "family home" (Section 194).[14] Regardless of what the matrimonial regime is between the spouses and regardless of how the property has been acquired, if the house is used as a "family home", it can be registered as such at any time during the continuation of the marriage.[15] This is a very significant move in Turkish Family Law. Now, one spouse cannot end a lease contract, or transfer the home, or limit the rights on it without the overt consent of the other. For instance,

---

13   On the whole these developments are positive. Unfortunately however, the gates are open for one spouse, usually the husband, to make the regime ineffective by contractual arrangement.
14   For other references to the "family home", see sections 240, 254, 279 and 652.
15   2. H.D. 2005/1615; 2005/4471; 22.3.2005, (2005) 31 *Yargıtay Kararlar Dergisi*, 1001.

according to the *Yargıtay*, if a house is used as a family home and the buyer knows this fact and the fact that one of the spouses does not agree to the sale, the court should annul the new title deed and decide on the registration of the house as the "family home".[16] The judge should be asked to intervene when consent cannot be obtained. The spouse who is not the owner can ask for an "entry of interest" into the land register that the house be designated therein as a "family home". This means that for this property the freedom and legal capacity of the owner-spouse to take effect needs the participation of the non-owner spouse. If the "family home" is rented, this fact can be written into the lease contract. Such designation entered into the property register can be repealed only following a law-suit, with the date of the trial intimated to the other party and after the evidence has been gathered.[17] These are most important new developments. In this way a spouse who does not pay the rent, cannot cause the eviction of the other, as long as that other does pay the rent. This protection also covers "family homes" acquired before 1 January 2002.

3.2. GROUNDS FOR DIVORCE

Divorce was previously covered by Sections 129–150 of the 1926 Civil Code. These have now become Sections 161 to 182, and grounds for divorce are largely unchanged except for their numberings. This area has not been modernised further than it was in 1988 when "irretrievable breakdown" was added as the main ground by the legislator.[18] Therefore, a multi-ground divorce system with the element of fault is still present. The grounds are the old grounds: adultery[19] (Section 161–old 129); threat to life, extreme cruelty or serious insult (Section 162–old 130); committing a humiliating crime, leading a dishonourable life (Section 163–old 131); desertion (Section 164–old 132); incurable mental illness (Section 165–old 133); and irretrievable breakdown and mutual consent (Section 166–old 134).

The list starts with adultery. This ground must be used within six months of the adultery coming to the knowledge of the other spouse and within five years of the adulterous act itself (Section 161). It is a breach of the marital duty of fidelity (Section 185). Adultery of either spouse is regarded in the same light and the adulter-

---

[16] 2. H.D. 2005/2547; 2005/7234; 3.5.2005, (2005) 31 *Yargıtay Kararlar Dergisi*, 1356.

[17] 2.H.D. 2005/7297; 2005/9634; 21.6.2005, (2005) 31 *Yargıtay Kararlar Dergisi*, 1533.

[18] See ÖRÜCÜ, E, "A Review of Turkish Divorce Law", in *Recht van de Islam: 8*, (RIMO 1991) pp. 47–62.

[19] The *Anayasa Mahkemesi* annulled the articles of the Penal Code regarding adultery as a criminal offence for the husband in 1996 and the wife in 1999. Thus here too equality was achieved. The new Penal Code of 2005 does not mention adultery as a punishable offence.

ous party and a spouse who forgives the other's adultery cannot bring a divorce suit to court on this ground. There is no definition of adultery in the Code, however, according to court decisions we observe that adultery involves sexual intercourse and anything less is not adultery; that the sexual intercourse of a husband in a brothel however, does not constitute adultery; that adultery can be considered to have taken place even when there is a separation decision.

Next to be covered is threat to life, extreme cruelty (severe maltreatment) or serious insult (Section 162). Physical violence or severe maltreatment in practice covers rape in marriage. In one case the *Yargıtay* stated that a husband, who had had anal intercourse with his wife without her consent, was guilty of "severe maltreatment of members of the family" as regulated by the Penal Code, and gave him a prison sentence of six months.[20] When "insult" is used as the ground, we see that according to court decisions, such treatment must be considered as "insult" by people living around the couple.[21] Such behaviour can also be referred to in conjunction with Section 166. These claims must be brought to the court within six months of the facts coming to the knowledge of the plaintiff and within five years of their occurrence. The spouse who forgives has no right to sue on this ground.

Committing a humiliating crime or leading a dishonourable life (Section 163) are regarded as eroding the moral basis of marriage. Both must, in addition, make life in common intolerable for the one who brings the law-suit. In both cases it is the judge who decides which offences are heinous and dishonourable as they are not defined in the Code. Court decisions indicate that theft, embezzlement, fraud, spying against the state, using drugs or trading in drugs, running a brothel or helping in illegal abortions are regarded as heinous offences. Drunkenness, gambling, homosexuality and anal intercourse with others are all viewed by courts as leading a dishonourable life. This ground can be used at any time.

Desertion is the next divorce ground in the Code when one spouse deserts the other to avoid marital duties and refuses without good cause to return (Section 164). What is important in these cases is the determination of the reason why the spouse left the matrimonial home. For instance, a husband cannot choose his parent's home as the matrimonial abode; therefore, a wife who refuses to come there cannot be blamed for desertion.[22] The home must be one chosen together by

---

[20] 94/5217; 7/7/1994.

[21] According to court decisions, examples of such behaviour are: if a husband tells his friends falsely that his wife was not a virgin when they married, his wife can sue for divorce on the ground of violation of her name and honour by insults. Other circumstances cited are beating, torturing and, as seen above, anal intercourse.

[22] See YHGK (General Civil Assembly of the *Yargıtay*) 1969/744/266, 21/4/1971 and 2HD 606/1198; 25/5/65. The Court, by regarding "not providing an independent home for the wife"

the spouses (Section 186) or by one of the spouses on certain conditions (Section 188) or determined by the judge (Section 195). The home must also be suitable for the circumstances of the spouses and independent. This is the kind of home to which the deserted spouse can invite the other, otherwise the desertion is regarded as being for good cause.[23] It must be noted that the durations for desertion have changed. Desertion should now last for 6 months rather than 3 months as formerly.[24] After at least 4 months of desertion, the judge is asked to issue a call to return to the marital home within 2 months.[25] If the spouse does not comply, then a divorce suit can be started at end of this period. The one who forces the other to leave the matrimonial home or prohibits the other from returning home without good cause is also considered to have deserted (Sections 164, 186/4). The deserter cannot sue for divorce on this ground.[26]

Another ground is mental illness (Section 165). Insanity is the only illness accepted as a ground.[27] There is no longer the requirement of duration as there was formerly (three years), however, it must be mental illness acquired after the marriage contract has been completed, be incurable and render life in common intolerable for the other spouse.

For our purposes, it is important to note the conditions for divorce for irretrievable breakdown and mutual consent. As mentioned above, the old Section 134 (now 166) had already been amended in 1988 when this no-fault ground was introduced. Before 1988 when the concept of mutual consent entered Turkish law

---

both as a reason for incompatibility and an acceptable reason for desertion, has taken a decisive step away from tradition, as in Turkish society the old tradition of the extended family approves of all sons bringing their wives into the household to live in the family home.

[23]   2.H.D. 2005/9764; 2005/12222; 19.9.2005 (2006) 32 *Yargıtay Kararlar Dergisi*, 374.

[24]   Before the amendment to section 134 (now 166) in 1988, the remarkably short period of time provided for in this ground amounted to divorce by mutual consent. Therefore it was frequently used by arrangement. However, this ground is sometimes used or abused when one of the spouses moves to a foreign country as a worker and does not ask the other to follow. This means that awareness of this ground is important for Turkish workers abroad, and especially for the spouse, usually the wife, left behind.

[25]   and the intimation that in case of non-compliance a divorce suit would ensue. See 2312/3130; 1/4/1994. A husband moved to a new address, but the wife did not follow. The husband immediately filed for divorce on the ground of desertion. The *Yargıtay* stated that an official warning from the court to the wife is a pre-condition of cognisance of a divorce case relying on this ground; that the warning should be sent upon the request of the husband and to be effective must include the following: the full address of the new home; the money for the costs involved for the wife in getting there; an invitation to the wife to come to the new matrimonial home within two months from the date of the warning;

[26]   2.H.D. 2004/4901; 2004/5829; 5.5.2004 (2005) 31 *Yargıtay Kararlar Dergisi*, 1717.

[27]   The inability to have children cannot be used as a ground for divorce under this heading, though there have been such demands; this could, however, lead to irretrievable breakdown of marriage under section 166.

for the first time, severe incompatibility (*şiddetli geçimsizlik*) had to make life in common intolerable and this had to be determined by the judge.[28] It was also the case that the spouse more responsible for incompatibility could not bring a divorce suit, one of the general principles of Turkish law being that no one can benefit from his or her own fault. The judge would balance the fault, making this general ground discretionary.

Titled "irretrievable breakdown of the marriage union"[29] since 1988, section 166 allows either spouse to sue for divorce if the marriage union is irretrievably broken down and they cannot be expected to live together. A marriage is regarded as having broken down if after one year of marriage spouses apply for divorce together, or one applies and the other accepts. Thus, when there is mutual consent, the underlying assumption is that the marriage union has broken down.[30] Mutual consent alone is not enough however. The following conditions must be fulfilled: the marriage must have lasted for at least a year, the judge must himself hear both parties individually, be convinced that they express their will freely, and endorse as acceptable the document prepared by the spouses for the arrangement of the financial consequences of divorce and the position of the children. These conditions have not changed and are regarded by the *Yargıtay* as part of public policy. As already mentioned, this is not the sole ground for divorce as is the case with recent developments in many other jurisdictions in Europe. Though the Turkish legislator regards Section 166 as the general ground, as stated in the general reasoning of the new Civil Code, the legislator is of the opinion that the present situation has not given rise to problems and that to remove especially "adultery" as a specific ground would lead to misunderstanding in Turkish society at large.

---

[28] Various circumstances were regarded by the judges as giving rise to incompatibility such as: extra-marital relationships, loss of trust, continual disagreements and arguments, a husband's being unable to provide an independent home, bad habits, refraining from sexual intercourse, impotence, hurting religious or national feelings, not looking after the house, maltreatment of stepchildren, gambling, a wife's staying overnight with a female friend of bad repute and wilful abortion.

[29] Or "impossibility of resuming life in common". The literal translation from Turkish "*temelinden sarsılmış*" is "shaken from its foundations".

[30] However, see this decision of the Second Civil Section of the *Yargıtay* 6979/8890; 2/10/1989: "Divorce by mutual consent is a new possibility not part of established tradition and therefore great care must be taken to see that justice is done. To this end, the parties should submit to the court a contract as to the arrangements of financial matters and children's welfare prior to any other process. The judge must take an active part in this settlement since the parties in their haste to end their relationship may be rash, For example, "one may give up everything" or "be under pressure or deceived". The judge must intervene and ensure reasonableness and justice. He is not bound by the facts as presented by the parties, but must directly investigate and determine the truth."

The *Yargıtay* has been extremely cautious in the application of divorce by mutual consent upon breakdown of marriage and tries to ensure that the above conditions of the provision are strictly met. As women, who are often the weaker partners in Turkish marriages, may be forced by their husbands to accept divorce under threat of, for example, their children being taken from them, divorces apparently based upon mutual consent may not be so. According to the *Yargıtay*, these conditions must also be fulfilled in divorces obtained abroad and therefore the *Yargıtay* does not recognise a divorce decree if the foreign judge has not ensured the existence of these conditions.[31] The *Yargıtay* Public Prosecutor of the Republic is extremely sensitive in this area and raises such issues using his power of *ex officio* objection.[32] Here we see the Court acting as the protector of women and children. This is an indication that the *Yargıtay* takes into consideration the needs of Turkish society rather than, for example, religious feelings which expect that divorce should be as easy as possible for men.

Thus we see that divorce by collusion or mutual consent has been made rather difficult. In addition to certain conditions having to be met, generally, the judge is not bound to accept the declaration of the spouses; he must be personally convinced that there is real incompatibility in the family and that the evidence is proven (intimate conviction = *vicdani kanaat*); and he has to certify the agreements reached (Section 184). As these agreements are regarded as vital, it is only the approval of the judge that gives them validity. The *Yargıtay* is of the opinion that the spouses cannot ask the judge to approve an agreement drawn up after the divorce case has been finalised, for instance.[33]

The less faulty spouse can contest the petition, as long as this objection is not regarded as an abuse of rights. If so regarded, or if there is no benefit worthy of protection in the continuation of marriage for the respondent and the children, then the divorce is granted. In the context of section 166, the rule that the judge is not bound by the declaration of the spouses does not apply, as long as they agree to the amendments he introduces into their financial arrangements.

Three years after an unsuccessful divorce suit on any of the grounds, divorce will be automatically granted in a second divorce suit upon the application of either spouse, that is unilateral divorce becomes possible as long as the spouses have not lived together during that time (Section 166/5). This option is available for initial divorce suits rejected on any of the grounds and therefore can be seen as an added

---

[31] See for a discussion of problems arising from this stance, ÖRÜCÜ, *supra* note 2 (1996), 32–34.
[32] A procedure borrowed from the French procedural system, as pointed out in 1997/6–175; 1997/196; 14/10/1997; 24 *Yargıtay Kararlar Dergisi* 1998.
[33] 2HD. 925/1772; 14/2/1995 (1995) 21 *Yargıtay Kararlar Dergisi*, 872.

possibility of divorce for couples whose earlier attempts at divorce have failed.[34] Fault is irrelevant.

A spouse can ask for separation instead of divorce (Section 167). The judge has discretion to decide for divorce or separation. If the suit is only for separation, he cannot decide for divorce, but if it is for divorce, he can decide for separation where he thinks there is a possibility of resumption of life in common (Section 170). It must be said that judicial separation is rather rare in Turkey. Separation can last for one to three years (Section 171) and at the end of that period one of the spouses can sue for divorce (Section 172). These sections are unchanged, except for their numbering.

In addition, Sections 197, 198 and 199 cover secession of living together, and related measures. If life in common threatens personality rights, economic security or family peace, a spouse has the right to a separate life. If the reasons are legitimate, the judge decides on the financial contribution of the other spouse to the one who has gained the right to live separately. He also decides on the use of furniture and managing property. If reasons are not legitimate, then the other spouse can demand the same. This is a new development. If one of the spouses does not fulfil his/ her obligations of contributing, then the judge can decide that persons owing money to him/ her pay their debts to the other spouse.

Thus the judge has considerable discretion in taking measures for the financial and economic protection of the family. The more vulnerable have gained more protection in the new Civil Code.

Another positive change comes with Section 240: in order to continue his or her existing life style, the surviving spouse can request either the right to live in, or the right to benefit from the fruits of the "family home" in which the couple were living before the death of the other spouse. The surviving spouse may have to make an additional payment if the value of the house is well beyond his/her contribution to acquisitions. The same applies to the ownership of the furniture. If there are legitimate reasons and agreement between the heirs, the surviving spouse can acquire ownership of the "family home". These developments are in the interest of women.

---

[34] However, according to the *Yargıtay*, where the parties had not asked to be and thus were not notified of the decree emanating from the *Yargıtay* given upon appeal against the original decision, this decree could not be regarded as final and therefore could not be taken as the starting point of the required three year period of actually living apart. According to the Court, in such cases the new divorce suit should be refused. 476/1005; 1/2/1994.

Before the amendments in 2002, a divorce suit had to be brought either to the court of the district where the couple had lived for the last six months or where the suing spouse lived. As the abode of the married woman was her husband's abode, this in fact was where the husband lived. Now, this court can be the court of the abode of the spouse bringing the suit. This change is in the interest of women.

3.3. CONSEQUENCES OF DIVORCE

Some of the consequences of divorce are personal, while others are financial. For instance, the divorced wife takes back her old surname, but may continue to use her married surname by a court decision if she has an interest in doing so and there is no damage to the interests of the husband (Section 173). Both spouses retain the age of the majority acquired by marriage. The wife may retain the nationality of her husband if she acquired it by marriage.

During the divorce or separation process, the judge will take ex officio the necessary steps (interim measures) to ensure housing and subsistence of the spouses, administration of the property and the caring and protection of the children (Section 169).

All rights to a law-suit lapse after one year of a final divorce judgement (Article 178). Previously, apart from suits for moral compensation, there was no time limit for bringing law-suits following divorce. Appropriate material compensation (*maddi tazminat*) is awarded for existing or expected interest, changed by the divorce. Moral compensation (*manevi tazminat*) is awarded if the claiming spouse is faultless, less faulty and if personality rights are damaged as a result of the events leading to divorce (Section 174). There are no time limits. If one of the divorced spouses falls destitute, maintenance (*yoksulluk nafakası*) for an unlimited period can be granted, on the condition that he or she is not the more faulty party.[35] This now applies equally to either spouse. Formerly, a husband could only ask for alimony from his wife if she had adequate means (Section 175). This is an

---

[35]   Note that, in addition to being a ground for divorce, adultery has consequences related to moral damages (sec 174), destitution alimony (sec 175, 176) and to matrimonial property (sec 236) In brief: an adulterous spouse cannot ask for moral damages unless he/she is the less faulty; neither can he/she ask for destitution alimony; alimony ends upon leading a dishonourable life, which could be adultery coming to light within five years of the act; also if death occurs while the divorce suit is pending and the heirs to the pursuer can prove that the defendant was at fault (e.g. adultery) then the defendant cannot inherit; and finally upon divorce based on adultery or threat to life, the judge may decide to reduce or remove the right on half the added value of the other's possessions, in keeping with the principle of fairness.

important change. It does fulfil the requirements of equality but may work to the detriment of Turkish women, most of whom do not have personal financial means.

Maintenance ends upon death, marriage to another, living with another as if married, or leading a dishonourable life (Section176). However if death occurs while the divorce suit is pending, the heirs to the pursuer can continue the suit and if they can prove that the defendant was at fault, then the defendant cannot inherit from the deceased pursuer. Previously, as the suit fell upon death, the defendant always inherited (Section 181/2). This is an important amendment and indicates a change in social policy.

If maintenance is demanded after the divorce, the competent court is the court of the abode of the spouse demanding alimony (Section 177). When so demanded, yearly increases in the alimony can be determined at the outset by the court (Article 176). This facility is in the interest of women and these are all new and positive possibilities. The judge cannot decide on these issues directly.

Child custody is decided upon after the parents have been heard (Section 182). The *Yargıtay* reiterates that according to the European Convention on the Use of the Rights of the Child Article 3, ratified by and put into effect in Turkey on 12 March 2002, a court can decide on custody only after a child, regarded by domestic law as having developed a sense of comprehension, is given the opportunity to receive all relevant information, is consulted and expresses his/her preference, and the opinion of an expert is taken.[36]

One spouse is given custody and relations with the other are determined in the best interest of the child, with health, education and moral welfare being considered. The spouse not granted custody has to contribute to the expenses of raising the child in proportion to his/ her means. If a child, having reached majority, is still in education, the parents have to support the child. This is "participatory alimony" (Section 328) and is distinct from "alimony for help" (Section 364), which is the obligation of someone to pay alimony (*nafaka*) to his/her ascendants, descendants and siblings who would fall into destitution without this help.[37]

---

[36]   2.H.D. 2005/12496; 2005/15273; 8.11.2005, (2006) 32 *Yargıtay Kararlar Dergisi*, 376.
[37]   12.H.D. 2005/12338, 2005/16008; 18.7.2005, (2005) 31 *Yargıtay KararlarDergisi*, 1760.

3.4. PARENTAL RIGHTS AND CUSTODY

While married, the spouses use parental rights together. If not married, the mother represents the child (Section 337).[38] Upon divorce, as stated above, one spouse gets the custody, the other, "personal relationship", parallel with the Convention on the Rights of the Child, which Turkey signed and ratified in 1995 (Section 324). Personal relationship can be ended if the child's well-being is under threat, if the parents abuse this right, do not take an interest in the child, or for other important reasons.[39] The mere existence of a blood tie will not give the right to abuse the rights of the child.[40] This is a very appropriate development.

Section 340 deals with the duty of the parents for the education of the child in accordance with their means. They must provide and protect the physical, mental, spiritual, moral and social development of the child. Section 341 deals with religious education, the determination of which is the right of the parents. Section 347 regulates fostering.

4. ASSESSMENT THUS FAR

In the new Civil Code, a husband will also be able to ask for maintenance from his wife regardless of her financial status. But, many women in Turkey are financially weak and they should be protected as they had been previously. Here we see a modern development that does not accord with the family realities of Turkish society.

As far as the legal status of children is concerned, the system has been simplified and the concepts of legitimate and illegitimate children have been abandoned. Instead the Code talks of children born in wedlock and out of wedlock. The word "*nesep*" (filiation or lineage) has been replaced by "*soybağı*" (family tie), which is a neutral concept.

---

[38] However, the *Yargıtay* is of the opinion that in paternity suits the mother may not always act in the best interests of the child and therefore immediately appoints a curator (*kayyim*) in such a suit. See *Yargıtay II. Hukuk Dairesi*, 2001/17671; 2002/781; 29/1/2002 (2002) 28 28 *Yargıtay Kararlar Dergisi*, p. 851–852.

[39] The *Yargıtay* alters the arrangements for custody when the child's relationship with the other parent is hampered, or his/her family ties or mental development are adversely affected. See *Yargıtay II. Hukuk Dairesi* 2002/3930; 2002/4731; 4/4/2002, (2003) 29 *Yargıtay Kararlar Dergisi*, pp. 356.

[40] If parents neglect their duties towards the child, the judge must decide on necessary measures for the protection of the child *ex officio*. See *Yargıtay II. Hukuk Dairesi* 2002/6834; 2002/7495; 4/6/2002 (2003) 29 *Yargıtay Kararlar Dergisi*, pp. 17–18

The matrimonial regime of "participation in acquisitions" is an extremely positive development, but is does not apply to marriages existing before 1 January 2002. This means that the unfair and unsatisfactory regime of "separation of property" of the past continues to apply to marriages concluded before that date. The new arrangement for existing marriages will create some practical problems. Spouses of existing marriages could have drawn up a contract between the period of 1 January 2002 and 1 January 2003, and decided that "participation in acquisitions" would apply to their property from the beginning of their marriage, regardless of when the marriage was contracted. Otherwise the new regime would apply to them only after that date, so that whatever they acquired after that date would fall into the new legal regime. This means that for spouses who have not by contract opted for the new regime, part of their goods will be subject to "separation of property" and part, that is, those acquired after 1 January 2002, to "participation in acquisitions". Upon death or divorce, this will create considerable problems. Not only is there the old inequality between men and women, but also new inequalities created between men and women married before 2002 and men and women married after 2002. In addition, the work of some women in the home is to be counted as a contribution to acquisitions only after 1 January 2002. It is also regrettable that it is extremely easy for spouses to opt out of the legal regime, which was an achievement after long years of struggle by the feminist camp.

On many of the issues arising under the provisions of Family Law, the newly set up Family Courts will have competence.[41] Family Courts will deal mostly with protective, educational and social aspects of family life, above all considering "the protection of mutual love, respect and tolerance within the family, determining the problems spouses and children face with a view to resolving them by peaceful means and encouraging such resolution by expert advice whenever necessary."[42] For instance, the *Yargıtay* decided that in cases where one spouse asks for the return of his/her goods in the possession of the other (Section 226), or the return of the dowry (*çeyiz*) and in assessing the increase in value of the goods by the contribution of the other (Section 227), the Family Court has competence.[43]

Prior to 2002, the Turkish family law was already in many ways quite similar to continental ones, the legal system being the product of global receptions of civilian law (Swiss, German, French and Italian). This resemblance is now closer. Though the Islamic law of the Ottoman Empire plays no part in the contempo-

---

[41] See Law No: 4787 of 9 January 2003 on the Establishment, Functions and Procedures of Family Courts (*Aile Mahkemelerinin Kuruluş, Görev ve Yargılama Usullerine Dair Kanun*) published on 18/1/2003 in *Resmi Gazete*: 24997.

[42] *Ibid,* Art. 7.

[43] 20.H.D. 2005/4426; 2005/5746; 2.5.2005, (2005) 31 *Yargıtay Kararlar Dergisi*, 1271.

rary Turkish legal framework, the traditional and religious sentiments of the people do not always coincide with the formal legal system. It must also be remembered that Turkish nationals differ from each other in many ways, such as religion, race, language, tradition, geography, education and wealth. It is therefore interesting to observe how the Turkish legislature and the courts deal with such social problems as they arise. The picture becomes even more interesting after the amendments in Family law. The majority of women in Turkey regard themselves as subservient to their husbands and regard the husband as the head of the family. Men definitely do so. Without further education, wide dissemination of information and a change in social norms, the new Civil Code will provide equality to enlightened families only. Such equality existed for them even before the changes.

The new Civil Code achieves formal equality in a society where women, especially those in traditional families, are not regarded as equal to men and do not have equal financial and professional status or means. The balance between the spouses, tilted previously in favour of the husband in the Civil Code of 1926, is now based on equality, but context may demand that it should be tilted in favour of the wife in order to achieve real equality. The courts work on this assumption. The law assumes equality where it does not in fact exist. Equality and rights may oversimplify complex power relations. The exercising of rights in the private sphere has little to do with legal rights. Turkish law is an example of a top-down model and there is no official recognition of pluralism.[44] Therefore the work done by the courts in everyday situations is of increased importance. The courts reformulating the law must tune the law to context to achieve the "best" substantive result for spouses and children.

Nonetheless, the amendments and the new provisions of the 2002 Civil Code do aim to bring Turkish Family Law into line with the laws of the member states of the European Union and give women the basic security of being able to rely on a law that gives them equality. We can only hope that in time, what is provided for by law becomes internalised by both sexes and the society at large.

---

[44]   See for a criticism of the non-recognition of Muslim legal pluralism in Turkey. YILMAZ, I, "Non-recognition of Post-modern Turkish Socio-legal Reality and the Predicament of Women" (2003) 30(1) *British Journal of Middle Eastern Studies*, pp. 25–41; and YILMAZ, I, *Muslim Laws, Politics and Society in Modern Nation States: Dynamic Legal Pluralisms in England, Turkey and Pakistan* Ch 5 "Muslim Legal Pluralism in Turkey " (Aldershot, Ashgate, 2005), pp. 83–123.

5. TURKISH FAMILY LAW JUXTAPOSED TO THE PRINCIPLES OF EUROPEAN FAMILY LAW

5.1. DIVORCE

5.1.1. General Principles

Principle 1:1 Permission of divorce:

Turkish law permits divorce on a number of grounds (Sections 161–184). For the general ground of irretrievable breakdown of marriage and mutual consent the marriage must have lasted for at least one year before divorce can be applied for. Here the Principle that "no duration of the marriage should be required" would not accord with Turkish law, neither therefore, would Turkish law accord with the CFEL Principles. Whether this provision of Turkish law can be changed is open to question in view of the courts' and the public prosecutors' sensitivity to the problems Turkish women may face, alluded to earlier (under 3.2).

Principle 1:2 Procedure by law and competent authority:

The divorce procedure is determined by law and divorce is granted by the competent judicial authority. Here there is complete accord between the approach adopted by the Principles and Turkish law. However, in Turkey administrative bodies are not involved in divorce cases.

Principle 1:3 Types of divorce:

Turkish law permits divorce by mutual consent (Section 166). Here too there is complete accord between the two approaches. However, behind divorce by mutual consent there is an assumption that the marriage union has been shaken to its very foundations, thus "divorce by mutual consent" is equated to "divorce for breakdown" and the courts are very cautious in the procedure to be followed, as they believe that divorce apparently by mutual consent might be taking place under pressure from the husband. The cases seen above (under 3.2) are indicative of this concern. If this procedure is not followed abroad in divorces granted to Turkish couples, then there is the serious problem of non-recognition of these decrees in Turkey.

5.1.2. Divorce by Mutual Consent

Principle 1:4 Mutual Consent:

Divorce can be granted on the basis of the spouses" mutual consent and there is no requirement for a period of separation (Section 166). Mutual consent is understood to be an agreement between the spouses that the marriage is broken down and therefore should be dissolved. The application to the court is made either by both spouses in agreement or one applies and the other accepts. There is accord here with the Principles. Additionally, however, the marriage must have lasted for one year.

Principle 1:5 Reflection period:

There is no reflection period in Turkish law. This is so whether the spouses have children under the age of sixteen or not, or have agreed on all aspects of the divorce or not. None of the requirements stated in this CEFL Principle find a place in Turkish law. In fact, if there is no total agreement on the financial consequences or divorce or issues related to the children, the divorce judge will refuse to grant divorce and can himself suggest arrangements which could be accepted by the spouses, in which case, he will grant divorce. If not accepted, he will not (Section 166:3). The judge has discretion on a number of issues and can use both his discretion and "intimate conviction" (*vicdani kanaat*) (Section 184).

Whether under Turkish law there is need for a reflection period is open to discussion. However, if the Principles were to become part of the European *acquis*, there would be no reason why Turkish law could not cater for this.

Principle 1:6 Content and form of the agreement:

A written agreement is to be submitted to the judge for approval, which should contain arrangements for the children and financial consequences of divorce. (Section 166:3) This is all that is overtly mentioned in the Code. Parental responsibility and custody is to be determined separately (Section 182), so are property rights (Section 179)

Principle 1:7 Determination of the consequences:

The judge has to approve of all the arrangements, as already mentioned. In this he will first consider the arrangements of the spouses and take into account the best interest of the spouses and the children. He is not only competent to scrutinise the contents of all agreements but is under an obligation to alter any arrangement as he sees fit. If there is no arrangement or no agreement, the judge would himself substitute for the parties. If they do not agree to his arrangements he will refuse divorce. This Principle is in accord with Turkish law, in the practice of which the judges are extremely sensitive.

The division of property and spousal maintenance are separate issues and are covered below under "Maintenance between former spouses".

5.1.3. Divorce without the consent of one of the spouses

Principle 1:8 Factual separation:

Divorce is permitted upon the application of one of the spouses if a previous divorce case on any of the grounds has failed, three years have elapsed since the date of that judgment and life in common has not been set up. This is an indication of irretrievable breakdown. This means that the separation period in this situation is three years (Section 166).

Factual separation is only mentioned in relation to the rights of a spouse to apply for the termination of marriage, in that, this spouse can ask either for divorce or for separation (Section 167). As long as the existence of a ground for divorce has been proven, the judge can decide either for divorce or, in cases where there is a possibility of resuming life in common, for separation (Section 170). However, if the petition was for separation he cannot decide for divorce. The decision for separation could be from one to three years (Section 171). When this period is over and life in common has not been resumed, then divorce will be granted upon the application of one of the spouses (Section 172). In a rather roundabout way this accords with CEFL Principle 1:8.

In cases where the grounds of divorce used are adultery (Section 161); threat to life, extreme cruelty and serious insult (Section 162); committing a humiliating crime, leading a dishonourable life (Section 163); or incurable mental illness (Section 165), divorce is granted on the application of one of the spouses with or without the consent of the other and there is no requirement for a one year or any other separation period. However, there may be other conditions attached, such as "making life in common intolerable" as in the case of committing a humiliating crime, leading a dishonourable life, or the need for a "medical report certifying the condition" as in incurable mental illness. In the case of desertion (Section 164), there are specific desertion and invitation periods such as six months, four months and two months (See 3.2 above). In addition, in adultery and threat to life, extreme cruelty and serious insult the spouse who has forgiven cannot then sue for divorce.

Principle 1:9 Exceptional hardship to the petitioner:

This principle has no application in Turkish law. It has no effect on the granting of the divorce. However, when a divorce or separation suit is brought to court, the judge will take necessary measures *ex officio* during the course of the suit, especially related to the housing, subsistence, management of the property of the spouses and the maintenance and protection of the children (Section 169). Such a spouse could also base the divorce petition on the ground of "threat to life, extreme cruelty or serious insult" (Section 162). There are no time limits here and the spouse has to bring this petition to court within six months of learning of the ground; the right to divorce elapses after five years of the occurrence of the events.

Principle 1:10 Determination of the consequences

The determination of the consequences are similar to that discussed under 1:7 above.

5.2. MAINTENANCE BETWEEN FORMER SPOUSES

5.2.1. General Principles

Since in the Principles the word "maintenance" is used for all kinds of monetary payments, I take it to cover both "material and moral compensation" and "destitution alimony" of Turkish Family law.

Principle 2:1 Relationship between maintenance and divorce:

Turkish law is on the whole in accord with this Principle in that the type of divorce has no impact on maintenance. However, the concept of fault has not lost its importance in maintenance claims. For instance, Section 174 states that the spouse who is not at fault or whose fault is the lesser can ask for appropriate material compensation from the faulty spouse if his or her existing or expected interest has been damages as a result of the divorce. For the spouse who has suffered damages to his or her personality rights, there is also the possibility to ask for appropriate moral compensation from the other spouse, if faulty. The title of this section is "Material and moral compensation". Again, the spouse who would fall into destitution as a result of the divorce, can claim alimony from the other for an indefinite period, as long as he/she is the less faulty (Section 175). The fault of the other is not taken into consideration, but the percentage of fault and the financial means of the other are. The title of the section is "Destitution alimony".

Thus, maintenance for destitution is subject to the same rules regardless of type of divorce, as in the Principles. However, for "compensation", fault plays a role. Whether the fault element can be totally and easily removed from Turkish law is open to discussion.

Principle 2:2 Self Sufficiency

When marriage comes to an end through divorce, all claim rights cease one year after the finalisation of the divorce decree. Thereafter the self-sufficiency rule applies, although this rule is not overtly stated anywhere in the Code. However, there is no mention of a time limit in compensatory maintenance. In addition, Turkish law does not accord with this Principle as an abstract principle, the exception to the rule being "destitution alimony" which could be for life. This is defendable in view of the weak position of Turkish women in marriages. However, the Code no longer uses the terms husband or wife but refers to spouses.

Nevertheless when the following Principles are considered, then there is some accord between Turkish law and the Principles.

5.2.2. Conditions for the attribution of maintenance

Principle 2:3 Conditions for maintenance

Maintenance after divorce is dependent on the creditor spouse being destitute and not the more faulty, as stated above. The ability of the debtor spouse to pay is not taken into account as such, however, Section 175 states that he or she has to pay maintenance in relation to his/her financial means. Section 176 can be regarded as pertinent here, as such maintenance ends upon death of either spouse, or marriage to another or living with another as if married or leading a dishonourable life by the creditor spouse.

The Principles mention the creditor spouse having "insufficient resources"—Turkish law uses the term "destitution", which may not mean exactly the same thing—and the debtor spouse's ability to satisfy these needs. In Turkish law this balance is struck by the judge. The conditions giving rise to "need" are not enumerated in the Code, but can be gleaned from court decisions. Child maintenance has also to be considered here.

Fault does play a role however, and this is not in accord with the Principles.

Principle 2:4 Determining claims for maintenance

In determining claims for maintenance, this CEFL Principle cites certain factors that may be taken into account by the court such as age, health, employability, care of children, duration of marriage and standard of living during the marriage. In Turkish law these are discretionary considerations. The Turkish Civil Code does not enumerate such factors and does not have a list of criteria, except standard of living during the marriage and legitimate expectations, and fault of the creditor spouse in the case of moral compensation and destitution alimony. In fault-based divorces the court may attach different weight to certain criteria.

Re-marriage of the creditor spouse would put an end to all claims, as would the death of one of the spouses. However, if during divorce proceedings one of the spouses dies then there are inheritance consequences, which have been discussed above (3.3). The re-marriage of the debtor spouse has no impact on maintenance claims. The length of marriage does not appear as one of the factors in Turkish law, though the judge, at his discretion, may pay attention to it.

Either spouse can return to the court to request a variation of a maintenance order on the basis of change of circumstances. If the financial circumstances of the parties change or if equity so demands, monthly payments could be increased or decreased (Section 176). Upon demand, the judge can decide how much the monthly payments will be in the future years according to the social and economic circumstances of the parties. The Principle does not play much of a role in this detail, as it assumes that these circumstances will be determined by national law.

Principle 2:5 Method of maintenance provisions

This Principle sets down that maintenance be provided at regular intervals and in advance. A lump sum payment may be ordered upon the request of either or both spouses according to the circumstances of the case. In Turkish law it is obligatory to pay moral compensation as a lump sum. Compensation for material damages and destitution alimony payments are to be made periodically as a monthly payment (Section 176) or as a lump sum. There is no payment in kind.

Monthly payments would automatically cease upon the re-marriage of the creditor spouse or the death of either spouse. Payments would cease following a judicial decision upon the creditor spouse living with another as if married, not being destitute any longer or leading a dishonourable life.

Principle 2:6 Exceptional hardship to the debtor spouse

Exceptional hardship of the debtor spouse will be taken into account by the court, especially if the creditor spouse was the more faulty party leading to divorce. Fault-based divorce has an impact on how the situation is viewed by the judge. However, even if divorce is not dependent upon fault, its existence is relevant in Turkish law.

In Turkish law, temporary measures during the divorce suit related to the housing and maintenance of the spouses, administration of the property and the care and protection of children, will be taken by the judge *ex officio*.

The maintenance Principles do not refer to fault and the Principles have also opted for no-fault divorce. Turkish law does not accord with either of these approaches.

5.2.3. Specific Issues

Principle 2:7 Multiplicity of maintenance claims

In determining the debtor spouse's ability to pay, the Principle asks the competent authority to give priority to any maintenance claim of a minor child and the obligations of the debtor spouse to maintain a new spouse.

There are no such requirements in the Turkish Civil Code, however, the judge always has discretion. In fact, the situation is unclear as there is no firm rule in a codal provision. By analogy to Section 364, which states that certain persons have a higher position for maintenance claims in the hierarchy of relationships such as ascendants and descendants, and siblings only where the obligation arises if the debtor is affluent, it can be said that children will have priority.

The obligations of the debtor spouse to maintain a new spouse does not have an impact on his or her previous obligations and will be covered by Section 186, which regulates the general obligation of spouses to contribute to household expenses with their work or property in accordance with their means.

These issues are left to the national law by the Principles.

Principle 2:8 Limitation in time

According to the Principles, maintenance is to be paid for a limited time, and only in exceptional circumstances without a time limit. In Turkey, there is no obligation to pay maintenance upon divorce unless it is material or moral compensation or destitution alimony. Only destitution alimony can be paid with no time limit. This unlimited obligation can cease only upon the occurrence of the conditions mentioned above (Principle 2.3).

Principle 2:9 Termination of the maintenance obligation

According to this Principle, maintenance obligation terminates when the creditor spouse re-marries, does not revive if that marriage ends, and terminates upon the death of either spouse. This principle is also followed in Turkey. Leading a dishonourable life is also mentioned in Turkish law, which has to be brought to the attention of the court in a claim for reduction of payments by the debtor spouse.

According to Section 182, the spouse who does not have custody has to contribute to the expenses incurred for the care and education of the child according to his/her means. On demand the judge can decide on the amount of future monthly payments in accordance with the social and economic circumstances of the parties. This obligation terminates when the child reaches the age of majority or continues until the end of his/her education (Section 328).

Principle 2:10 Maintenance agreement

According to this Principle, spouses should be permitted to make an agreement and in writing and the judge should at least scrutinise the validity of this arrangement. In Turkey, courts may take such arrangements into consideration but are not obliged to do so. The judge has wide discretion in balancing the financial interests of the spouses. All situations envisaged under this Principle are covered by Turkish law and practice, and accord with the Principle.

6.   CONCLUDING REMARKS

As all changes and developments in Family law in Turkey have been effected since 1926 in the name of modernisation, westernisation and secularisation (laicism) without taking much notice of the socio-cultural fabric, and reception was used as the means of achieving these goals, it would be easy to assume that the changes in Turkish law required in order to accommodate the "common cores" or the "better laws" envisaged by the Principles of European Family Law could also be put into effect without much difficulty. Even those who do not believe that harmonisation is possible, concede that eventually, virtual convergence could be brought about by legislators enacting very similar or the same normative repertoire, though such enactments would not reflect reality or bring about immediate actual convergence.

However, in view of the many recent changes introduced into Turkish law as late as 2002, the legislator and the legal actors may be reluctant to undertake further changes. Moreover, these changes too would not fit the socio-cultural fabric, which is made up of a very varied weave. The wisdom of making yet further top-down interference may be questionable, unless the European vision is fully embraced regardless of "fit".

Additional concerns would be that the Principles do not offer women, the weaker party in Turkey, sufficient protection. On the other hand, the requirement of a reflection period before divorce and consideration of multiple maintenance claims could be regarded to do so. The fact that the Principles are rather general and vague and leave certain issues to be determined by national laws can prove to be weakness as well as strength.

Many of the Principles fit Turkish law and Turkish law already fits many of the Principles. The ones that may prove more difficult to find acceptance are the removal of adultery, and generally fault, as a ground of divorce and the reflection period of three months, which may be regarded as unnecessary. Exceptional hardship to the petitioner in divorce cases, which is not considered in Turkish law, could be a positive development, though the same result might be achieved under Section 162.

Maintenance obligation has been consistently reduced in Turkish law to cover only instances of compensation for damages caused by the divorce and destitution, and a reversal of this trend and insistence on self-sufficiency would not be timely.

PART FOUR
COMPARATIVE ASSESSMENT

THE NATIONAL LEGAL SYSTEMS JUXTAPOSED TO THE CEFL PRINCIPLES: HARMONIOUS IDEALS?

JANE MAIR

The Commission on European Family Law's main goal is the creation of Principles of European Family Law that are thought to be most suitable for the harmonisation of family law in Europe.[1]

The purpose of this chapter is, for the moment, to accept that the Commission has achieved its goal and that the Principles set out an ideal for European family law in respect of divorce and maintenance. How ready are the national systems to receive and accommodate this new framework? The process of devising the Principles had its basis in the rules of the 22 individual jurisdictions and therefore there should be some expectation of a reasonable fit but the cultural and legal diversity of the systems together with the natural "chaos"[2] of family law suggests that the process of harmonisation faces significant challenges. Many of the individual legal systems which have been considered in this study formed part of the original research which contributed to the Principles. Others for a variety of reasons[3] are being considered in this context for the first time.

In devising principles of family law for Europe, the CEFL "has tried to propose rules which are functionally common to a significant majority of the legal systems involved"—the "common core" approach.[4] Their project however has been not simply to restate the common approach—where one exists—but to evaluate the national systems and to seek to move forward and modernise where that is thought to be the "better" approach. So even where the genesis of a Principle may be familiar to a national system, the final format may have changed. In other areas, no common approach could be discerned and there the Commission sought to evaluate all of the national rules and follow the "better law method" which "[I]t

---

[1]   *CEFL Principles*, p. 1.
[2]   DEWAR, "The Normal Chaos of Family Law" (1998) *Modern Law Review* 467.
[3]   See the Introductory Overview of this volume.
[4]   *CEFL Principles*, p. 2.

goes without saying ... is much more complicated than that of the common core".[5]

While the Commission faced the difficulty of trying to find common ground within such diversity they had the great benefit of a fresh start. The Principles represent the first stage in a proposed code of family law and, as the first step, there is no need or attempt to fit within a wider system. Although it is hoped that the Principles might be used "as a frame of reference for national, European and international legislators alike"[6], this is primarily an academic exercise and as such the Commission was not hindered by the need to devise politically acceptable proposals.

Family law reform in the national context faces many problems because of the sensitive nature of the subject matter. Strong cultural, religious and emotional reactions are caught up with legal concerns and the process of modernisation and change must respect the needs and expectations of the individuals who live out family life. National legislatures seeking to amend family law may be hampered in their legal aims by the need to reflect the expectations and aspirations of a diverse range of family members. The Commission, in their project, are to a large extent protected from this interaction with the human subject of family law and are free to engage in pure legal debate. The human tensions are much more striking in the national systems where the influence of personal sensibilities and not just legal reasoning are clear.

Divorce was chosen as the subject for the first part of the CEFL's work, partly on the basis that it is an area where there are certain common trends and where there is already some evidence of similarity in national developments and patterns of reform. Perhaps the common trend which is most striking is the rising divorce rate throughout Europe which may also have contributed to the choice of this as the initial area for consideration. Common trends may be evident at first glance but deeper analysis soon discloses the national peculiarities in which these common trends are situated and the difficulties inherent in harmonisation quickly emerge.

---

[5]   *Principles*, p. 2.
[6]   *Principles*, p. 3.

1. CHAPTER I: DIVORCE

1.1. PART I: GENERAL PRINCIPLES

1.1.1. Principle 1:1

With respect to the first general Principle, that divorce should be permissible, there is almost unanimous agreement. All 22 of the countries which submitted reports for consideration by the CEFL matched this Principle with ease and shared in common statistical trends of rising divorce applications. On this at least there was uniformity. With the inclusion of Malta in our study, however, the universality of the first Principle is already challenged. Although the Marriage Act of 1975 represented a move away from religious control in relation to family law, by means of the introduction of civil marriage, the position that marriage is indissoluble and that divorce is not available in Malta continued. Maltese law does, however, permit recognition of foreign divorce and it makes provision for both judicial separation and nullity of marriage and in these areas of family law there is evidence of similar trends and concerns as arise elsewhere in relation to divorce. While clearly recognising that Malta alone cannot currently meet the most fundamental of the Principles, its provision in other respects to the breakdown of marriage will be considered.

The histories of the various national systems of divorce have much in common and trends, though they may have emerged at different times, are familiar through many of the jurisdictions. The decline of religious law to be replaced with a civil law of divorce can be seen in all but the case of Malta. As the only jurisdiction in Europe which does not permit divorce, the influence of the church in law and society remains very strong as seen in the statement that "[D]ivorce has been said to be deemed to be incompatible with Maltese culture and religious tradition which is founded deeply in Roman Catholicism."[7] Commenting on the position in England, it was stated that the legal permission of "divorce is now uncontroversial, since it is no longer feasible to believe that marriages can be saved in any real sense by restricting divorce."[8] The availability of separation, both interim and permanent, of nullity and the recognition of foreign divorces in Malta would seem to suggest that marriages there are not necessarily more stable as other methods of giving legal recognition to marital breakdown exist. The feasibility of this continued denial of divorce must be questioned.

---

[7]   At p. 103.

[8]   At p. 56.

The extent to which individual states have fully accepted the futility of "restricting divorce" is less clear when the second part of the Principle is considered; that divorce should be available without a minimum period of marriage. Many systems, with the exception of Estonia, require a minimum period of marriage at least in respect of some forms of divorce. Lithuania permits divorce by mutual consent but only where the marriage has lasted for at least one year. Turkey, for example, only permits divorce on the ground of irretrievable breakdown where the marriage has lasted for a minimum of one year and in Scotland, although there is no absolute minimum requirement in order to establish irretrievable breakdown, the most frequently used method of showing that a marriage has broken down irretrievably is by means of one year's non-cohabitation. Various justifications are given for restricting the availability of divorce in very short marriages; for example in France, in divorces other than those based on mutual consent, the parties are called to a conciliation hearing which in practice prevents immediate divorce. In England, a minimum period of one year must elapse between marriage and the petition for divorce, which was introduced in order to prevent divorce from being too easily available. Statistics suggest that where no minimum period of marriage is required the number of divorces in the case of very short marriages is extremely low and therefore it could be argued that the minimum period serves little purpose.

If it is accepted that common principles are to be adopted then, in recognition of the shared trend towards marriage breakdown, it seems clear that divorce must be available in all countries. In those countries where divorce is currently permitted but there is a required minimum duration of marriage, there is little evidence of justification for it and therefore compliance with Principle 1:1(2) is also to be commended.

1.1.2. Principle 1:2

With the exception of Malta, which does not permit divorce at all, all of the systems meet principle 1.2 to the effect that divorce procedure should be set by law and that divorce should be granted by a competent legal or administrative authority. Although divorce itself is not recognised in Malta, the systems which exist for judicial separation, nullity and recognition of foreign divorce clearly meet the principle. Most of the national systems permit only judicial divorce, although the existence of simplified procedures in undefended actions where no other disputes exist, suggests a move towards a quasi-administrative process. Rebecca Probert goes further and suggests that Principle 1.2 should be more radical by providing that divorce should be available as an administrative procedure. She gives as an example the "special procedure" in England which is, "judicial in form but administrative in nature, since the parties are not required to attend court and the judge only has the information supplied by the parties when deciding whether or not to grant a divorce."[9]

1.1.3. Principle 1:3

A move towards divorce as an administrative, or at least as a very straightforward judicial process, is clearly achievable in terms of Principle 1:3 which requires that divorce should be available in two ways—either with or without consent. The structure of the Principles for divorce, which offer only two possible types of divorce, is attractive in its simplicity. A move towards divorce by mutual consent fits well with modern notions of marriage as a personal and private relationship with very little opportunity for public scrutiny. A general trend towards deregulation of the marriage relationship is reflected in a shift towards personal choice being at the heart of divorce. The model of two types of divorce, where the central issue is whether or not the parties consent, signifies a clean break from the notion of divorce as legal recognition of marital breakdown. It shifts focus entirely from the past matrimonial relationship to the present wishes of the parties.

The simple choice in Principle 1:3 represents a fresh start, not only for the couple, but also in terms of legal frameworks for divorce. Unlike the national systems which are the product of diverse historical and cultural traditions and which demonstrate attempts to balance personal freedom with the desire to promote matrimonial stability, the CEFL Principle is firmly grounded in legal clarity. It is, therefore, perhaps not surprising that, while many of the national systems present elements in common with Principle 1:3, they tend to lack its simplicity.

1.2. CHAPTER II

1.2.1. Principle 1:4

In Chapter II of the Principles, the detailed structure for divorce by mutual consent is set out with Principle 1:4 establishing first that divorce should be available by mutual consent with no period of separation required. It goes on to clarify the meaning of mutual consent, which is that the spouses agree to the dissolution of the marriage, and to confirm that such agreement may be shown either by a joint application for divorce or by application by one party with acceptance by the other. In this Principle, the CEFL makes it clear that a distinction is being drawn between the divorce itself and its consequences. The parties may disagree on

---

9   At p. 59.

aspects of the outcome of their relationship breakdown but what is required is simply that they agree to be divorced. Principle 1:4 grants some flexibility as to how this agreement may be expressed but it is the simple fact of agreement which matters and it cannot be based on other external evidence of matrimonial break-down—in particular there must be no required period of separation.

In considering the national reports, the CEFL recognised that there were three main groupings within the domestic systems. In the Nordic countries, there is provision for " 'unilateral divorce' according to which the request for a divorce of one spouse will suffice".[10] A second group of countries currently recognise "mutual consent as an autonomous ground for divorce"[11] and in a third group there is provision for divorce on the basis of irretrievable breakdown although "mutual consent as such is not explicitly recognised as a ground for divorce".[12]

The provision for divorce is relatively liberal in the Scandinavian countries and here divorce is available by mutual consent, without the need for any period of separation. An interesting distinction, however, is drawn between the "right to give a petition for divorce immediately after the solemnisation of marriage and the right to get divorce immediately after the rapid divorce process".[13] Within the separate Scandinavian countries there is a range of measures designed to provide for mutual consent divorce without a period of separation but also to seek to avoid overly hasty action by the parties. Estonia appears to reflect closely the distinction between consent and no consent in Principle 1:4 by providing that divorce is available administratively by joint petition to a vital statistics office or judicially, without consent, as a result of the "impossibility of continuation of the marriage"[14]

The types of divorce which are available in France can be divided into consent and no consent but the system lacks the simplicity of the CEFL Principles, providing as it does for four types of divorce. Divorce by mutual consent was permitted in France following the secularisation of marriage and divorce at the time of the Revolution. Divorce was later abolished, reintroduced but only in the case of fault and finally re-established on the basis of mutual consent in 1975. Following the most recent major reform of divorce law in France in 2004, there now exist four separate types of divorce. Of these, two may be described as being based on mutual consent: divorce by mutual consent where the parties agree on both the

---

[10] *Principles*, p. 27.
[11] *Principles*, p. 28.
[12] *Ibid.*
[13] At p. 40.
[14] At p. 41.

divorce and its effects, and accepted divorce where "the spouses agree on the principle of the breakdown of the marriage with the judge ruling on its consequences".[15]

England, Scotland and Turkey are similar in their approach in that divorce is available with the mutual consent of the parties but only where there is also irretrievable breakdown of the marriage. As such they fall within the category identified by the CEFL where the consent to divorce itself is not being acknowledged as sufficient to permit divorce but instead it is "proof or an indication that the marriage has irretrievably broken down".[16] English law at present only permits divorce by consent where there has been two years' non-cohabitation, whereas Scotland has recently reduced the requirement to one year. In Turkey, mutual consent is relevant it is still regarded as "divorce for breakdown"[17] and the marriage must have lasted for at least one year. In Lithuania too there is provision of divorce mutual consent but in this system a number of conditions must also be met including the existence of the marriage for a minimum period of one year.

The notion of consent within the context of divorce is not necessarily comfortably accommodated within all of the national systems. Writing about English law, Rebeccah Probert makes the point that "English law was for long suspicious of any hint of agreement between the parties; prior to 1963 any agreement between the parties would have been termed collusion and—if discovered—would have led to a divorce being refused."[18] Collusion too operated as a bar to divorce in Scotland until the reforms in the 2006 Family Law (Scotland) Act. Consent can also be a controversial concept within relationships where there may be doubts as to the relative bargaining power of the spouses. The point is made in respect of Turkey that the courts are cautious to ensure that there really is mutual consent and not undue pressure from the husband.[19]

In many of the national systems, consent forms a part of the divorce process but the structure is rarely as clear as that proposed in Principle 1:4. For many states, the role of consent is situated within the framework of the irretrievable breakdown of marriage, a system which clings to the notion of marriage as an institution, meriting some protection, beyond the individual spouses who are involved in it. Consent itself is not sufficient to permit divorce but is interpreted as signal-

---

[15]   At p. 22.
[16]   *Principles*, p. 28.
[17]   At p. 202.
[18]   At p. 60.
[19]   At p. 202.

ling the breakdown of the relationship and in this respect most systems fail to match the clear and simple requirements of Principle 1:4.

In order to comply with Principle 1:4, most of the jurisdictions considered will require to acknowledge openly that divorce should be available on demand where both parties consent to it and further, to ensure that this mechanism for access to divorce is isolated from the notion of irretrievable breakdown. The consent of the parties must be recognised as the trigger for divorce rather than simply as evidence of their acceptance of the fact that their relationship is at an end. The clarity of the role of consent needs also to be accompanied by a simplification of the framework for divorce into a binary system where divorce by consent is one of only two types of divorce, if the national systems are to be fully compliant with the Principles.

1.2.2. Principle 1:5

Many of the systems considered require a period of non-cohabitation as an element in establishing the breakdown of a marriage. Others, while providing for divorce by mutual consent, require a period of delay as part of the divorce procedure. None however provide specifically for a "reflection period" as set out in Principle 1:5. Provision is made for a reduction in the reflection period where there are no children under the age of 16 and where the parties have reached agreement on all of the consequences of the divorce. Where the parties have in fact been separated for six months, then no further period of reflection will be required.

The contents of Principle 1:5 suggest that the period of reflection is intended primarily as an opportunity to reflect on the consequences of the divorce rather than as a period for reconsidering the decision to divorce itself. It is reflection on the effects of divorce rather than an attempt at reconciliation and this clear distinction between establishment of the grounds for divorce and attempts to reach agreement about the consequences is to be welcomed. It is, however, not entirely clear how the period of reflection fits with Principle 1:4, which allows divorce on demand. In all of the systems considered, there is some evidence of a range of methods of attempting to find a balance between facilitating divorce and protecting the solemnity of marriage or at least guarding against unduly rash or hasty decisions. Perhaps before encouraging domestic systems to accept this Principle, further consideration of this balance is needed.

1.2.3. Principle 1:6

The remaining two Principles in Chapter II on divorce by mutual consent deal with the matters to be considered in any agreement between the parties and on the method for determining the consequences of the divorce. In Principle 1:6, the CEFL outlines the issues on which the parties should seek to reach agreement during their period of reflection. There is little that is controversial here and there is considerable harmony between Principle 1:6 and the provisions in the various national systems. Increasingly in divorce, attention has focused less on the divorce itself and more on the legal consequences—children and money. With regard to children, agreement is sought in respect of parental rights and responsibilities including residence and contact arrangements and in respect of child mainte-nance. Agreement is also sought in respect of the economic consequences of divorce and in particular with regard to the division of property and spousal maintenance. In all of the national systems, the concerns over the consequences of divorce focus on children and finance and to this extent Principle 1:6 fits well within existing domestic laws. The benefits of agreement as opposed to judicial determination are also widely recognised although, in the detail of how these dif-ferent approaches to resolution of the problems which may arise from marital breakdown are accommodated in national frameworks, there is considerable diversity and flexibility.

Principle 1:6 is, however, deliberately wide and leaves determination of the exact process and form of the agreement to the individual legal systems. Beyond speci-fying that any agreement must be in writing, there is no prescribed format. Simi-larly, the Principle makes no provision as to the nature or scope of parental responsibility beyond acknowledging the particular relevance of residence and contact arrangements post-divorce. The need to resolve issues of property and maintenance is also highlighted by Principle 1:6 but again it is left to the indi-vidual systems to set out the detail of entitlements.

To a large extent, issues surrounding the matters listed in Principle 1:6 will arise because of the non-cohabitation of a couple rather than strictly as a consequence of their divorce. Matters of where a child should live, the division of property and of financial support have as much to do with the practicalities of separate house-holds as with a change in legal status. It is therefore not surprising that in Malta, even though divorce itself is not permitted by domestic law, provision for dealing with the consequences of separation would be similar: "It is not possible to effect a legal separation in the absence of an agreement or judicial decree detailing all the elements listed in the said Principle."[20]

---

[20]   At p. 122.

The emphasis on agreement in Principle 1:6 fits well with the emphasis on agreement as the basis for divorce with mutual consent and, the benefits of this linkage, are well rehearsed in the Estonian chapter which acknowledges that Estonian law does not currently reflect the interdependence of divorce and its consequences where the divorce is by mutual consent. In some other systems, the link is made much clearer in, for example, the French system of mutual consent divorce where what is required is agreement as to both the divorce itself and its consequences. In Lithuania too, it is a condition of divorce by mutual consent that an agreement has been concluded by the parties as to the consequences of the divorce with regards to financial matters and children.

Compliance with Principle 1:6 is therefore relatively unproblematic, reflecting the common practical consequences of relationship breakdown which are experienced regardless of nationality or culture together with the level of national discretion which is inherent in this Principle.

1.2.4. Principle 1:7

The difficulties and disputes which are likely to result from the breakdown of marriage are universal. Splitting a household creates the same problems of shared responsibilities and liabilities regardless of nationality. There is also widespread evidence of the importance of encouraging agreement and self-regulation but at the same time recognition of vulnerability and unequal bargaining power. While the individual countries are largely in agreement as to the issues to be resolved, there is less consensus as to the means of resolution. In the event of divorce by mutual consent, Principle 1:7 sets out three guidelines for determining the consequences of divorce which represent seeking a balance between self-regulation and judicial (or other approved) supervision.

The consequences for children are ultimately regarded as too important to be left entirely to the negotiations of their parents and while the competent national authority should take into account the terms of any agreement made by the parties, the authority should have the power to determine the consequences for the children. Account can only be taken of an agreement to the extent that this is consistent with the child's best interests. As the CEFL recognises, this is an area where "there is clearly a common core"[21] which is to a large extent a reflection of the fact that there has already been considerable harmonisation in respect of the rights of the child resulting from international documents such as the UN Convention on the Rights of the Child.

---

[21] *Principles*, p. 48.

For Scots law, parties have the opportunity to regulate their relationships with their children through private agreement although application may also be made to the court for regulation of parental rights and responsibilities.[22] The principle of non-intervention will apply with the court only making an order where it would be better to do so than not to act.[23] In making any decision concerning the child, the court will be guided by the primary consideration of the welfare of the child.[24] In England and Wales there is similar encouragement for self regulation although the courts also have authority to disregard any such agreement. As stated, such an approach is likely to fit with Principle 1:7 "since although agreement is encouraged, whether or not such agreements are binding ... is left to national authorities to decide."[25]

In France, divorce by mutual consent matches well with, and even exceeds, the emphasis of principle 1:7 on agreement. To fall within the scope of divorce by mutual consent, the parties must submit both their agreement to divorce and their written agreement as to the financial consequences of the divorce and arrangements for the children. The court can approve the agreement as to consequences and thereupon grant the divorce or where "the agreement does not sufficiently protect the interests of the children or one of the spouses, or if the rights and obligations of the spouses are inequitably determined" the court does not substitute its own determination but instead gives the parties a further six months in which to present a new agreement. Ultimately if there is no acceptable agreement this divorce procedure will fail. In this way divorce by mutual consent in France places even more emphasis on the central role of consent, while retaining some limited protective role for the court. There is a similar requirement in Lithuania where divorce by mutual consent requires that the parties have reached agreement on the consequences of the divorce.

Principle 1:7 places considerable emphasis on consent but problems of inequality within marriage are well known and are openly acknowledged in the approach of the Turkish courts. In matters of consent, it is recognised that "women, who are often the weaker partners in Turkish marriages, may be forced by their husbands to accept divorce under threat of ... taking the children from them."[26] The need for true agreement is also expressly recognised in the French system where, prior to approving the agreement as to consequences, the judge must be satisfied that

---

[22]   Children (Scotland) Act 1995, s.11.
[23]   *Ibid,* s.11(7)(a).
[24]   *Ibid,* s.11.
[25]   At p. 62.
[26]   At p. 194.

"the will of each spouse is real, and ... their consent is free and well understood."[27]

As previously indicated, Estonian law is more liberal in its approach to divorce itself, allowing for "divorce by mutual consent even if the spouses have a dispute concerning the legal consequences of the divorce" but in commenting on the Principles, the authors view the linkage between agreement as to divorce and consequences as being a positive step which should be recommended for Estonian law. From the Scandinavian viewpoint however there is some scepticism as to the practical value of reflection and linkage, which may be "noble at the level of ideas" but nonetheless better kept separate.[28]

1.3. CHAPTER III

1.3.1. Principle 1:8

Chapter III deals with the second type of divorce, that is divorce without the consent of one of the spouses. Such divorce should be available where the parties have been separated for a period of one year. In developing this principle, the CEFL adopted a common core approach and sought "to provide a simple objective test"[29] which can be viewed as a compromise "between the overwhelming majority of jurisdictions" which permit divorce without consent following a period of separation "and the minority 'Scandinavian' position" which permits unilateral divorce without a requirement of separation, although with a compulsory period of reflection.[30]

It is therefore not surprising to find that the countries which have been considered in this book match well with the basic idea of this Principle but with considerable diversity in the detail. In reviewing the national systems, two principal issues emerge—the need for and length of the period of separation and the relationship between non-consensual divorce and fault. In respect of non-consensual divorce, France provides for both fault-based, divorce which has no separation requirement, and divorce on the grounds of irretrievable breakdown, where there is a minimum of two years' separation, representing a significant reduction from the previous requirement of six years. [see French chapter p6]. For Turkey, Scotland, England and Estonia there is a combination of the concepts of fault and

---

[27] At p. 23.
[28] At p. 44.
[29] *Principles* p. 55.
[30] *Principles* p. 55.

irretrievable breakdown with a range of periods of separation. The period of separation is generally regarded as a means of proving the irretrievable breakdown of the relationship and whereas there is some evidence of a gradual reduction in the periods of non-cohabitation required,[31] none of these systems currently meets Principle 1:8. Only in the Scandinavian systems is there evidence of a real rejection of fault in the absence of consent and even there the position is "not coherent at all".

In order for the national systems to meet the requirements of Principle 1:8, widespread reconsideration of the framework of divorce would be required. In particular, the notions of fault and irretrievable breakdown require to be finally abandoned and replaced instead with a simple provision for divorce without mutual consent based on a relatively short period of non-cohabitation.

1.3.2. Principle 1:9

The general provision for non-consensual divorce provides only for divorce following a period of one year's separation. Unlike many of the national systems, "instant divorce on grounds of fault or reprehensible behaviour"[32] is not permissible which thus necessitates provision for exceptional circumstances. This is the goal of Principle 1:9 which permits non-consensual divorce without one year's separation "in cases of exceptional hardship". In the Commentary on this Principle it is stressed that this provision should be restricted to extreme circumstances. For most of the national systems, this principle has no place in that they permit non-consensual divorce in the event of irretrievable breakdown which may be established by either fault or a period of separation. By separating out these two situations, few of the systems strictly speaking meet Principles 1:8 and 1:9. In respect of these provisions, not only is there a difference in the detail between the ideal European Principle and the national rules but there appears to be a more fundamental philosophical split. Although in this chapter the starting point is to accept the Principles as ideal and assess the national systems accordingly, the considerable gap between the ideal and the national reality points towards the need for further consideration in this area.

1.3.3. Principle 1:10

As Chapter II emphasised the consistency between consent to divorce and consensual arrangement of the consequences, so Chapter III is consistent in down-

---

[31] See eg France, as discussed above and Scotland where the Family Law (Scotland) Act 2006 has reduced the period of non-cohabitation from five years to two.
[32] *Principles,* pp. 55–56.

grading the role of agreement as to consequences where one party refuses consent to the divorce. Principle 1:10 provides that the consequences of divorce in respect of parental responsibilities, child maintenance and economic arrangements for the spouses should be determined by the competent national authority. The possibility of agreement between the spouses is acknowledged to the extent that the authority should take any such agreement into account.

This is to a large extent an uncontroversial Principle, which following on from the much more divisive treatment of non-consensual divorce seems relatively easily accommodated in each of the national systems. Any differences which do exist between the Principle and national rules are minor in nature.

2. PART II: MAINTENANCE

The CEFL Principles in Part II, while based on the self-sufficiency principle, recognise that in some situations post-spousal maintenance may be justified. The purpose of the Principles is to avoid any unfair economic consequences of a divorce but while identifying a variety of justifications for post-divorce spousal maintenance the Principles do not attempt to distinguish between these different purposes. In devising principles for maintenance, the CEFL has taken the preliminary decision to distinguish between maintenance and property settlement. This reflects a similar distinction in the majority of the jurisdictions which were considered by CEFL. As with the preliminary decisions of the CEFL which informed the detailed Principles of divorce, it is to a large extent these fundamental aspects of the Principles which influence their applicability within national systems.

2.1. CHAPTER I: GENERAL PRINCIPLES

2.1.1. Principle 2:1

Having divided Part I into two sections depending on mutual consent or absence of consent to divorce, the starting point for maintenance is that there should be no distinction in the rules that apply. This Principle "reflects the common core approach and provides for a single maintenance regime regardless of the type of divorce" and as such fits well with the trend in most jurisdictions towards the irrelevance of fault in decisions as to the economic consequences of divorce.

Despite a general consensus in favour of this Principle there remains some evidence of divergence with Turkish law, for example, distinguishing between two types of payment: compensation in the assessment of which fault is relevant and destitution alimony where fault is not considered and which consequently matches the CEFL Principle. In Malta, in relation to separation, there is considerable distance from Principle 2:1 where maintenance is "dependent on apportionment of fault unless the parties reach an amicable settlement".[33] In Lithuania, the spouse responsible for the breakdown of the marriage has no right to maintenance, which reflects the continuation of fault-based divorce and allows for no exceptions. For France, the starting point is that the consequences of divorce should be the same regardless of the type of divorce. Compensation may however be granted in certain circumstances on the basis of fault in order to address "the disparity that breakdown of the marriage creates in the respective lifestyles".[34] In both England and Wales and Scotland, although the frameworks are significantly different, the approach to maintenance is similar in that there is no distinction depending on the specific method of proving irretrievable breakdown and fault will only be taken into account where it would be grossly unfair to ignore it.

Recognising a common trend towards limiting the role of fault in divorce in all the systems which have been considered, this Principle seems appropriate. If the national systems accept the Principles in Part I and provide for divorce only with or without consent, then it is entirely consistent that they should apply the same Principles for maintenance in both types of divorce.

2.1.2. Principle 2:2 Self Sufficiency

In commenting on principle 2:2, it is noted that "few jurisdictions have a statutorily expressed self-sufficiency principle"[35] although in some systems there is a clear preference for a 'clean break' approach which is in harmony with the principle. Several authors emphasise that in their legal system the obligation of maintenance ends on divorce[36] and in respect of Estonia it is commented that "the principle of self-sufficiency is such a widespread concept that it has not even been written down in law in black and white".[37] It should also be noted however that for several of the national systems considered, it is difficult to analyse the provision of maintenance without placing it in the broader context of financial provision on divorce. In considering the specific detail of the principles which follow,

---

[33]   At p. 123.
[34]   At p. 29.
[35]   *Principles*, p. 78.
[36]   See eg Scotland and France.
[37]   At p. 148.

in Chapter II on the Conditions for Attribution of Maintenance, this caveat must be borne in mind.

2.2. CHAPTER II: CONDITIONS FOR THE ATTRIBUTION OF MAINTENANCE

2.2.1. Principle 2:3

There is general agreement amongst the separate states that maintenance should be dependent upon an assessment of need on the part of the "creditor spouse" and ability to pay on the part of the "debtor spouse". For Turkey, needs and resources form the basis of an obligation to pay but fault remains a consideration which "is not in accord with the Principles"[38] and for Estonia there are much more specific requirements[39] which reflect the situation of spousal maintenance within a model of social justice according to which "everyone has in principle three sources of income for meeting his/her need: income earned from work, maintenance received from members of the family and social benefits."[40] The linkage in Lithuania of the quantification of maintenance payments to the Minimum Monthly Wage[41] highlights the important interaction of work and family. These insights, together with comments about the relatively weak economic position of married women in Turkey, highlight the difficulties inherent in assessing the extent to which states meet the principles without considering the principles themselves in a broader social and economic context.

The danger of viewing the obligation of maintenance in isolation is also highlighted in a number of chapters which emphasise that in their legal system, maintenance is only a part, and often a minor part, of a more comprehensive framework of financial settlement on divorce. In England, for example, a periodical allowance may include maintenance which is intended to support an ex-spouse and is therefore based on need whereas it might also be used as a form of compensation or in order to leave "the parties on an equal footing". [42]In Scotland, while the principle of maintenance being based on needs and resources is acceptable it must be emphasised, such assessment can only be made following the division of matrimonial property on divorce with the hope that such allocation will replace the need for any ongoing support.

---

[38]   At p. 206.
[39]   Discussed at pp. 147–152.
[40]   At p. 147.
[41]   See p. 176.
[42]   At p. 67.

While broadly accepting this Principle as suitable and appropriate, there is an important caveat to the effect that the economic function of the family cannot be viewed in isolation from the economic structure of the society within which it is situated, The public/private distinction has long been identified as a potential source of discrimination against women, in particular, and it is therefore recommended that careful consideration should be given to the interaction of public and private economies in the application of this Principle in the national context.

2.2.2. Principles 2:4- 2:7

In this group of Principles, the CEFL sets out a general framework for the assessment of maintenance. It provides a list of factors to be considered; states that payments should be monthly in advance although accepting an alternative lump sum payment and sets out a hierarchy to be followed when dealing with a multiplicity of claims. To a large extent the various jurisdictions considered conform to these principles. The factors listed in Principle 2:4 are almost all considered in all of the countries although not necessarily specifically in the context of maintenance. For example, in Scotland, these factors are variously considered in the application of the principles in section 9 of the Family Law (Scotland) Act in relation to financial settlement upon divorce, within which ongoing maintenance is intended to play a very limited part.

There is some national variation in dealing with multiplicity of claims, although there is general approval of Principle 2:7. The provision as to payment in Principle 2:5 is accepted by all of the countries in that where maintenance is payable it is paid monthly although some jurisdictions, for example Scotland and France, have a strong statutory preference for a capital sum payment. In Turkey, there is a distinction between the two types of payment which are described as maintenance, with moral compensation being paid in a lump sum and compensation for material damages and destitution alimony being paid by monthly payment.[43] These Principles however are intended to promote partial harmonisation and therefore appear able to accommodate this national diversity.

Of this group of Principles, Principle 2:6 is perhaps the most controversial although even there the various systems are able to meet it. Having set out from the position that fault is not relevant to consideration of maintenance, this Principle allows it be taken into account in cases of exceptional hardship to the debtor spouse. All of the jurisdictions considered permit some account to be taken of conduct where it would be manifestly unfair to ignore it, with the exception of

---

[43]   At p. 207.

Sweden and Finland which are truly no-fault systems and therefore, while this does not meet the Principle, it appears to be consistent within the overall national scheme. The Scandinavian commentator does however question the reintroduction of conduct at this stage. As previously discussed, Turkey continues to allow consideration of fault in the assessment of some aspects of maintenance and to by not limiting it to cases of exceptional hardship it does not currently satisfy Principle 2:6. This is indicative of the underlying tension in relation to the role of fault within divorce which survives to some extent in most of the systems considered. As indicated elsewhere, compliance with these more minor Principles requires first that national systems engage in wider debate as to fault-based divorce.

2.2.3. Principles 2:8 and 2:9

These Principles seek to limit the period during which maintenance should be paid and provide for circumstances in which the obligation will terminate. There is again general compliance with these provisions, with many countries having stricter time limits. Again consideration of the extent to which some countries meet these principles is rather artificial due to the consideration of maintenance within a broader framework for financial settlement and property division. Arguably the Principles are more generous than some domestic systems but the broadness of the Principles appears to accommodate these stricter national rules. In countries such as France and Scotland, there is a strong preference for financial settlement by means of capital sum payments or property transfers in which case issues of time limits and the termination of maintenance are of limited relevance.

2.2.4. Principle 2:10

In respect of the final Principle, which provides for the use of maintenance agreements, there is widespread compliance. In France and Lithuania, for example, agreement is compulsory for mutual consent divorce and is possible for other types. There is again, some diversity in the form of agreement and the provision for consideration of it by the competent national authority but in general compliance with this Principle can be identified in each of the states.

3. CONCLUSIONS

In the detail of the national systems considered, there is considerable diversity. Even within states which have broad similarities, there are significant distinctions. To some extent such diversity can be accommodated within the CEFL Principles which primarily aim to create partial harmonisation by setting out a framework within which national systems have some element of flexibility. There is therefore, in some areas, a reasonable match between the Principles and the existing national rules and where there is currently divergence there is, however, a positive reception for the CEFL framework.

In assessing the fit between national laws and the European Principles, however, two principal issues emerge. The first, relating to divorce itself, concerns the apparent split between a legal system which provides for consensual and non-consensual divorce and one which is based on the fault/non-fault dichotomy. This could alternatively be conceived of as a division between divorce on demand and divorce where the marriage can be shown to have irretrievably broken down. Before the detail of the Principles can be accommodated within individual European states this much more fundamental debate needs to develop.

With regard to Part II of the Principles on post-divorce maintenance, the principal issue is the extent to which the individual jurisdictions consider maintenance within the context of property division and financial settlement or deal with it separately. It is in this bigger picture that significant diversity exists. In the detail and in the identification of issues to be considered there is broad agreement. In the present structure of the CEFL Principles, however, maintenance appears to have a primacy which it does not hold in some countries and to that extent, until the CEFL situates its Principles within a fuller framework of property and economic consequences it remains difficult to assess fully the fit between national systems and the common Principles.

THE PRINCIPLES OF EUROPEAN FAMILY LAW PUT TO THE TEST: DIVERSITY IN HARMONY OR HARMONY IN DIVERSITY?

Esin Örücü

1. INTRODUCTION

The Principles were presented in the previous section as ideal formulations towards which legal systems of the member states of the EU and those countries wishing to join the EU should strive, thereby indicating the shortcomings of those legal systems juxtaposed to the Principles.

This assessment is the other side of the coin pointing out the shortcomings of the Principles in view of the reality of the legal systems covered in this study. The stance here will be two-pronged. One will be that though a top-down model and harmonisation of family law in Europe may be necessary, feasible and desirable, what has been produced by the CEFL does not live up to expectations. Even where harmony might be desirable, this cannot be achieved by having a number of issues either vaguely regulated or left to the will of domestic legislators, thus leading to fragmentation. The second is total rejection of a top-down model, even one such as these Principles, which leave the regulation of a number of issues to the will of the national legislators. Cultural, political and economic contexts demand that diversity in this field should be maintained. Therefore, this is a futile exercise.

This inquity will point to the sections of the Principles that do not fit the aims and aspirations of the legal systems covered in this study. When seven out of the eight systems[1] looked at share a solution, it will be accepted that there is a "common-core" and therefore scope for a general European Principle, but the concept of the "better law" will be rejected when there is no such "common core". "Better law" is regarded in this assessment as a value-based choice on the part of the drafters that

---

[1] Though eight main legal systems are covered, in fact the actual number of legal systems is eleven in view of the contribution on Scandinavia which includes four, and at times five, legal systems.

cannot be presented to the legal systems these Principles address, since the legal systems themselves have no agreed goal.

2. HARMONY MAY BE NECESSARY BUT CEFL PRINCIPLES HAVE SHORT-FALLS

Though harmony may be regarded as necessary, the Principles are not sufficient for this purpose, being often vague, leaving many issues to the national legislators or, not having reached a common core, proposing an unsatisfactory "better law".[2]

A *Preamble* is always valuable in understanding the direction Principles take. Here, the basic *raison d'etre* of the Principles is to facilitate free-movement of persons in Europe which is hindered by the existing diversity. When changing residence, people should be able to rely on the unchanging nature of personal relationships. However, other considerations such as human rights or European citizenship could also have been the basic movers for harmonisation. In fact, these would have been more noble causes, as they would apply regardless of the existence of the EU. To achieve gender equality is another aim, so is to promote and protect the best interests of the child. Not all legal systems would cover the latter in relation to divorce. Parental responsibility and child maintenance are generally covered by statutory provisions and not by agreement. This might have been a better approach.

The Principles aim at fast track, easy, uncomplicated divorces. The Principles related to divorce have been over-simplified and do not seem to reflect the present, only aiming at a future based on a specific vision. In the area of maintenance, regarded as a post-divorce economic consequence, the fundamental purpose is stated as self-sufficiency. Providing economic support for the dependent spouse is still a serious concern in our societies where many women are housewives or part-time workers in poorly paid jobs. The Principles accept this but only as "specific situations". Since no common-core was found in the type of maintenance payments available in the legal systems looked at, the Principles do not make a distinction. The overall purpose is to avoid unfair economic consequences of divorce. The word chosen is "maintenance" for all kinds of monetary payments between former spouses for the purpose of support, and other words follow such as "debtor spouse", "creditor spouse", "maintenance claim" and "obligation".

---

[2]   From time to time we have also considered the Model Family Code (hereafter MFC) both for inspiration and for a base for criticism. See SCHWENZER, I and DIMSEY, M, *Model Family Code from a Global Perspective* (Antwerpen, Intersentia, 2006).

The Principles do not consider matrimonial property law, though the division of such is an essential aspect of relationships after divorce. Neither do they consider pension sharing or issues arising out of taxation.[3] The criteria used are "need" and "ability to pay".

2.1. DIVORCE

2.1.1. General Principles

Principle 1. 1(1): There is a common core in the area of acceptance of divorce in the systems under consideration here except in Malta.[4] In Malta separation seems to rely on comparable grounds to divorce and produce comparable results, save the possibility of a second marriage, and divorces obtained abroad are recognised. Thus by our criteria, seven out of eight legal systems agree here. The Principle is acceptable. Nonetheless, it reads as a very odd first Principle since it does not carry much meaning to deserve to be a separate principle; it is superfluous.[5]

Principle 1(2) rejects any requirement of duration of marriage before divorce. The legal systems under consideration do not all agree on this point, some requiring a certain period of being married at least for certain types of divorce as none of such systems follow a monistic divorce system. No divorce suit based on mutual consent or breakdown of marriage can be pursued within the first year of marriage in at least three of our systems with an absolute bar (England and Wales, Lithuania, and Turkey). In systems where separation is used as a ground, there are also time limits, such as five years (with no consent) in England and Wales, three years in Turkey, two years in France, one year in Finland, Sweden, Norway, Iceland and Scotland (though, in divorce without consent a separation of two years is necessary), and six months in Denmark. In Malta to ask for separation, spouses must have been married for four years. In desertion cases, there are other time limits.

The time bar reflects a specific social policy and indicates the aim of supporting marriage A minimum duration of marriage as a requirement justifies the differentiation between marriage and cohabitation without marriage. If one can marry

---

3   Whereas the MFC includes some of these and has twenty provisions on 'financial relief' compared to ten of the Principles (See *ibid*).

4   Malta would find justification in *Johnson v Johnson* (1986) 9 ECtHR 203, which has not yet been superseded.

5   For instance, the first article to deal with divorce (Art. 1.9) in the MFC says that divorce is granted upon either the joint application of both spouses or the unilateral application of one spouse (See *supra* note 2).

today and divorce tomorrow, this makes a mockery of the distinction. In addition, if the Principles are going to introduce a period of reflection before divorce is granted (1:5), then, it seems as if what is refused entry at the front door is allowed in from the back one.

Since the drafters admit that there was no common core on "mutual consent" as the sole ground and as there was quite a varied list of different periods required attached to different grounds in different systems, and as this is also the case under the legal systems surveyed in this research, we do not think that 1(2) is an acceptable Principle. This is a "better law" solution and in this part of the assessment we decline the use of "better law" choices. We also feel that this Principle is irreconcilable with, or at least contradicts Principle 1:5 on "reflection period" and Principle 1:8 introducing "separation for one year".

Principle 1:2. That divorce procedure should be determined by law (1:2 (1)) is a common core and our legal systems all adhere to this Principle. Judicial authority should always remain the basic authority and the administrative body would only be acceptable in exceptional circumstances. This is the outcome we see in surveying our eight systems. Thus, to reflect the reality of the legal systems, the wording of the Principle should not be "or", but "or in exceptional circumstances by". An "either or" presentation in the Principle is too general. Since what one gathers from the comparative overview and the comments attached to the Principle would not be part of the law, we feel that this Principle could be abused in systems such as Turkey and the jurisdiction of the courts may be avoided bringing more arbitrariness into the divorce procedure. Therefore, to be acceptable the Principle should have embodied the circumstances under which this type of procedure could be available. In any event, at present in Lithuania, Finland, France, England and Wales, Scotland, Sweden, and Turkey, administrative bodies cannot grant divorce, though at times judicial bodies may be acting as administrative bodies in nature. Thus, only an amended version of this Principle would be acceptable.[6]

Principle 1:2(2) suffers from vagueness and therefore is not satisfactory. In any event, there is no common core for 1:2(2). If in uncontested divorces the courts act as administrative bodies, this would still count for us as judicial authority.

The comments on 1:2 (1) exclude private divorce and this is a common core, but 1:2(2) leaves the matter to national legislation. We feel that this method dilutes

---

6   For instance, the MFC does not allow administrative divorce if the marriage has lasted for more than ten years (Art. 1.13) and also caters for the possibility of alternative dispute resolution (Art. 1.14). See *supra* note 2.

any Principle and that at least guidance should appear in the Principle, as it does, for example, in 1:6.

Principle 1:3. Divorce by mutual consent and divorce without the consent of one of the spouses are the two options. From the comparative overview and the comments, we understand that divorce for irretrievable breakdown (which could be considered to be the common core in our group—even mentioned as a ground for separation in Malta) is considered to be different from mutual consent and rejected. However, mutual consent as such is not a common core. It can only be presented as an aspiration. In England and Wales for instance, mutual consent is only allowed when parties have been separated for two years and in Scotland for one year; in France there is mutual consent but also irretrievable breakdown and fault grounds, as is the case in Lithuania and in Turkey. In Malta mutual consent alone is not acceptable in separation cases, though in non-contested cases joint application is acceptable.

Divorce grounds could have been reduced to one ground: breakdown of marriage. This is a common core.[7] The reasons for the breakdown seem to be many in the legal systems under consideration ranging from assault, threats to life, adultery, behaviour and desertion. The least is the claim that there is an impossibility to continue the marriage (Estonia). The spouses could agree on the breakdown by mutual consent, if possible, in which case we would be talking of uncontested divorce. Since other types of divorce are not shared by all systems under review here, they should not be considered either.

2.1.2. Divorce by mutual consent

Principle 1:4. Mutual consent is the basis of this Principle and no factual separation is required. Request for divorce by one spouse (unless accepted by the other) cannot prevail as a Principle, since unilateral divorce is not a shared principle among the legal systems surveyed. Even under most Scandinavian legal systems—which seem to be the ones predominantly preferred by the Principles—when there is no mutual consent a unilateral divorce can only be possible after two years of separation.

Mutual consent is an indication that the marriage is broken down, so although it is significant, it is not an autonomous ground shared by the legal systems under

---

[7]   The MFC also rejects "breakdown" as a ground on the force of the argument that the institution of marriage should not be placed above the actual will of the spouses (See *supra* note 2, p. 22). The will of the parties as the sole ground for divorce is dubbed as the "modern approach", but does not accord with the realities of the legal systems under consideration.

consideration here (England and Wales, Lithuania, Malta, Scotland and Turkey). There is no common core for factual separation either.

In certain circumstances consent may appear to be there, but may have been obtained under pressure. It may give unequal parties the semblance of equality. Moreover, the spouse who wants to get out of the marriage may be prepared to pay a high price to obtain the consent of the other spouse. Thus though mutual consent with no period of separation or any other additional requirements sounds progressive and civilised, and may be welcome, it cannot be the sole option in the form proposed and drafted.

Principle 1:5. The general point to make is that the term "period of reflection" is inappropriate in the circumstances. If the Principles prefer mutual consent as the basis of divorce and after divorce proceedings start there could be a delay to sort out the financial consequences and the position of children under sixteen, this period could have been called a three or six months of "delay of proceedings". "Reflection" implies that the consent may not have been genuine.[8] This period is not required if the spouses have already been separated for six months. But what if they have agreed on nothing? How and when will this be resolved?

As the Principles aim at fast track and easy, uncomplicated divorces (no require-ment of duration of marriage, administrative authority with competence to grant divorce, main ground of mutual consent and no requirement of separation) a reflection period presents a step back in the process. In effect, it delays divorce in certain cases, maybe in the majority of cases. In any event, many of our systems have no reflection period (England and Wales, Estonia, France, Scotland and Tur-key). Such a period may be introduced by the court for conciliation, which has a different purpose than the "reflection period" envisaged by the Principles.

Principle 1:6. The consequences on which an agreement is needed are enumerated in this Principle. These arise from a common core in our survey, although no shared principle is seen in the original survey.[9] One of the requirements men-tioned is the division or reallocation of property, which then, unfortunately, is not covered by the CEFL Principles.

---

[8] The MFC also uses this term, but the reasoning behind it seems different. One sees in Art. 1:10, that a reflection period and a renewal of application after six months from the first application is required if there are minor children or where one of the spouses does not agree on the divorce or any of its consequences. This would also mean that in contested unilateral applica-tions, there is need for a six months period after which the spouse wishing to divorce must re-apply (See *supra* note 2).

[9] The *CEFL Principles*, p. 38.

The statement "should be agreed" is said not to be binding[10] and the regulation of this is left to national laws. But the consequences of divorce related to financial arrangements and arrangements for the children and parental responsibility are the most important aspects of divorce. It is a fact that although leaving issues to be decided by national legislators makes for easier acceptance of the Principles, nonetheless it detracts from the value of one law for European spouses and would lead again to fragmentation.

The most important issue of "division and reallocation of property" has been left out because this was a difficult issue to resolve. This is a "cop-out" on the part of the CEFL. However, as there is no common core, for the purposes of this assessment, all we can say is that the legal systems in our survey consider this to be a most significant consequence of divorce.

The freedom to decide whether or not one pays additional maintenance to the other should not be part of divorce proceedings, or replace the maintenance requirements as arranged by the Principles. It should be a matter to be covered by the law of obligations, a contractual matter, not one to be covered by family law.

Principle 1:7. This Principle introducing the scrutiny of the agreement by the court is a safeguard. The systems in our survey all agree on this. This is especially the case related to the agreement concerning the children. What should be the scope of this review however?

Although any maintenance agreement beyond the one regulated by statute is a contractual matter, the financial agreement foreseen by legislation should also be scrutinised by the judge. Scrutinising frustrates consensual divorce. However, since on this issue there is no common core, the Principles leave all the detail to national law. But in this way, some legal systems could introduce stringent measures and thus go against the spirit of the Principles.

Partial agreement, similar to non-agreement, leads to a consensual divorce being treated as a non-consensual one in relation to the role of the court related to consequences. Too much is left to national laws, which would again lead to serious diversity and fragmentation.

---

10   *Ibid*, p. 40.

2.1.3. Divorce without the consent of one of the spouses

Principle 1:8 deals with divorce without consent, which the CEFL equates with factual separation. If there is no mutual consent, then there must be separation for one year, whereupon there is unilateral divorce without the consent of the other spouse. Why should this be the case? This is quite an intriguing Principle, not based on a common core, but on an amalgam of various approaches to separation seen in legal systems. Mostly, separation is linked to irretrievable breakdown however, being an indication of a breakdown, but not in these Principles.

In our systems under review, there are grounds for divorce other than mutual consent and separation, such as adultery, behaviour (fault) or mental illness. The Principles followed the "better law" approach, which we do not allow in this assessment. Irretrievable breakdown encompassing mutual consent is the common core.

The period of one year is quite short but may be acceptable since some of the legal systems under survey have already reduced this period since the Principles were drafted (France, Scotland, and Turkey). However, though this period may be too short for some, it is too long for others.

Principle 1:9 provides what can be regarded as in effect, a third ground. In case of exceptional hardship to the petitioner, divorce will be granted without factual separation. This is not a common core and very few systems include this among the grounds cited, though they may have an implied hardship clause (e.g. behaviour).[11] Though it is stressed in the comments that fault is not necessary, it could be taken as such in order to meet the existing laws in the legal systems under review here, and may be seen as a compromise offered to the legal systems that have fault based divorce. However, "hardship" could also be understood to be financial and as a term is confusing.

Principle 1:10. In non-consensual divorce, consequences to be determined, where necessary, by the competent authority are related to parental responsibility and child maintenance. Agreements can be taken into account. The competent authority may also determine the economic consequences. This Principle is only meant to provide guidance. Different standards are used in different legal systems. Laws differ; there is no common core here, so in order to be acceptable, these consequences should have been given as examples only of what could be taken into consideration.

---

[11]   *Ibid* p. 58.

2.1.4. Boiled down to the bare bones, it has to be admitted that where the drafters are not opting for "better law" based on the belief of a quick and painless divorce, they would not have been able to draft many Principles of family law based on "common core" research. This might explain why there are quite a number of "better law" choices and quite a number of vague and general principles with a number of issues left to the national legislators. Does this really mean that it is nearly impossible to harmonise family law for Europe even in the area of divorce and its consequences?

In most of the Principles, the North seems to trump the South, so though one legal system is not taken as a model, the "better law" is inspired by Scandinavian solutions. As we decided in our survey to go for seven out of eight shared answers to form the basis of a Principle and we treat the Scandinavian approach as one system (though with variations, to which can be added at times Estonia), discrepancies arise in many issues. Most of the existing laws in this field reflect compromises catering for the views of the conservative and the progressive, ever-present in all societies. Considering this fact, the Principles only reflect an aspiration for the future of Europe, not necessarily shared by even the majority of its peoples.

2.2. MAINTENANCE

2.2.1. General Principles

Principle 2:1: Here we see the first maxim: there is no connection between maintenance[12] and type of divorce. This is consistent with the Principles related to divorce. The concept of the "innocent" spouse is rejected. The principle that the creditor spouse should be innocent of fault has only recently been removed from some of the legal systems, and in some countries the basic distinctions remain. Though fault has not retained its historic importance either as a ground of divorce or maintenance, nevertheless, the protection of the "innocent" spouse still prevails if not in legislation, then in court decisions. However on the criteria of calculation used by the Principles, a common core exists here. For our purposes however, there is no common core since in the legal systems we cover we still see that the connection exists in a number of systems. For instance in France, *prestation compensatoire* is not related to fault but compensates also for moral wrong. In Lithuania, the spouse who is at fault for the breakdown of marriage gets no maintenance. In Turkey, there is even a balance of "more or less faulty" in claims for

---

12   The MFC uses the term "financial relief" and has a rather extensive discussion on the issue (See *supra* note 2, pp. 40–43).

maintenance for material and moral compensation and destitution alimony. In Malta fault is paramount in maintenance arrangements.

Principle 2:2 contains the second maxim: self-sufficiency. Each spouse should provide for his or her own support after divorce.[13] This Principle has not entered individual statutory laws overtly, however, it reflects the de facto position in nearly all cases by the fact of maintenance being limited to a short period of time. However, since the reality of the position of the spouse is to be taken into consideration, this general Principle will be riddled with exceptions. The drafters claim to be looking to the future and not the past, and possibly also, not to the present! This is not a workable Principle.

The "clean break" principle seen in England and Wales and Scotland, and also preferred in France, must be the best example of a belief in self-sufficiency. However, in France for instance, self-sufficiency is not the basis, neither is it in Lithuania, Norway or Turkey, or obviously in Malta, since in spite of separation, marriage continues. In Malta maintenance payments must be seen as a way of penalising the guilty spouse (the debtor); since, if there is no fault, then the self-sufficiency principle applies.

2.2.2. Conditions for the attribution of maintenance

Principle 2:3. The payment of maintenance relies on two criteria: the creditor spouse having insufficient resources to meet his or her needs, and the debtor spouse's ability to meet these needs. This is the common basis seen overtly or covertly in most jurisdictions; however, different approaches have been adopted. In some jurisdictions, the courts have discretion to make the necessary adjustments (Denmark, England and Wales, Finland and Scotland). In Scotland, the judge's discretion is limited by five principles: fair sharing of matrimonial property (deferred community); economic advantages and disadvantages during marriage; care of a child under 16, readjustment to lack of support subject to a maximum of three years; and serious financial hardship caused by divorce, in which case, the maintenance has no time limit. In England and Wales, though "ability" is regarded as an objective factor, "need" is a debatable issue and the system is discretionary. In Norway, the Code gives guidance to the judge, such as caring for children and distribution of tasks during marriage. In France, it is a matter of compensating for any economic imbalance caused by divorce. Turkey is similar with the additional "destitution" alimony.

---

[13]   The wording of the MFC Article 1.20 on the principle of self-sufficiency, "The parties shall be placed in a position to become self-sufficient as soon as possible" is both more realistic and more equitable (See *supra* note 2, p. 45).

In most legal systems, the calculation of income and assets are closely linked to social security and tax laws as well as judicial tradition and socio-economic perceptions. For example, in Estonia, State benefits either substitute or supplement the income, reducing the need for maintenance from the other spouse. In both Estonia and Lithuania the maxim for maintenance can be the government's calculation of Minimum Monthly Wages. In Lithuania courts look at the duration of marriage, need, assets of the debtor spouse, health, age and capacity for employment. In Estonia three issues are taken into account: incapacity to work, disability occurring within three years of divorce in marriages lasting 25 years and pregnancy and child care until the child reaches the age of three.

In view of the complexity of the situation, no maintenance calculation table is proposed by the Principles. Though this seems to be the only feasible approach, it does not create harmonisation. Thus, this is a very basic, basic Principle!

In the long run, courts will calculate maintenance, and the general guideline suggested by the Principles is "need" and "ability". Each spouse's income and assets have to be considered in the broad category of "income". "Needs" are reasonable living expenses. Additional factors are to be found in Principle 2:4.

Principle 2:4 sets the following conditions that should be taken into account when determining a maintenance claim: the spouses' employment ability, age and health; the care of children; the division of duties during the marriage; the duration of marriage; the standard of living during the marriage; and any new marriage or long-term relationship.

Lists of criteria are provided in some of our legal systems: For instance in Norway and Sweden, the Codes have a list of factors. In France courts look into the effects of liquidation of the matrimonial regime, succession and pension rights and consider age, health, duration of marriage, time devoted to child-care, and professional qualifications. These conditions are taken into account also in England and Wales. Some jurisdictions are more vague such as Finland and Turkey. Courts have wide discretion in some, such as Denmark, England and Wales, Finland, and Scotland though limited by the five principles noted above under Principle 2:3. Other jurisdictions demand that the need should arise because of either the marriage or the divorce, for certain types of maintenance claims; for instance Scotland and Turkey opt for divorce, Sweden and Norway for marriage.

Fault of either spouse can also be a determinant (Lithuania, Malta and Turkey).

In Norway and Sweden for instance, needs are related to division of spousal duties such as child caring. This duty is taken into consideration in all jurisdictions.

The duration of marriage is a factor in Denmark, England and Wales, Estonia, Finland, France, Lithuania, Iceland and Sweden, but is irrelevant in Estonia, Turkey and Scotland, although the judge may consider this, especially in case of marriages of short duration.

The standard of living during marriage, sometimes expressed as "legitimate expectations" such as in Turkey, should be maintained (England and Wales, France, Turkey, and in Malta for the "innocent" spouse).

Marriage of the creditor spouse ends maintenance claims. Most legal systems accept this. The debtor spouse's new marriage however, is problematic.[14] He or she may face multiplicity of claims (Principle 2:7), but should this matter? Normally this has no impact on his or her ability to pay; it could have gone up or down. The new spouse's means, which may improve the position of the debtor spouse, has an impact in England and Wales, France and Scotland, but is not considered in Denmark, Estonia, Finland, Norway, Sweden or Turkey. Thus there is no common core.

This Principle is regarded as a clarifying Principle additional to 2:3, the list of circumstances being inexhaustible. Additionally, when circumstances change, either spouse can return to the competent authorities, except in Lithuania, where spouses who may not have arranged or asked for maintenance in the agreement of mutual consent, cannot do so later even if circumstances change.

Principle 2:5 (1) mentions that payments must be made at regular intervals and in advance. 2:5 (2) states that a lump sum may be ordered upon request.

As a general rule payments are monetary and periodic, usually monthly. For instance, in Estonia there is no lump sum payment since maintenance payments are not seen as compensation. A lump sum as a one-off or in addition to periodic payment is also possible. The courts can order this form of payment in England and Wales, Finland, Scotland and Sweden. It is possible in Norway, but rare. In England and Wales, and Scotland this is actually the preferred method since the basic principle is "clean break". In France, in case of *prestation compensatoire* a capital sum is payable or property transferable, whereas in Turkey a lump sum is acceptable only in case of moral damages. Usually this possibility arises following the request of either spouse (France and Norway) or the creditor spouse (Fin-

---

14   Also see under Principle 2:9.

land). Sometimes, the court can so decide (England and Wales, Finland, Norway and Sweden).

In most systems courts have discretion both as to the form and to the amount payable. Lump sum payments bring a clean break and if so demanded by either spouse, should be respected. But as seen this is not a common core.

This Principle does not take into account immovable (real) property adjustments (however, see France, Lithuania, Scotland and Turkey), the family home, or division of pension rights. Therefore, it does not deal with the whole issue.[15]

Principle 2:6 determines that if maintenance payments create exceptional hardship to the debtor spouse, the competent authority can deny or limit maintenance or terminate maintenance owing to the conduct of the creditor spouse. In this case, as in the case of divorce Principle 1:9, we object to the term chosen since "hardship" implies financial difficulty. We feel that this Principle is there partly to appease those legal systems in which fault still plays a role. Though it is said in the comments that the fault of the debtor is excluded, the conduct of the creditor spouse is considered when there is hardship to the debtor. This is a hypocritical Principle.

Factors of hardship are not cited in 2:6, but from the comments we can gather that this is not financial; factors such as attempted murder of the spouse, misconduct, mistreatment, domestic violence, financial misconduct could play a role in the reduction or termination of payments. Although the comments indicate that hardship is exceptional and fault should not re-enter the system,[16] 90% of the examples indicate fault in the sense that they emanate from wilful acts.[17]

In fault-based divorces—not part of the Principles—we know that fault leads to at least a reduction in the amount of payments in Lithuania and Turkey, and in France, although the judge cannot terminate maintenance relying on "conduct". If the system opts for non-fault based divorce, then this Principle again applies in maintenance claims as in Denmark, Finland, Norway, Sweden and Estonia. In Scotland for instance, misconduct during marriage is only important if it is ineq-

---

[15]   On this point again, a look at the MFC may be profitable. See *supra* n. 2, Articles 1.15–1.39, especially Articles 1.33–1.37.

[16]   The CEFL *Principles* p. 105.

[17]   Here it is also intriguing to observe that the MFC when citing exceptions, i.e. factors that the court may take into account to depart from the principle of equal division of benefits and detriments (Art. 1.28), brings in (j) financial misconduct, and (k) domestic violence. Thus we see "fault" lurking in the shadows, in spite of the fact that the consideration of "fault" is vehemently denied by these drafters also (See *ibid*).

uitable to leave it out of account. In England and Wales courts take conduct into account, though fault is not considered. In Estonia, courts can restrict maintenance payments on the ground of indecent behaviour. In Denmark, Norway and Iceland exceptional hardship serves as a ground for divorce. In Malta, where domestic violence is regarded as faulty conduct, maintenance is withheld. So, fault has not altogether disappeared in most of the legal systems under consideration here. The Principle has to come clean!

2.2.3. Specific issues

Principle 2:7 considers multiplicity of claims. The competent authority should give priority (a) to a minor child of the debtor spouse and (b) the obligation to maintain a new spouse.

A minor child comes before a spouse in Denmark, England and Wales, Finland, Malta, Norway, and Sweden although there is no such codal rule. Courts may take other factors into account. In Estonia, court practice is to protect the minor child first. In Sweden a child is considered to be a minor up to the age of 21 and this is the cut off age. England and Wales only mention "ongoing education" not the age, and the primary carer. The solution is unclear in France, Turkey and Scotland where the rule is "orders must be reasonable". There is a kind of common core then to protect the children first.

The prioritisation between the ex-spouse and the new spouse is more problematic. Do they have the same ranking? If there is a lack of means, in England and Wales the new spouse is preferred, though there is no ranking. There is no rule on prioritisation in Estonia and no ranking. The situation is unclear in France, Scotland, Norway and Turkey, where multiple claims are not regulated.

The ranking of ex-spouse and other relatives such as parents is not settled in the legal systems under consideration either. In England and Wales and Scandinavia for instance, other relatives are not recognised for ranking. There is no clear rule in France or Turkey.

Even if we can regard Principle 2:7 (a) as the common core, we cannot do so for 2:7 (b). Maintenance obligation between spouses is accepted in all legal systems as part of solidarity, but not to be regulated among divorce principles.

Principle 2:8 introduces the general principle that maintenance is to be for a limited period, and only exceptionally without a time limit.[18] Although we could expect a common core here, there is no common practice. It is true that in most legal systems the duration of maintenance is limited, though the length of the period varies; for instance, in Norway and Scotland it is for no longer than three years, while in Sweden for four years and Denmark for ten years. This seems to be left usually to the discretion of the competent authority in individual cases and related to the length of the relationship and the overall situation of the creditor spouse. We see, for example a transitional period mentioned in Denmark, England and Wales, Norway and Sweden. In France there is an exceptional *pension alimentaire,* which is a one off payment or payments for eight years with no conditions attached; in Turkey maintenance could be life-long. In France in *prestation compensatoire,* the period is fixed by spousal agreement. No time limit is prescribed in Denmark, Norway and Sweden, where if need be, a new period may be added at the end of the first period. In England and Wales courts can specify a term but a one off lump sum is preferred. In compelling circumstances, there would be no time limit. In Estonia, maintenance would be paid for an unspecified time or until the cessation of the grounds for payment, seen above under Principle 2:4. This is the case in Lithuania also. In Malta there can be no time bar since the spouses are still married.

Case by case fixing of the period is recommended. This is a good recommendation but does not fit the practice where periods are fixed by statute, though it is possible that the competent authorities do have a say even in those systems. However, the Principle as is, is a common core of a very general kind; it states the obvious.

Principle 2:9 has three sub-principles: (1) Maintenance will cease when the creditor spouse remarries; (2) it does not revive if the new marriage ends; (3) it ceases upon the death of either spouse.

All change of circumstances effects maintenance. So, what happens when the creditor spouse's conduct is considered unworthy (See Principle 2:6)? This is not covered.

Principle 2.9 (1) is a common core (Denmark, England and Wales, Finland, France, Norway, Scotland and Turkey). However, in Sweden an adjustment is made. and in France *prestation compensatoire* continues and in cases of entering a *pacte civil de solidarité* where *pension alimentaire* is received, the debtor spouse

---

18   The MFC in Art 1.32 limits the time to that necessary to allow the other partner reasonable time to adjust to the new circumstances (*ibid*). This wording is more elegant.

must request termination; in case the payment is a capital sum it goes to the creditor's heirs.

Principle 2:9 should be considered together with 2:4. There is an overlap here.

Long-term relationships may be considered as a change of circumstance by courts and therefore rely on judge-made rules in England and Wales, France, Norway, Scotland and Sweden, but is not so considered in Estonia. However, in Finland maintenance cannot be denied on this ground. In Denmark, the debtor spouse has to request it.

Principle 2:9 (2) is also a common core. However in Lithuanian law maintenance can revive if the creditor spouse is caring for a child from the first marriage. The Principles do not seem to have considered this possibility.

Principle 2:9 (3) is controversial and there is no common core. This is not a well thought out Principle. Though there is agreement that the death of the creditor spouse puts an end to maintenance (though what happens to the maintenance of the children in this case has also to be determined), there is no agreement on the impact of the death of the debtor spouse. This has an impact in Denmark, Finland, Norway and Sweden, not always in England and Wales, and the obligation is devolved to the debtor's estate in France, but not to the heirs since 2004, and to the payee's successors in Lithuania and Scotland. In Estonia the debtor's obligation may be replaced by other incomes, through State benefits, for instance. So this Principle introduces fundamental change and would not be acceptable in this assessment.

Principle 2:10 (1) states that the spouses can make a maintenance agreement, (2) it should be in writing; (3) the competent authority should at least scrutinise its validity.

There is a common core for 2:10 (1) in that Denmark, England and Wales, Finland, Norway, Scotland, Sweden and Turkey all allow maintenance agreements. In France agreement is compulsory in divorces by mutual consent (*divorce sur requete conjoints*), in other instances, though possible, not binding on the court. The judge must ratify agreements. In Estonia such agreements are rare since it is the Code that determines maintenance obligations and the right to receive maintenance cannot be waived by agreement.

There is no common core for 2:10 (2) as for instance, in Denmark no special form is needed, a notary public is necessary in Norway, Scotland and Turkey; in France a notary public is needed if real property is an issue. In Sweden the agreement must be in writing.

Similarly there is no common core in 2:10 (3). For example, no scrutiny or approval is needed in Denmark and Norway, however, in Sweden, Iceland and Norway the courts can adjust maintenance if an agreement is found to be unreasonable or for change of circumstances. In Finland and Denmark, confirmation is needed from the Board of Social Welfare. In Scotland where couples are encouraged to make their own agreements, if such agreement is reached after the divorce, no scrutiny is needed otherwise courts can scrutinise and alter the agreement. In England and Wales though judicial scrutiny is limited, it cannot be ousted by agreement. The competent authority has control over the agreement in Finland, France and Turkey, especially that related to the protection of the interests of the children. In Turkey, the judge can replace an agreement drawn up by the spouses and if they do not accept his version, the divorce will not be granted. In Malta agreements related to the consequences of separation cannot be made prior to breakdown.

2.2.4. Overall the verdict must be that the Principles on maintenance, merely ten, addressing the most important issue of divorce, that is its consequences, cover this area only partially, do not reflect the reality of the legal systems under consideration in our research and do not provide solutions that correspond to their needs. Compared for example, to the Model Family Code[19]—with its twenty provisions on "financial relief"—which we also reject as being even more firmly based on the "better law", if not the "best law" approach stemming from an idiosyncratic value based choice on the part of the drafters, the CEFL Principles are even more unsuitable. The CEFL Principles cover far less, they lack detail, and, in being incomplete, cannot be used for replacing the existing provisions in the legal systems they aim to address and help.

It must be admitted that if one looks for perfection, one can never harmonise in a field full of such diversity where, though basic concerns may be shared, solutions offer a myriad of possibilities. To draft a Principle on each item out of such a number would remain unsatisfactory. However, these Principles are too vague, too general and, by allowing national legislators to go their own way on quite a number of issues, defeat their purpose and can only support fragmentation rather than lead to unification. One can be justified in asking whether, since the only harmonisation possible is at the "lowest common denominator", this project can please any of the legal systems addressed.

---

19   See *supra* note 2.

3. HARMONISATION IS REJECTED AS A TOP-DOWN MODEL

Let us first take note of the fact that in family law the so-called common law/civil law divide is not a determinant as far as values are concerned, and family law is predominantly about values. This divide is reflected only in the role and the discretionary powers of the courts. What is crucial is religion. In secular societies moral values which reflect religious positions, do not disappear. Differing political economies do have a role to play in choices made by top-down models, but overall this is of lesser importance to the people.

Although it may be said that in our day religion is on the decline in Western Europe, this is happening at best in different speeds in different societies. In Eastern and Central Europe however, the direction is not the same in some of the ex-socialist republics, if not the reverse. It is also worth remembering that religion has been traditionally a major source of conflict between European countries historically. Protestant, Catholic and Eastern Orthodox Christianity divided Europe into North and South, and East and West. In many of the countries in Europe today, in spite of secularism at the level of the legal systems, there are divided religious structures following the patterns of multi-culturalism.

To put it crudely, as religion reflects into the concept of the family, we see that in the predominantly Lutheran North, family ties are weak and welfare systems are strong, whereas in the mostly Catholic and Eastern Orthodox South, family ties are strong and welfare systems are weak. It is also the fact that in Northern Lutheran countries and Britain divorce rates are higher than in the Southern Catholic countries. The number of births outside marriage also follows a similar trend, being high in the North and Britain and low in the South.[20] In Turkey with a secular legal system, and a family law derived originally from Switzerland (reflecting the Swiss divided religious structure) yet quite similar to the Southern Catholic and Eastern Orthodox countries, we observe that the predominant values held by the people are traditional and conservative, 98% of the population being Muslims of different traditions, sects and schools.

An interesting scale of values comes to light in this survey. It ranges from a Lutheran population with an ex-socialist secular legal system (Estonia), a number of secular legal systems with Evangelical Lutheran populations (the Scandinavian countries), a predominantly Roman Catholic population with a secular legal sys-

---

[20] See further on what factors divide Europeans, GUIBERNAU, M, "Introduction: Unity and Diversity in Europe", in GUIBERNAU, M (ed) *Governing European Diversity* (London, Sage Publishers, 2001), pp. 1–34 at 14–19.

tem (France), a Roman Catholic population with an ex-socialist legal system (Lithuania), a predominantly Protestant Anglican population with a secular legal system (England and Wales), a mixed Presbyterian Protestant—Roman Catholic population with a secular legal system (Scotland), a Roman Catholic population without a secular legal system (Malta), to a Muslim population with a secular legal system (Turkey). The impact of the values these beliefs embody can be traced in their present family laws, secular or not, and regardless of their membership of the civil law or common law families. However, all these countries are on the path of modernisation but within their own circumstances, definitely at different speeds and not necessarily in the same direction.[21]

Culture, and legal culture which to a certain extent reflects general culture, are widely used terms which have no agreed definition. Here is an attempt to define legal culture, which can be regarded as a starting point:

Legal culture, in its most general sense, should be seen as one way of describing relatively stable patterns of legally oriented social behaviour and attitudes. The identifying elements of legal culture range from facts about institutions such as the number and role of lawyers or the ways judges are appointed and controlled, to various forms of behaviour such as litigation or prison rates, and, at the other extreme, more nebulous aspects of ideas, values, aspirations and mentalities. *Like culture itself, legal culture is about who we are, not just what we do.*[22] [Emphasis added]

For the people then, the family, with its values, aspirations and mentalities, is responsible for all its members and especially those who cannot be in paid employment: the young, the elderly, the infirm and those in full-time education. Different societies however, organise these tasks in many different ways, with significant variations. In order to appreciate the differences, different historical, political, socio-economic and, above all, cultural and religious contexts must be borne in mind.

Culture is the product of historical influences, it is not uniform but hybrid. Obviously long-standing historical patterns can be altered, otherwise there would be no room for reform. To the extent that cultures remain closed or are self-referential, they become mummified. However, though cultures can be dynamic and be influenced by evolutionary change, this change should be spontaneous and

---

21   See for a different view ANTOKOLSKAIA, MV "The Process of Modernisation of Family Law in Eastern and Western Europe: Difference in Timing, Resemblance in Substance" (2000) 4.2 *EJCL* <http://law.kub.nl/ejcl/42/art42–1.html>

22   NELKEN, D "Using the Concept of Legal Culture", (2004) *Australian Journal of Legal Philosophy*, 1–28.

autonomous to be healthy, internalised and continuous to be effective, and a bottom-up development to be acceptable.

Although Masha Antokolskaia regards CEFL as providing a model for the voluntary bottom-up harmonisation of family law,[23] this assessment can be challenged by the fact that, since CEFL targets national legislators—even if only hoping to be a source of information and inspiration—this can only bring about a top-down method of harmonisation. There is no suggestion here of a spontaneous bottom-up convergence.

There is always tension between tradition and transformation which "almost invariably leads to conflict between the two, and it is only after negotiation that consensus can be achieved." However, "certain positions are not open to negotiation and dialogue".[24] When considering family life in Europe, diversity comes to the fore though there are some signs of commonality in the development of societies. The European context is shifting, countries being transformed broadly in the same direction such as in fertility and divorce, says Catherine Lloyd.[25] However, she also points out that, "political and social developments in different countries have followed very different trajectories."[26]

For instance, over the centuries, divorce laws have evolved in Europe, from no-divorce, divorce as sanction, divorce as remedy, divorce as a spousal decision, to divorce as a right. These options reflect different visions of family, marriage and morality, and different balances between the intervention of the state and the church, and spousal autonomy.[27] Today, divorce remains based on fault, on irretrievable breakdown, on separation, on consent and on demand. Some legal systems use a combination of these bases. Some use one or two. Some have difficult procedures and time limits while others have easy procedures. A few which appear to provide for easy and quick divorce have surrounded it by unforeseeable restrictions. The differences reflect historical developments, cultural and religious differences and ideological preferences. All that this tells us is that the common core

---

[23] ANTOKOLSKAIA, MV *Harmonisation of Family Law in Europe: A Historical perspective – A Tale of Two Millennia*, European Family Law Series, Volume 13 (Antwerp, Intersentia, 2006), p. 362.

[24] LLOYD, C "The Transformation of family life and sexual politics", in GUIBERNAU (ed) *supra* note 20, pp. 139–168 at 165.

[25] *Ibid.*

[26] *Ibid.* For the historical development of divorce in Europe from the sixteenth century onwards see, ANTOKOLSKAIA, *supra* note 23.

[27] See for an analysis of these trends ANTOKOLSKAIA, MV "Convergence and Divergence of Divorce Laws in Europe!" (2006) 18:3 *Child and Family Law Quarterly*, pp. 307–330 at p. 308; and for a helpful concise history of developments, pp. 309–323. For a more thorough coverage of historical developments see *supra* note 23.

is very limited and any Principles to harmonise family law in Europe relying on common core research will be of very little use. The only effective type of harmonisation today can be top-down intervention reflecting a vision for the future with provisions based on the "better law" approach, which we find unacceptable in this assessment.

Cultural diversity necessitates that legal diversity should be maintained. Why should people amend their laws in order to meet the requirements of a vision which they do not share? Comparing Estonia and Lithuania for example, we see the typical phenomenon of convergence under pressure during 1940–1991, followed by a spontaneous divergence reflecting the different cultural/religious contexts under which the majority of the population live.

Assumptions relying on: working women, equality, women capable of supporting the family and self-sufficiency, relate to the realities of some societies and not to all, and we might consider these as desirable. However, even if that were the case, what is the justification for outside interference in democratic societies? An additional concern must be: Why should some set of values trump others? Especially in systems where considerable public consultation takes place so that laws more or less match public opinion and expectations, top-down intervention of this sort would be totally unacceptable. In pressing for transformation of family life, bottom-up strategies are crucial. For this, internally organised social movements are more effective than external interference or even internal legislative enactment. As rightly stated, "integration may involve the development of rules and repertoires or processes of autonomous adjustment."[28]

This assessment can happily endorse and echo Josep Llobera's remarks:

> National identities are here to stay. Any forward-looking perspective has to come to terms with the persistence of some very basic categories such as kinship, language, culture, religion and historical memory. The importance of any of the categories may vary from place to place; what matters is the specific combination that occurs in each nation, and which makes it different from others. It is probable that a kind of 'European identity' will be on the increase along with, but not against or as a substitute for, national identities.[29]

There might very well be an eventual "norms diffusion" and "identity change" and European integration may have a transformative effect on the laws of the member states. However, first, there is as yet no formal harmonisation of family

---

28   LLOYD, *supra* note 24.
29   LLOBERA, JR "What Unites Europeans", in GUIBERNAU (ed) *supra* note 20, pp. 169–194 at 193.

law, and second, even if there were such harmonisation, empirical research suggests that, because of "differentiated integration", "partial implementation" and "flexibility" arrangements inherent in the EU structure, "convergence " is absent, though there is evidence of "mutual influence" and "interdependence". Antoaneta Dimitrova and Bernard Steunenberg show that "no clear and unambiguous trend towards convergence due to the influence of European integration can be found."[30]

Family life and family law may have an instrumental dimension but their emotional dimension is more prominent. The famous EU slogan, "unity in diversity" means that there must be a mutual understanding and acceptance of this diversity. In the type of project we are dealing with here, it would be difficult to generate a popular response in favour of a harmonised Europe-wide family law, harmonised through Principles drafted by a committee of legal experts, with the gaps to be filled in by national legislators—Principles that seemingly reflect the value system of a particular world view. There is no indication that these Principles reflect what the majority of the population in the legal systems under review would regard as desirable to replace the product of their own legal cultures.

Antokolskaia concludes her research into convergence and divergence of divorce law in Europe, by saying that all "will unavoidably meet each other at the finish line",[31] and suggests that "administrative divorce on demand" might be the "final point" for developments in divorce law, thus implying that the "modernisation trend" coincides with a "convergence tendency". This for her would be "uniformity by way of a spontaneous modernisation/convergence process". Maybe one day we will end up at another "final point", whereby one spouse grants divorce to the other without the involvement of the state in any form or fashion. Maybe one day "marriage and divorce will not be regulated by law at all"! She does admit however, that such futuristic interpretations seem "far too speculative".[32]

Reality has it however, that the legal systems we looked at in this study are not in line with the CEFL Principles, and certainly not with the "final points".

---

[30]   DIMITROVA, A and STEUNENBERG, B "The Search for Convergence of National Policies in the European Union", (2000) 1(2) *European Union Politics*, pp. 201–226.
[31]   ANTOKOLSKAIA, *supra* note 27, p. 329. She uses Zeno's paradox on the race between Achilles and the tortoise, which in her metaphoric example become Achilleses and the tortoises.
[32]   *Ibid.*

ANNEXES:
THE QUESTIONNAIRE
AND THE PRINCIPLES

QUESTIONNAIRE
GROUNDS FOR DIVORCE AND
MAINTENANCE BETWEEN
FORMER SPOUSES

September 2002

A. GENERAL

1. What is the current source of law for divorce?
2. Give a brief history of the main developments of your divorce law.
3. Have there been proposals to reform your current divorce law?

B. GROUNDS FOR DIVORCE

I. GENERAL

4. What are the grounds for divorce?
5. Provide the most recent statistics on the different bases for which divorce was granted.
6. How frequently are divorce applications refused?
7. Is divorce obtained through a judicial process, or is there also an administrative procedure?
8. Does a specific competent authority have jurisdiction over divorce proceedings?
9. How are divorce proceedings initiated? (e.g. Is a special form required? Do you need a lawyer? Can the individual go to the competent authority personally?)
10. When does the divorce finally dissolve the marriage?

If under your system the sole ground for divorce is the irretrievable breakdown of marriage answer part II only. If not, answer part III only.

II. DIVORCE ON THE SOLE GROUND OF IRRETRIEVABLE BREAKDOWN OF THE MARRIAGE

11. How is irretrievable breakdown established? Are there presumptions of irretrievable breakdown?
12. Can one truly speak of a non-fault-based divorce or is the idea of fault still of some relevance?
13. To obtain the divorce, is it necessary that the marriage was of a certain duration?
14. Is a period of separation generally required before filing the divorce papers? If not, go to question 16. If so, will this period be shorter if the respondent consents than if he/she does not? Are there other exceptions?
15. Does this separation suffice as evidence of the irretrievable breakdown?
16. In so far as separation is relied upon to prove irretrievable breakdown:
    (a) Which circumstances suspend the term of separation?
    (b) Does the separation need to be intentional?
    (c) Is the use of a separate matrimonial home required?
17. Are attempts at conciliation, information meetings or mediation attempts required?
18. Is a period for reflection and consideration required?
19. Do the spouses need to reach an agreement or to make a proposal on certain subjects? If so, when should this agreement be reached? If not, may the competent authority determine the consequences of the divorce?
20. To what extent must the competent authority scrutinize the reached agreement?
21. Can the divorce application be rejected or postponed due to the fact that the dissolution of the marriage would result in grave financial or moral hardship to one spouse or the children? If so, can the competent authority invoke this on its own motion?

III. MULTIPLE GROUNDS FOR DIVORCE

1. Divorce by consent

22. Does divorce by consent exist as an autonomous ground for divorce, or is it based on the ground of irretrievable breakdown?
23. Do both spouses need to apply for a divorce together, and if not, how do the divorce proceedings vary according to whether one or both spouses apply for a divorce?
24. Is a period of separation required before filing the divorce papers?

25. Is it necessary that the marriage was of a certain duration?
26. Is a minimum age of the spouses required?
27. Are attempts at conciliation, information meetings or mediation attempts required?
28. What (formal) procedure is required? (e.g. How many times do the spouses need to appear before the competent authority?)
29. Do the spouses need to reach an agreement or to make a proposal, or may the competent authority determine the consequences of the divorce?
30. If they need to reach an agreement, does it need to be exhaustive or is a partial agreement sufficient? On what subjects should it be, and when should this agreement be reached?
31. To what extent must the competent authority scrutinize the reached agreement?
32. Is it possible to convert divorce proceedings, initiated on another ground, to proceedings on the ground of mutual consent, or must new proceedings be commenced? Or, vice versa, is it possible to convert divorce proceedings on the ground of mutual consent, to proceedings based on other grounds?

2. *Divorce on the ground of fault/ matrimonial offence*

33. What are the fault grounds for divorce?
34. If adultery is a ground what behaviour does it constitute?
35. In what circumstances can injury or false accusation provide a ground for divorce?
36. Is an intentional fault required?
37. Should the fault be offensive to the other spouse? Does the prior fault of one spouse, deprive the guilty / fault-based nature of the shortcomings of the other?
38. To obtain a divorce, is it necessary that the marriage was of a certain duration?
39. Does the parties' reconciliation prevent the innocent spouse from relying upon earlier facts as a ground for divorce?
40. How is the fault proved?
41. Are attempts at conciliation, information meetings or mediation attempts required?
42. Can the divorce application be rejected or postponed due to the fact that the dissolution of the marriage would result in grave financial or moral hardship to one spouse or the children? If so, may the competent authority invoke this on its own motion?
43. Is it possible to pronounce a judgment against both parties, even if there was no counterclaim by the respondent?

*3.   Divorce on the ground of irretrievable breakdown of the marriage and/or
        separation*

44. How is irretrievable breakdown established? Are there presumptions of irre-
     trievable breakdown?
45. Can one truly speak of a non-fault-based divorce or is the idea of fault still of
     some relevance?
46. To obtain the divorce, is it necessary that the marriage was of a certain dura-
     tion?
47. How long must the separation last before divorce is possible?
48. Does this separation suffice as evidence of the irretrievable breakdown?
49. In so far as separation is relied upon to prove irretrievable breakdown,
(a) Which circumstances suspend the term of separation?
(b) Does the separation need to be intentional?
(c) Is the use of a separate matrimonial home required?
50. Are attempts at conciliation, information meetings or mediation attempts
     required?
51. Is a period for reflection and consideration required?
52. Do the spouses need to reach an agreement or to make a proposal on certain
     subjects? If so, when should this agreement be reached? If not, may the com-
     petent authority determine the consequences of the divorce?
53. To what extent must the competent authority scrutinize the reached agree-
     ment?
54. Can the divorce application be rejected or postponed due to the fact that the
     dissolution of the marriage would result in grave financial or moral hardship
     to one spouse or the children? If so, can the competent authority invoke this
     on its own motion?

C.   SPOUSAL MAINTENANCE AFTER DIVORCE

I.   GENERAL

55. What is the current source of private law for maintenance of spouses after
     divorce?
56. Give a brief history of the main developments of your private law regarding
     maintenance of spouses after divorce.
57. Have there been proposals to reform your current private law regarding
     maintenance of spouses after divorce?
58. Upon divorce, does the law grant maintenance to the former spouse?

59. Are the rules relating to maintenance upon divorce connected with the rules relating to other post-marital financial consequences, especially to the rules of matrimonial property law? To what extent do the rules of (matrimonial) property law fulfil a function of support?

60. Do provisions on the distribution of property or pension rights (including social security expectancies where relevant) have an influence on maintenance after divorce?

61. Can compensation (damages) for the divorced spouse be claimed in addition to or instead of maintenance payments? Does maintenance also have the function of compensation?

62. Is there only one type of maintenance claim after divorce or are there, according to the type of divorce (e.g. fault, breakdown), several claims of a different nature? If there are different claims explain their bases and extent.

63. Are the divorced spouses obliged to provide information to each other spouse and/or to the competent authority on their income and assets? Is this right to information enforceable? What are the consequences of a spouse's refusal to provide such information?

II.   CONDITIONS UNDER WHICH MAINTENANCE IS PAID

64. Do general conditions such as a lack of means and ability to pay suffice for a general maintenance grant or do you need specific conditions such as age, illness, duration of the marriage and the raising of children? Please explain.

65. To what extent does maintenance depend on reproachable behaviour or fault on the part of the debtor during the marriage?

66. Is it relevant whether the lack of means has been caused by the marriage (e.g. if one of the spouses has give up his/her work during the marriage)?

67. Must the claimant's lack of means exist at the moment of divorce or at another specific time?

III.   CONTENT AND EXTENT OF THE MAINTENANCE CLAIM

68. Can maintenance be claimed for a limited time-period only or may the claim exist over a long period of time, maybe even lifelong?

69. Is the amount of the maintenance granted determined according to the standard of living during the marriage or according to, e.g. essential needs?

70. How is maintenance calculated? Are there rules relating to percentages or fractional shares according to which the ex-spouses' income is divided? Is there a model prescribed by law or competent authority practice?

71. What costs other than the normal costs of life may be demanded by the claimant? (e.g. Necessary further professional qualifications? Costs of health insurance? Costs of insurance for age or disability?)

72. Is there a maximum limit to the maintenance that can be ordered?

73. Does the law provide for a reduction in the level of maintenance after a certain time?

74. In which way is the maintenance to be paid (periodical payments? payment in kind? lump sum?)?

75. Is the lump sum prescribed by law, can it be imposed by a court order or may the claimant or the debtor opt for such a payment?

76. Is there an (automatic) indexation of maintenance?

77. How can the amount of maintenance be adjusted to changed circumstances?

IV. DETAILS OF CALCULATING MAINTENANCE: FINANCIAL CAPACITY OF THE DEBTOR

78. Do special rules exist according to which the debtor may always retain a certain amount even if this means that he or she will not fully fulfil his maintenance obligations?

79. To what extent, if at all, is an increase of the debtor's income a) since the separation, b) since the divorce, taken into account when calculating the maintenance claim?

80. How far do debts affect the debtor's liability to pay maintenance?

81. Can the debtor only rely on his or her other legal obligations or can he or she also rely on his or her moral obligations in respect of other persons, e.g. a de facto partner or a stepchild?

82. Can the debtor be asked to use his or her capital assets in order to fulfil his or her maintenance obligations?

83. Can a "fictional" income be taken into account where the debtor is refusing possible and reasonable gainful employment or where he or she has deliberately given up such employment?

84. Does the debtor's social security benefits, which he or she receives or could receive, have to be used for the performance of his/her maintenance obligation? Which kinds of benefits have to be used for this purpose?

85. In respect of the debtor's ability to pay, does the income (means) of his or her new spouse, registered partner or de facto partner have to be taken into account?

V.   DETAILS OF CALCULATING MAINTENANCE: THE CLAIMANT'S LACK OF OWN MEANS

86. In what way will the claimant's own income reduce his or her maintenance claim? Is it relevant whether the income is derived, on the one hand, from employment which can be reasonably expected or, on the other, from employment which goes beyond what is reasonably expected?
87. To what extent can the claimant be asked to seek gainful employment before he or she may claim maintenance from the divorced spouse?
88. Can the claimant be asked to use his or her capital assets, before he or she may claim maintenance from the divorced spouse?
89. When calculating the claimant's income and assets, to what extent are the maintenance obligations of the claimant in relation to third persons (e.g. children from an earlier marriage) taken into account?
90. Are there social security benefits (e.g. income support, pensions) the claimant receives which exclude his or her need according to the legal rules and/or court practice? Where does the divorced spouse's duty to maintain rank in relation to the possibility for the claimant to seek social security benefits?

VI.   QUESTIONS OF PRIORITY OF MAINTENANCE CLAIMS

91. How is the relationship between different maintenance claims determined? Are there rules on the priority of claims?
92. Does the divorced spouse's claim for maintenance rank ahead of the claim of a new spouse (or registered partner) of the debtor?
93. Does the claim of a child of the debtor, if that child has not yet come of age, rank ahead of the claim of a divorced spouse?
94. What is the position if that child has reached the age of majority?
95. Does the divorced spouse's claim for maintenance rank ahead of the claims of other relatives of the debtor?
96. What effect, if any, does the duty of relatives or other relations of the claimant to maintain him or her have on the ex-spouse's duty to maintain him or her?

VII. LIMITATIONS AND END OF THE MAINTENANCE OBLIGATION

97. Is the maintenance claim extinguished upon the claimant's remarriage or entering into a registered partnership? If so: may the claim revive under certain conditions?

98. Are there rules according to which maintenance may be denied or reduced if the claimant enters into an informal long-term relationship with another person?
99. Can the maintenance claim be denied because the marriage was of short duration?
100. Can the maintenance claim be denied or reduced for other reasons such as the claimant's conduct during the marriage or the facts in relation to the ground for divorce?
101. Does the maintenance claim end with the death of the debtor?

VIII. MAINTENANCE AGREEMENTS

102. May the spouses (before or after the divorce or during the divorce proceedings) enter into binding agreements on maintenance in the case of (an eventual) divorce?
103. May a spouse agree to renounce his/her future right to maintenance? If so, are there limits on that agreement's validity?
104. Is there a prescribed form for such agreements?
105. Do such agreements need the approval of a competent authority?

PRINCIPLES OF EUROPEAN FAMILY LAW REGARDING DIVORCE AND MAINTENANCE BETWEEN FORMER SPOUSES

PART I: DIVORCE

CHAPTER I: GENERAL PRINCIPLES

Principle 1:1 Permission of divorce
(1) The law should permit divorce.
(2) No duration of the marriage should be required.

Principle 1:2 Procedure by law and competent authority
(1) The divorce procedure should be determined by law.
(2) Divorce should be granted by the competent authority which can either be a judicial or an administrative body.

Principle 1:3 Types of divorce
The law should permit both divorce by mutual consent and divorce without consent of one of the spouses.

CHAPTER II: DIVORCE BY MUTUAL CONSENT

Principle 1:4 Mutual consent
(1) Divorce should be permitted upon the basis of the spouses' mutual consent. No period of factual separation should be required.
(2) Mutual consent is to be understood as an agreement between the spouses that their marriage should be dissolved.
(3) This agreement may be expressed either by a joint application of the spouses or by an application by one spouse with the acceptance of the other spouse.

Principle 1:5 Reflection period
(1) If, at the commencement of the divorce proceedings, the spouses have children under the age of sixteen years and they have agreed upon all the consequences of the divorce as defined by Principle 1:6, a three-month

period of reflection shall be required. If they have not agreed upon all the consequences, then a six-month period shall be required.

(2) If, at the commencement of the divorce proceedings, the spouses have no children under the age of sixteen years and they have agreed upon all the consequences of the divorce as defined by Principle 1:6(d) and (e), no period of reflection shall be required. If they have not agreed upon all the consequences, a three-month period of reflection shall be required.

(3) No period of reflection shall be required, if, at the commencement of the divorce proceedings, the spouses have been factually separated for six months.

Principle 1:6 Content and form of the agreement

(1) The consequences upon which the spouses should have reached an agreement are:
  (a) their parental responsibility, where necessary, including the residence of and the contact arrangements for the children,
  (b) child maintenance, where necessary,
  (c) the division or reallocation of property, and
  (d) spousal maintenance.

(2) Such an agreement should be in writing.

Principle 1:7 Determination of the consequences

(1) In all cases the competent authority should determine the consequences for the children as mentioned in Principle 1:6(a) and (b), but any admissible agreement of the spouses should be taken into account insofar as it is consistent with the best interests of the child.

(2) The competent authority should at least scrutinise the validity of the agreement on the matters mentioned in Principle 1:6(c) and (d).

(3) If the spouses have not made an agreement or reached only a partial agreement on the matters mentioned in Principle 1:6(c) and (d), the competent authority may determine these consequences.

CHAPTER III: DIVORCE WITHOUT THE CONSENT OF ONE OF THE SPOUSES

Principle 1:8 Factual separation

The divorce should be permitted without consent of one of the spouses if they have been factually separated for one year.

Principle 1:9 Exceptional hardship to the petitioner

In cases of exceptional hardship to the petitioner the competent authority may grant a divorce where the spouses have not been factually separated for one year.

Principle 1:10 Determination of the consequences

(1) Where necessary, the competent authority should determine:

    (a)   parental responsibility, including residence and contact arrangements for the children, and

    (b)   child maintenance.

Any admissible agreement of the spouses should be taken into account insofar as it is consistent with the best interests of the child.

(2) On or after granting the divorce the competent authority may determine the economic consequences for the spouses taking into account any admissible agreement made between them.

PART II: MAINTENANCE BETWEEN FORMER SPOUSES

CHAPTER I: GENERAL PRINCIPLES

Principle 2:1 Relationship between maintenance and divorce

Maintenance between former spouses should be subject to the same rules regardless of the type of divorce.

Principle 2:2 Self sufficiency

Subject to the following Principles, each spouse should provide for his or her own support after divorce.

CHAPTER II: CONDITIONS FOR THE ATTRIBUTION OF MAINTENANCE

Principle 2:3 Conditions for maintenance

Maintenance after divorce should be dependent upon the creditor spouse having insufficient resources to meet his or her needs and the debtor spouse's ability to satisfy those needs.

Principle 2:4 Determining claims for maintenance

In determining a claim for maintenance, account should be taken in particular of factors such as:

– the spouses' employment ability, age and health;
– the care of children;
– the division of duties during the marriage;
– the duration of the marriage;
– the standard of living during the marriage and
– any new marriage or long-term relationship.

Principle 2:5 Method of maintenance provision

(1) Maintenance should be provided at regular intervals and in advance

(2) The competent authority may order a lump sum payment upon request of either or both spouses taking into account the circumstances of the case.

Principle 2:6 Exceptional hardship

In cases of exceptional hardship to the debtor spouse the competent authority may deny, limit or terminate maintenance because of the creditor spouse's conduct.

CHAPTER III: SPECIFIC ISSUES

Principle 2:7 Multiplicity of maintenance claims

In determining the debtor spouse's ability to satisfy the needs of the creditor spouse, the competent authority should

(a) give priority to any maintenance claim of a minor child of the debtor spouse;

(b) take into account any obligation of the debtor spouse to maintain a new spouse.

Principle 2:8 Limitation in time

The competent authority should grant maintenance for a limited period, but exceptionally may do so without time limit.

Principle 2:9 Termination of the maintenance obligation

(1) The maintenance obligation should cease if the creditor spouse remarries or establishes a long-term relationship.

(2) After its cessation according to paragraph 1 the maintenance obligation does not revive if the new marriage or long-term relationship ends.

(3) The maintenance obligation should cease upon the death of either the creditor or the debtor spouse.

Principle 2:10 Maintenance agreement

(1) Spouses should be permitted to make an agreement about maintenance after divorce. The agreement may concern the extent, performance, duration and termination of the maintenance obligation and the possible renouncement of the claim to maintenance.

(2) Such an agreement should be in writing.

(3) Notwithstanding paragraph 1, the competent authority should at least scrutinise the validity of the maintenance agreement.

EUROPEAN FAMILY LAW SERIES

1. *Legal Recognition of Same-Sex Couples in Europe*, K. Boele-Woelki and A. Fuchs (eds.)
2. *European Family Law in Action Volume I: Grounds for divorce*, K. Boele-Woelki, B. Braat and I. Sumner (eds.)
3. *European Family Law in Action Volume II: Maintenance Between Former Spouses*, K. Boele-Woelki, B. Braat and I. Sumner (eds.)
4. *Perspectives for the Unification and Harmonisation of Family Law in Europe*, K. Boele-Woelki (ed.)
5. *Family Law Legislation of the Netherlands*, I. Sumner and H. Warendorf
6. *Indépendance et interdépendance patrimoniales des époux dans le régime matrimonial légal des droits néerlandais, français et suisse*, B. Braat
7. *Principles of European Family Law Regarding Divorce and Maintenance Between Former Spouses*, K. Boele-Woelki, F. Ferrand, C. González Beilfuss, M. Jänterä-Jareborg, N. Lowe, D. Martiny and W. Pintens
8. *Inheritance Law Legislation of the Netherlands*, I. Sumner and H. Warendorf
9. *European Family Law in Action Volume III: Parental Responsibilities*, K. Boele-oelki, B. Braat and I. Curry Sumner (eds.)
10. *Common Core and Better Law in European Family Law*, K. Boele-Woelki (ed.)
11. *All's well that ends registered?*, I. Curry-Sumner (ed.)
12. *Model Family Code – From a global perspective*, I. Schwenzer and M. Dimsey
13. *Harmonisation of Family Law in Europe. A Historical Perspective*, M. Antokolskaia
14. *Brussels II bis: Its Impact and Application in the Member States*, K. Boele-Woelki and C. González Beilfuss (eds.)
15. *Tensions between Legal, Biological and Social Conceptions of Parentage*, I. Schwenzer (ed.)
16. *Principles of European Family Law Regarding Parental Responsibilities*, K. Boele-Woelki, F. Ferrand, C. González Beilfuss, M. Jänterä-Jareborg, N. Lowe, D. Martiny and W. Pintens (eds.)
17. *Juxtaposing Legal Systems and the Principles of European Family Law on Divorce and Maintenance*, E. Örücü and J. Mair (eds.)